A Short History of Espionage

A Short History
of Espionage

By

COLONEL ALLISON IND
United States Army Intelligence, Ret.

DAVID McKAY COMPANY, INC.

New York

A SHORT HISTORY OF ESPIONAGE

COPYRIGHT © 1963 BY COLONEL ALLISON IND

LIBRARY OF CONGRESS CATALOG CARD NUMBER: 63-11581

MANUFACTURED IN THE UNITED STATES OF AMERICA

VAN REES PRESS • NEW YORK

1461448

for Helen

Among the many whose friendly cooperation and help have gone into the preparation of this book, it is desired to mention especially Miss R. E. B. Coombs, Librarian, Imperial War Museum Library, London, England, Dr. J. Lawrence Evans, Jr., of Englewood, New Jersey, and Curtis Carroll Davis of Baltimore, Maryland.

CONTENTS

A Short History of Espionage

I

The Spy

LA ROCHEFOUCAULD, who knew much of intrigue in his life, was close to truth when he said: "There are two sorts of curiosity; one is from interest, which makes us desire to know what may be useful to us; another is from pride and arises from a desire of knowing what others are ignorant of." The former—that which might be useful to us, even essential to our self-preservation—would seem to establish the *raison d'être* and the nature of intelligence apparatuses among nations. For only as this curiosity is graduated from something personal and is amplified into something impersonal, organized, and for the good of the state, is it seen in the perspective that applies to national intelligence matters.

Such universality demands respect. Nations that did not spy went down into the dust of oblivion because they didn't; other nations, ancient and modern, waxed fat on the fruits of espionage. In the United States, the adoption of espionage as an instrument of survival was a natural, necessary concomitant of our emergence into national maturity. Pearl Harbor taught us that foreknowledge is a possible guarantor of survival.

Spying as a contributory means to foreknowledge is a function of self-preservation. Spying is at least the second oldest profession—and when rulers of nations protest wrathfully against it, they indulge in hypocrisy that fools only the naïve.

It would seem, then, that naïveté in the matter of modern-day espionage or in that far wider field of human endeavor from which espionage derives—"intelligence"—is foolish, unnecessary, and can be dangerous. In these days intelligence is big business. Espionage in one form or another is vital for protection—as much against acts of treason from within, as against acts of subversion from without.

The U-2 incident brought the official announcement, surprising, even shocking to many, that the United States was engaging in spying. Intelligence with its specialized facet of spying excited public interest well before the U-2, but that fiasco and the fact that it was *our* spy shot interest to an all-time high.

It also generated sober thinking about what seemed to be a lack of familiarity, on high levels as well as low, as to the true nature of intelligence and how its objectives should be accomplished.

For an activity of such major national concern there is a surprising amount of misinformation, or at least fanciful distortion, about intelligence. Some is deliberate. Some results because the word "intelligence" means both the total apparatus and the specialized information it produces. There is understandable overemphasis on the "cloak-and-dagger" aspect of what is really a many-sided activity, most of it not secret at all. The public is further confused because an honest disagreement exists among Government agencies about what is safe to discuss freely and what should be revealed for public understanding and support. This has resulted in half-truths half told—or diplomatic untruths that occasionally have had severe repercussions.

It is well to keep in mind, too, that not all secret agents are

2

spies. They may on the other hand be spy catchers, or "plants," to uncover disaffection or subversion, sometimes in surprisingly high places. Or they may be saboteurs, or code snatchers, or function in numbers of other ways.

The United States of America was a long time emerging from amateur status in the field of intelligence. But, characteristically, having made the decision to develop an intelligence force, Washington performed prodigiously. It was as though that American technique, mass production, had been applied to the business of intelligence—with its dangers of confusing quantity with quality and of assuming that greater dollar appropriations would be commensurate with results. Sometimes this failure of discrimination has contributed to some unpleasant surprises. None has been quite as disastrous as Pearl Harbor, although our obtuseness in high places prior to the Battle of the Bulge and in Korea during the Chinese Communist build-up certainly approached it.

The Hawaii disaster came about because in 1941 we had no intelligence apparatus worthy of the name. We still operated in an atmosphere of adolescent chivalry, to the amusement and contempt of other nations, aware that national existence depended upon recognition of jungle rule in the world of diplomacy. One of the principal reasons why we had no hint of Japan's naval capability for simultaneously exploding war over a fifth of the earth's surface was because one of our Secretaries of State had, in a burst of quixotic zeal, blinded us a dozen years before. In 1929, it was explained to the late Henry L. Stimson why we were so well prepared for the forthcoming Naval Limitations Conference. Our experts had succeeded in breaking the Japanese diplomatic cipher system and we thus knew Tokyo's instructions to its delegates. "Code breaking" had been practiced by all nations clever enough to do it for hundreds of years before we were even a colony. But when Secretary Stimson was informed of the United States'

3

activities in the field, he was so outraged at our "reading the other gentleman's mail" that overnight he acted to destroy invaluable machinery and scatter the experts.

Since Stimson's day we have gone far and fast—maybe too fast. Perhaps a cool appraisal of our intelligence apparatus, or apparatuses, for there are many of them, is in order. Such a survey will help to dispel naïveté, will teach us to discriminate between protection and mere organization, between effectiveness and massiveness.

It is axiomatic that the more advanced and complex the civilization, the wider must be the spectrum from which information is derived to satisfy a state's requirements for useful knowledge of its neighbors in an uncertain world. It also follows that the collectors and processors of that information must be more specialized, more highly trained.

The overwhelming bulk of intelligence information is the result of dogged, day-to-day routine compilation by myriad specialists, military and civilian. They work in a perfectly open and aboveboard manner. An encyclopedic mass of facts results, covering every phase of human activity, from religion to racial characteristics, from geography to geophysics, from political theory to political poltergeists. Inspiring? Adventurous? Hardly. Yet something like ninety per cent of the intelligence compiled by modern nations is put together by such overt means.

To gain a proper perspective on the subject of modern intelligence information and intelligence apparatuses, then, it is necessary to know that something less than ten per cent of all intelligence results from the activities of men and women employing covert, or underground, means. Upon the doings of those men and women whole dynasties have fallen and others have risen in their stead. When intelligence activities move into the covert, or clandestine, things become mysterious, sinister. These things pique us, of course, and arouse our sense of the dramatic. We like to identify our prosaic selves with them, to

4

share in the dangers, albeit vicariously. Burton said in *Anatomy of Melancholy:* "An itching humor or kind of longing to see that which is not to be seen, to do that which ought not to be done, to know that secret which should not be known . . ."

Public interest is sharpened when indications of the grim, continuous, subterranean warfare that is international secret service suddenly break to the surface in newspaper headlines. A one-time West German intelligence chief who only a short time before was given the red-carpet treatment in Washington intelligence installations, disappears through mysteriously opened barriers into Red Germany. A one-time Soviet intelligence agent breaks away from his Kremlin masters, tells us all, and now lives in deepest anonymity some place in the West. The body of a sergeant of the U.S. Army's Counter Intelligence Corps is found floating in a filthy canal in the heart of Tokyo, Far East hot spot for operatives of many nations. Two highly-regarded civilian clerks in a most carefully secured Army agency near Washington turn up missing one day and a few days later are seen smugly smiling on a Moscow TV screen. There is a public outcry as to how such things can happen to us. And again, a dingy little man makes an appointment to get some vital data from an officer of one of our armed services. They are to meet at the base of the Washington Monument, one of our symbols of democratic freedoms. Some months later the little man tries to take his life in a federal prison because the "officer" actually was a carefully prepared agent of the Federal Bureau of Investigation.

So it goes, and likely will go as long as there are men and women willing and able to pit their wits against unseen "opposite numbers" quite as determined, as ruthless, and as ingenious as themselves. It is these who have given history some of its most violent turns (and their absence at critical times has been quite as disruptive). Nor will the sophistication of electronic spy gadgets reduce the importance of the man on the spot. The gadget remains to be envisioned that can peer into men's minds—or better, their hearts—to synthesize fleeting elements of thought and emotion into a foreseeable course of action and then report that probable action when it is still in gestation and before it can become significant.

In the final count, human eyes and ears serving a discerning, analytical brain, still must remain the collectors of the intangibles that underlie decisive human behavior. Tenuous dreams, curdling ambition, corrosive greed, enduring love—whether of man or country—make the world go round. These motivations, good or bad, develop only in the association of human beings. Whether we are concerned with the so-called positive aspect of intelligence work, that is, the aggressive collection of information, or the security phase that would protect us against the machinations of others on positive missions against us, it is the same. The purposeful brain is at work, acting and reacting with infinite flexibility to meet, then beat, play for play, the maneuverings of the opponent to gain the ultimate objective. True, these men and women operatives may employ technical aids of marvelous complexity and great potential. But in the long run, results depend upon the resourcefulness, the thoroughness, the determination, the love, hate, idealism, the deceptiveness, and the saintliness of that ultimate in unpredictable variables: the human being.

Intelligence Is . . .

SECRET operators may have secret assignments as varied and numerous as are they themselves. But the spy has one mission—to gain information. It is data that the overall intelligence apparatus will use to supplement other information on the subject, relate it, and from this grist, produce intelligence.

Misunderstanding arising from general and specific meanings of the word "intelligence" is easily resolved. In the broad sense intelligence is the whole apparatus: collectors (including

6

spies), researchers, compilers, evaluators, relators, estimators, writers, disseminators, and a host of others, together with all their gadgets, communication systems, libraries, laboratories, files, and production plants. On the protective side there are: the spy catchers, censors, code makers and breakers, loyalty checkers, plant security experts, and many others, with their own accessories and equipment.

In its limited sense, intelligence is simply properly processed information, but it is the essence of information. Some thousands of years before Christ, Sun Tsu, a famous Chinese general summed it up:

> . . . what enables the wise sovereign and good general to strike and conquer and achieve things beyond the reach of ordinary men, is foreknowledge.

A generation or two ago it was not uncommon to refer to any piece of news as intelligence and many newspapers called themselves "intelligencers" of one kind or another. (Some still do, as the *Seattle Post-Intelligencer*.) But in the modern apparatus we speak of here, information is not generally regarded as intelligence until it has been subjected to certain tests and processing to make it as reliable and pertinent as possible— to give it maximum utility for the need in hand.

Many acts of daily living illustrate these points. For instance, if you plan a trip by automobile into a mountain area you have never visited before, you might prepare by doing such things as calling your automobile club office to determine the best route, the condition of roads in the mountains, and to obtain a list of recommended inns and their rates. You might get in touch with friends who have been in the area for their opinions on the same questions. You might buy a newspaper to get the five-day weather forecast, inquire of your photographic dealer as to the type of film and exposures recommended for high, clear mountain atmosphere at the particular time of year, buy a film exposure guide, listen to the late radio or TV weather forecast, and so forth. You will have availed yourself of all pertinent information: you take what the auto club said and compare it with what your friends who have been there have said; you check the photo expert's advice against the data in the guide; you analyze the long-range forecast and relate it with the late forecast. Then you evaluate your various sources, deciding which ones are probably the more reliable. Then you assemble your tested data. And presently you come up with, not isolated pieces of information, but a tested, evaluated, and comprehensive piece of intelligence that would serve you to the maximum. If there was doubt in your mind as to the advisability of making the trip, you have provided yourself with an "intelligence estimate" that should enable you to make your decision.

It is all simple enough, but let us inject some special conditions and see how quickly the situation can become complicated.

Let us assume that there is a war on and that that particular part of the country has experienced sabotage incidents in war industry plants. There have been aerial bombing alerts, too.

Now what the weather is going to be can be of utmost importance to enemy squadrons carrying heavy bomb loads over the mountainous areas you're interested in. And the condition of the roads in the mountains and which of them is closed for military reasons can be of vital interest to saboteurs who plan to traverse the area during the night in order to arrive at a certain hydroelectric installation before dawn.

You discover that the information you need for your innocent jaunt is flatly denied you by the authorities. The information is "classified." You consider it bureaucratic abuse of power against a taxpaying citizen. Well, suppose you have a friend who knows someone who can get the information for you because he's in a position to do so by posing as a government official. You ask, and your friend and his friend comply.

Thus the line between the simple acquisition of information

8

and the acquiring of it under certain special conditions blurs into the difference between lawful gaining of data and becoming involved in espionage activities! You actually have become one of a chain or network whose objective is the acquiring of prohibited information, and people can be shot for things like that.

So, in spying, or espionage, a pivotal point is *prohibited* information. International espionage can, in fact, be defined as the "attempt to obtain clandestinely or under false pretenses denied information concerning one government for transmission to another government." In our illustrative case, all the conditions are not met since you plan to use the information yourself and have no notion whatever of being disloyal. But while the Hague provisions on international rules of war clearly recognize the rights of belligerents to employ spies to get information, individual nations protect themselves by passing their own laws making it a crime even to *seek* classified information in peace or war. We do so ourselves. Then there is an additional clause which makes it a further crime to try to transmit that information to another government.

Information can be classified as *prohibited* because of the subject it deals with, such as anything concerning nuclear fission for weaponry in World War II and thereafter in this country. Or it might be simply because the information sought is obtainable only from a prohibited area, some other country, for instance, which insists that it has the full right to protect its own secrets, regardless of what they're about, or how silly it may seem to other countries that they are considered secrets at all. When it comes to that, how could the United States in World War II declare as "top secret" scientific data on nuclear fission that had been worked out by the scientists of a dozen nations and which was available in the public libraries of scores of cities throughout the world?

It appears then that the ethics of spying may be concerned less with moral issues than with national laws. Is it espionage or ultrasecrecy, then, that is the real offender against the welfare of mankind?

In 1960 Khrushchev protested, with vocal clamor and beating shoe, against the "crime of espionage" in the U-2 case. (The Hague Agreements make no mention of espionage as an international crime in time of peace. The President's rebuttal was that Soviet Russia's inordinate secrecy made such surreptitious seeking of information necessary—there's that "necessary" again—to the continued well-being of this country.

This is a pragmatic concept but not an unknown one in man's code of ethics throughout the ages. The end justifies the means—and the dishonor lies not in the commission of the act, but only in its failure. This ethical nicety is still further refined among governments in the cases of such protocol individuals as army, navy, and air attachés, and others enjoying diplomatic status in other countries. Attachés, for instance, are accepted, even honored, by host governments as official observers (although what they may seek to observe another man might well risk his neck for), and they are actually accorded the diplomatic pouch for transmitting their data back to their own governments. But, should one betray such bad manners as to be uncovered in dubious practice while acquiring information concerning the host country, he becomes *persona non grata* and is handed his exit visa to be used with all possible speed. He has then "acted under false pretenses" for getting data and has abused the hospitality of a host.

The fact is that we are confronted with a grim reality: The employment of espionage for the production of needed intelligence information must be accepted as standard survival procedure among the nations of the earth, regardless of ethics, ego, or cultural embellishment.

We have spoken of various broad categories of intelligence. Generally these are considered from the standpoint of who is to be the ultimate user. These users are classified according to

10

interest, the one having the broadest interests at the top. This usually results in a split into political and military intelligence.

Obviously the "summit" individuals of a nation, the policy-makers who frame the destinies of a country, would have little need for a report on the road conditions in a given mountain area, but they *would* be vitally concerned with the rise of a radical political faction in a country that had become belligerent toward its neighbors in recent years. They would seek the most profound studies on the political philosophy of that group, its aspirations, its means and methods of winning converts, and the characteristics of those playing dominant roles. They would want the most careful assessments of political strength and projections for the future. The political strategy for alignment with other nations would receive top attention. There would be economic reports, sociological surveys to include such things as the literacy rate, health studies, and an examination into the financial structure, and all things entering into the war-making potential of the country. On the basis of all this policy intelligence the rulers of a nation would formulate their own policy.

On a somewhat lower level would be the military planners who might have to implement action to enforce those national policies once they had been determined by the executive or legislative group. The military planners would seek strategic intelligence on every conceivable subject concerned with war planning, whether defensive or aggressive in nature, or both. They would want to have, for instance, the most accurate surveys on natural resources of the subject country; they would want the location of every steel-producing unit of importance, and exact data on the transportation capacity of the railroads and highways serving those centers. They would require every iota of information, processed into comprehensive intelligence reports, upon the armed forces of that land, as well as data concerning seasonal weather and how it affected the land and the population. Then, when their data was as complete as it could be, they could plan field campaigns.

Campaigns are carried out by field commanders. And now the condition of particular roads becomes a matter of prime importance, for certain commanders might have to move elements of an army over key highways within a specified time. Can those roads accommodate the traffic? And how much of a force will have to be overcome to insure use of those roads? What kind of a force? Commanded by whom? What is the state of the terrain over which that force and possible friendly co-operating forces will have to operate? And what is the weather likely to be? All this, and much more, is tactical intelligence. Its requirements can go right down to the smallest platoon whose leader wonders what enemy, if any, occupies the woods in the darkness off to his right.

The platoon leader's needs come down to the barest elements: he wants information. There is no time for an intelligence study, or any use for it. He must know immediately who is out there, if anyone, so he can plan how to stay alive through the night. He sends a reconnaissance patrol to find out.

Now the process reverses itself.

His patrol comes back. They have a prisoner. He is cold, disgruntled—and talkative. He gives his name, rank, and serial number, but he also mentions that he is of the Seventy-fifth Regiment of the Ninth Mountain Division. The information goes to company headquarters. The company intelligence officer has another report from a different patrol that would seem to confirm the existence of Seventy-fifth elements out in front. The report goes to battalion, to regiment, to division, to corps, to Army. Army has had it from eight different sources and by pinpointing the map knows pretty well the general disposition of the Ninth Mountain Division. And now we are dealing, not with mere information, but with processed information to make intelligence, in this case tactical, or combat intelligence.

But we have an additional report from the platoon right out on the line. The prisoner was talkative. In addition to giving his name, rank, and serial number, and the fact that he belonged to the Seventy-fifth Regiment, he let slip during subsequent interrogation that he had been transferred to that place on the line from a comfortable job in a super-secret plant far back in his homeland because he had gotten a little drunk one night after working overtime for five straight months and talked a little too much. The job? Technician in a gigantic bacterial warfare laboratory. What is this?

It comprises the first intimation to *strategic* intelligence analysts of a potential threat of bacteriological warfare by the enemy. The next step is to bring that prisoner of war to higher levels for thorough interrogation by specialists who know that part of the enemy country and by others versed in techniques of bacteriological warfare. The subsequent findings seem sound. But is the man a "plant"? Or is he a convincing liar enjoying the attention he is getting?

Many things must be done to check his story. One of them is to ask the highest-level positive intelligence people to send out carefully briefed operatives to try to penetrate that very area and confirm the existence of the installation the soldier claims exists. Another is for high altitude planes to make electronic camera photographs.

Then bit by bit scattered returns of information come in. Most of it tends to confirm. Some is contradictory. More attempts must be made: more spies, more dangerous overflights, more studies of every kind. The last would include locating the whereabouts of all prominent bacteriologists in the enemy's country to determine whether they are at their usual tasks (as determined by the never-ceasing overt collection work done in peacetime), or engaged in another, and more sinister task.

Finally the reports are all evaluated and related to each other, or collated, as it is called. Then the analysts go to work and come up with their estimate. Their consensus proves to

13

be a staggering piece of news for both the strategic authorities and for the national policy-makers. Now the problem is how to meet and defeat the threat of mass extermination by germ warfare.

Counterintelligence Is ...

Now that we know what intelligence is, it should be no problem to infer a definition of counterintelligence. Alas for those who seek orderliness in their approach to things and in the things themselves! There is a curious and enduring disagreement among various intelligence organizations as to which is which. Each of them, such as the Army, which is the senior service in this regard, has its own glossary of terms. And it might be added that even within any single organization, the glossary in use represents something of a compromise among its own compilers. For instance, an "agent" to Central Intelligence Agency (CIA) is a foreign agent of one kind or another, a spy, if you will, whom Washington would like to lay hands on. The principal spy-catching organization within the United States proper is the Federal Bureau of Investigation. How would FBI apprehend this menace to national security? Send out an "agent"? Only the FBI man would be considered a top-notch American of sterling character and patriotism. The semantics can be quite baffling at times to the uninitiated.

In summary, it is both workable and accurate simply to classify intelligence, as either positive or negative. Positive would refer to the collection, evaluation, and processing of information. Negative would refer to protecting our secrets and our material: Censorship to protect against carelessness among our own people on the inside, and actual detective work to spot and apprehend spies working against us from the outside. (Some in the sensitive and chancy work of spy-catching

14

are understandably hostile to the term "negative.") It is generally agreed that counterintelligence is the negative side of the coin, meaning, of course, the reverse side.

Since spies perform espionage, it can be said that counterespionage is the business of frustrating them, catching them if possible, the catchers being counterespionage agents.

The ultimate factor is the human being who is a spy. And how does one define him? The total overt intelligence apparatus towers over the lone secret operative like an inverted pyramid. But he is the darling of the drama-loving public as he stalks through the pages of its books and glides across television picture tubes. Because he really exists and has existed since the first caveman peered from behind a boulder to inform himself of the size and number of clubs his shaggy neighbor could employ to make an attack, or repel one (tactical intelligence!), perhaps a comprehensive working knowledge of the subject could be gained by following him, the secret agent, through the ages.

II

Antiquity Speaks

ARCHEOLOGISTS have been picking the bones of antiquity at the site of the city of Ur in ancient Chaldea with interesting results. It has been hinted that the ancient Sumerians who lived there may have known the rudiments of psychological warfare three or four thousand years before Christ —an enormous span in terms of human experience. In the year 1245 B.C., for example, recorded in the Book of Judges, Gideon extricated himself and his Israelite hosts from a strategically bad plight before the Midianites. He artfully created fright so demoralizing in Midianite ranks that their warriors slaughtered each other, allowing Gideon to put the rest to rout. He had secretly equipped three hundred soldiers with trumpets and torches. Since torches could not be controlled for simultaneous lighting at the right moment, Gideon thought to mask their flames in pitchers. The soldiers stole in the darkness to positions surrounding the enemy encampment. At a signal, they smashed their pitchers. The raw flames sprang out. At the same time, each man blew his trumpet with all the force of his lungs. The flames and the din of the three hundred was psychologically thirty thousand in the jangled minds of the rudely awakened defenders.

In these ancient lands many events occurred which today would be classified as intelligence, or espionage.

Mithridates VI, King of Pontus, who lived a century before Christ, qualifies as one of the most accomplished military and political spies of all ages. By the time he was fourteen he was performing systematic espionage in countries he intended to bring under his control. Let us examine his methods, for the agent-training schools of today, from Washington to London to Moscow, use him as a case study.

To learn the lands he intended to subjugate and the people in them, this child-man became one with them. His demand upon himself (as it would be for the Soviets' "Gordon Lonsdale" in London more than two thousand years later) was: be one of them, speak as they speak, think as they think. If you would know them, know their strengths and weaknesses (and one was quite as important as the other). Mithridates did just this. Even while he was in his teens he had mastered all their languages until he was literally and linguistically "one of them." No one knows how many agents in modern espionage have ended up before a firing squad or dangled at a rope's end because their trainers failed to emphasize dialects, then on top of dialects, colloquialisms—and on top of those, the colloquialisms peculiar to a given small section of a target area. The people of fishing hamlets on the coast detect quickly that a stranger comes from inland plains, and the people of both detect at once, by his speech, the intrusion of one from the hill country. Mithridates provided against such detection in his rigorous self-training. From a safe site he studied the garb of the people and their habits before he moved in among them. Thus, as apparently just another urchin, he got no attention while he went his sinister way, hearing all and seeing all, politically, socially, and militarily. Before he left he knew when and how the thrust should be delivered.

17

Back in Pontus, he was ready. His intelligence estimates were flawless. And he struck, one after the other, the countries he had penetrated and surveyed. They fell as he had seen they had to fall.

But the warped mind of the child became the contorted mind of the adult. So suspicious was this man who had devoted his childhood to deceit that he trusted no man, feared poisoning from all. He probably qualified as the world's first immunologist, treating himself first with miniature doses of known poisons and then bigger doses to build up an immunity to all of them. His insanity progressed. He killed his mother, brothers, lovers, friends, and eventually contemplated killing himself. He took poisons, all of them, but his immunities mocked him. At this point, history is not clear whether he ordered a soldier to kill him with his sword, or seized the weapon and destroyed himself.

The common attitude toward the Trojan Horse is that it was a classic example of espionage. Actually, it is no such thing. As a brilliantly planned and faultlessly executed *ruse de guerre,* it is unsurpassed. But that phase of it that involved the use of a secret agent was concerned with espionage in only an incidental way, if at all. A more accurate classification today would be that of a commando operation in two phases. The first phase dealt with the horse and its viscera of armed men; the second concerned Sinon. It was his mission to make certain that the Trojans elected to get the horse inside Troy. Details of the operational plan called for Sinon to get himself "captured" by the Trojans and then to simulate a bitter, disillusioned outcast from the Greek ranks. He was then to tell the Trojans the meaning of the horse. It was a propitiation built by the Greeks to the gods and purposely made too large for the Trojans to get it within their gates. If this were accomplished, its protective powers would be transferred to the Trojans. The Trojans, rejoicing at the apparent departure of the

18

Greek fleet, breached their own walls and hauled in the horse. The Greek mission was successful and history has its eternal symbol of the *ruse de guerre*.

Postal censorship also had its inception prior to the birth of Christ. Alexander the Great made use of it to detect the disloyal or unreliable in his army. Wise in the evil ways of men, he sensed disloyalty among the mercenaries recruited from defeated but still proud Athens. Who was false? He must know before battle. He devised a plan that would make them betray themselves. From his command tent he issued unaccustomed utterances about home ties and the enforced separations required by duty. Then came a promise to suspend all censorship of one last letter home. Couriers would hurry the post to Athens as the march to new conquests began. But the couriers were hardly out of sight with their burdens before they were hauled in by Alexander's agents. He himself became the chief censor and grim tribunal.

It might be mentioned in passing that to Alexander, too, goes credit for the first extensive use of a cipher device for secret communication. It was a scroll-and-cylinder contrivance. Sender and recipient possessed baton-like cylinders, or staffs, identical in size and markings. When a scroll was received from headquarters, it was wrapped around the baton. The coincidence of inscribed characters showed which characters were meaningful.

Secret doings naturally require secret means of communication. Herodotus tells of one of the most ingenious. Five hundred years before Christ, Histiaeus governed the city of Miletus in Asia Minor, then dominated by Darius of Persia. Histiaeus, disaffected, plotted the overthrow of Darius but he knew that without a strong fleet he could not hope to succeed. As things developed, one Aristagoras, who had similar designs against Darius, found himself in a position to create a mutiny in the Ionian fleet and thereby convert it to his own purposes. Histiaeus and Aristagoras joined forces. To know

19

the proper moment for the commencement of the mutiny, it became necessary for the pair to have a secret means of communication. Histiaeus summoned one of his most trusted slaves and had the man's hair shaved from his head. A message was tattooed onto the scalp. He then was held in secure retirement until the hair had grown back. Subsequently he went through the Persian lines with no more than cursory challenge. Arriving, he had only to say to Aristagoras, "Master, shave my head." The whole power of Persia was absorbed for the next six years putting down the subsequent rebellion.

Throughout the history of espionage, resourcefulness has been a prerequisite for an agent. Laelius displayed it when ordered by the Roman general, Scipio Africanus, to lead a "political deputation" into the opposing camp of the Numidians. This was, of course, cover for an espionage penetration. But Laelius had to make sure of personally seeing enough of the camp into which he had come under truce conditions to enable him to make an authentic estimate. The trick lay in another horse, a live one this time. At an appropriate moment, the animal apparently bolted. It was hotly—but not too hotly—pursued by the Romans and caught only after it had somehow traversed much of the Numidian military installation. Laelius relaxed; he knew all he wanted to know. But relaxation was premature. He saw a Numidian officer staring at one of his "retainers." Then he saw perplexity change to conviction in the other's mind. The "slave," said the Numidian, was no slave at all, but a Roman officer with whom he had once shared training. (In our own system we have had occasions to regret our generosity in training at our own facilities members of foreign staffs who later turned against us when their political policies changed.) The quick-thinking Laelius snorted in disgust and delivered such a blow to his "slave" that the man went sprawling in the dust. The Numidian was convinced. Such treatment of a true Roman officer would have resulted in a prompt demand for satisfaction. The Numid-

20

ian failed to recognize that the discipline of a well-trained espionage agent can hold in check a desire for honor that would imperil an entire operation.

It was about this time that Sextus Julius Frontinus produced his amazing compendium of more than nine hundred tricks which might be used by a resourceful commander. Frontinus pointed out that his *Stratagems* were equally useful in peace and war, thus forecasting another discovery of the present generation, the cold war.

The various Caesars extensively developed internal spy nets, or *espionnage civile*, the Gestapo of those times. But curiously enough, Julius Caesar was history's most famous exception. Had he known what was going on around him, *"Et tu, Brute?"* would likely have been uttered from the security of his throne to a prisoner kneeling helpless between two of the Emperor's previously alerted police agents.

Vox Clandestina

THE knocking on the door in the dead of night has been the summons of doom to countless secret police victims through the centuries. In our times, it has been the Gestapo and the gas ovens or the Russian OGPU and the grim techniques of Lubyanka prison; in days gone by, the followers of Robespierre and the guillotine. But none exceeded in sinister depravity those who acted in the name of the Christian religion at the time of the Inquisition.

Whether or not bigotry and lust for power were the motivations of the Inquisition, it was ruthless.

The Inquisition has been defined as "the systematic pursuit of heresy and the punishment of heretics." Therein lies the essence of one of history's greatest developments of internal spying, that is, spying by a people on its own citizens rather than upon those of another nation.

21

For a hundred years and more following the latter part of the 15th century the Inquisition spread terror over European Christendom, with cruelty so bizarre and diabolical that its torture engines are still displayed as maximum achievements of human ingenuity. The headquarters were the Holy Offices in Rome. The members of the inner chamber were named by the Church and were required to serve without question. In Spain the *corps d'espionnage* was the *Hermandad,* or brotherhood. The members were specially qualified: even in childhood they had been distinguished by their excesses against animals or schoolmates. No crime was beyond their powers—or their willingness—to assist the Holy Office in accusing anyone considered necessary to be liquidated, however innocent he may have been. The historian, Infussoria, records that these spies and *agents provocateurs* were required to have another qualification, to prove that they were descended from a line of "perfect Christians" and were, accordingly, perfect Christians in their own right. They took an oath never to reveal the identity of their employers, if they knew them, and to keep secret their *modus operandi.* There was no adulation if they succeeded in a mission, however risky, and no sentiment if they were so clumsy as to wind up in the dungeon of an intended victim.

While the poor as well as the rich were targets, victims were more often those whose wealth could contribute to the greater glory of the Church. But men of wealth often possessed great influence and formidable numbers of armed retainers as well. The end results were the same. It meant only a greater investment of spies and *agents provocateurs,* with a greater expenditure of patience, flattery, cajolery, and a dangling of more refined baits over a greater period of time. Once the *Hermandad* had fixed upon the objective, the result was inevitable: the joints of noble skeletons would be torn asunder by the rack or blood pressed from noble veins by the iron maiden. That way

22

another convert could be made with no possibility of back-sliding.

No account of religious and diplomatic spying can ignore the serpentine network established by the French Cardinal Richelieu. In 1624 he established himself as virtually the chief minister of France and gave that troubled country its first organized system of both internal and external spying. Although a cardinal of the Church of Rome, this schemer *par excellence* exhibited few Christlike qualities to his friends and none whatsoever to those who opposed his public and private ambitions. Seeking to make France politically powerful and to maintain himself as the pillar of such a state, the "Red Cardinal" was not above secretly aligning himself with a Protestant leader, Gustavus Adolphus of Sweden, in order to vanquish one of the most successful Catholic field generals in modern history, Wallenstein, who was becoming too successful and popular for Richelieu's taste. Such duplicities as these required Richelieu to know at all times what was in the minds of all men. His spies were everywhere. So numerous and so productive were they that Richelieu required an efficient full-time intelligence chief. He epitomized the iron fist in the velvet glove; the soft word was as deadly as the rapier and the abhorrence of violence more destructive in its final effects than open brutality. Cruelty of a sleek, feline kind characterized his schemings. It was natural that he should shun the police type for so vital a post and turn instead to the brotherhood. The Capuchin father, Joseph du Tremblay, so closely mirrored the mannerisms and the very thoughts of his famous employer that he, in turn, became the "Grey Cardinal." Served to perfection by this ideal leader for his vast network, Richelieu succeeded in his aspirations and established the Bourbons upon the French throne, a dynasty that would thrive until dissolved in the blood bath of the French Revolution.

It should be noted that this espionage system was one of the first to include an analysis and production organization to process the huge intake of information into intelligence. It is also unique in that the successor to the Red Cardinal was also a cardinal, the Italian, Mazarin. He, however, lacked the benefit of the soft-spoken, mild-mannered du Tremblay and, as time went on, Richelieu's once great organization lapsed into essentially a counterintelligence operation, almost internal in coverage.

The English Stamp

INTELLIGENCE authorities are often asked for an opinion as to which nationality is considered the most able in secret service matters. Judgments vary, even when strongly documented. But in any popularity vote, the English invariably rate high, although many of the most accomplished in Whitehall's silent ranks themselves will make bows in the direction of the Polish.

Perhaps concentration of effort through England's long history has had something to do with it. But surely of importance is the British capacity for infinite patience coupled with even temper, whatever the immediate situation.

Some authorities credit Sir Francis Walsingham with being the founder of modern secret service, a child of necessity, really, born of the anxiety-laden days when the Armada was being assembled for the final subjugation of England by Spain. There is much to sustain the view.

But if one can separate myth and folklore from authentic history of that stormy island in the ninth century, one might hold that Alfred the Great laid the foundation through his own activities as a spy against the Danes, who then held southern England in thralldom.

Following disastrous clashes Alfred had at last been compelled to take refuge in a wretched, frozen swampland in the southwest known as the Isle of Athelney. His mind seethed with plans for his return, although to many he appeared pre-occupied by idle pursuits. Minstrelsy and tumbling were hardly occupations for a king, said his critics. The faithful knew better. Traditionally minstrels and tumblers roamed the countryside entertaining churl and peasant alike. If they were good, they might be invited into the great houses—even the sprawling camp of Guthrum the Dane, conqueror of the land. The gay minstrel and his small company entertained well indeed. But as they gave out, they took in. And when Alfred returned to his frozen marshes, he knew how and when and where to campaign against Guthrum. The assaults began in 878 and though they went on for years, England was proof against the Danes. Alfred had proved as efficient a spy as he was a commander.

Four hundred and fifty years later Edward III established British secret service as an organized effort. The foundations were laid, but it remained for Henry VII to develop secret intelligence as a court policy. This was a combination of military and *espionnage civile* by which he sought to keep abreast of the schemings that followed his efforts to unite the houses of York and Lancaster. Especially designing was Margaret, duchess dowager of Burgundy, sister of Edward IV. Henry's agents kept her under closest surveillance, but so devious was the political situation that it was impossible to determine at all times who was watching whom.

Despite the difficulties, Henry was advised by several observers as to Margaret's latest scheme for setting up a pretender to the English throne. A principal in the plot was Francis Viscount Lovell. Henry required that Lovell be brought in dead or alive. Excited scouts then alerted Henry to an invading force of mercenaries paid for by Margaret and led by a group including Lord Lovell. Henry, being a man of action, headed the army himself and routed the invaders at Stoke-on-Trent.

As for Lovell—but where was he? He was not among the

fallen. Henry's agents scoured the neighborhood. They brought back unconvincing reports of Lovell's having been drowned in the Trent as he tried to escape: there was no confirmation and no body. Henry was furious. His orders to find Lovell were sent throughout the country.

But to his dying day Henry never knew what had become of Lovell. More than a hundred and fifty years later workmen were demolishing walls of a fortified manor on the banks of the Trent. Suddenly all work stopped. They had come upon a secret room and, sitting at a table, his head resting on his hand, was a man in rich garb. As they stared, a current of air stirred the dry mortar dust. The man trembled, shriveled, and slowly crumbled into dust as dry and powdery as that of the mortar. Lord Lovell had found sanctuary from Henry's wrath. He had also found starvation and death in a room so secret that none who survived the battle had known of its existence.

Served well by his agents otherwise, Henry expanded his system and was the first English king to apply secret service as a policy against a foreign state with which he was not at war. Thus he actually set the formal pattern for Wolsey, Burleigh, Walsingham, and Cecil. Henry "got what he desired and many other mysteries were revealed." In pious judgment on such methods, Bacon wrote: "He had such moles working to undermine him."

Could Henry have read the account of Laelius beating one of his own brother officers in order to discredit him in the eyes of the suspicious Numidians? Bacon recounts that Henry "for the better credit of his espials (agents) abroad, with the contrary side, did use to have them cursed at Paul's amongst the Bead-roll of his enemies according to the custom of the times." But if he directed harsh treatment in public, he "furnished his employed men liberally with money to draw out and reward intelligence." For this he expected them to "report what they found out and nevertheless still go on . . . to discover to the bottom."

26

From such beginnings developed the formidable British agent throughout the centuries. Curiously, to be found in these ancient records are definitions that hold good today: secret agent—a resident person in good position; informer—anyone, often of low birth, who is paid for information; spy—an intelligencer by profession, having some connections with public calling, as priest, monk, friar, barber-surgeon, scrivener, or clerk ... and without fixed abode ... and be sufficiently respectable to be a hanger-on of courts, royal, church, civil, etc.

Henry VIII carried on where his father left off. But to do this, he put in charge a man of police-state mentality. In the ten years following 1530, Thomas Cromwell saturated all England with paid agents of both sexes. Truly, a "scorpion lay under every stone." The odium reeked to heaven, and gave rise to the question of whether plotters or spies establish the initiative. Scheming theoretically demands protective spying, but excessive spying tends to make men plot in self-defence.

Walsingham

WALSINGHAM'S reputation as a spymaster is most luminous. King Philip II of Spain is alleged to have complained that his state secrets for unhorsing Queen Elizabeth went to England via Walsingham's agents, were conned by the "Beloved Gloriana," and were back in his own court circulating as gossip before he had time to acquaint his ministers with the official information.

Ordinarily parsimonious, Elizabeth nevertheless believed wholeheartedly in secret intelligence and lavished funds on this activity. Hardly was she on the throne at twenty-five before she ordered every ambassador overseas to submit secret reports on all and sundry. Possibly her amazing foresight already was warning her of dark things to come from Spain and Rome. Walsingham's association with her secret service dates from 1568. Then he made arrangements "with the Lord Mayor of London to make weekly reports of all strangers who took lodgings in the city." He was an exceptionally well-educated man who combined keen observation with an orderly, index-type mind. Walsingham infiltrated the top levels of Catholic King Philip's court. He had observers of high caliber in the Vatican itself. But if highest Rome was under observation, so were the most modest of the brotherhood; he insinuated pretenders to the faith among the student body in the Catholic seminary at Rheims in France. Among these agents in all probability was the young poet, Christopher Marlowe. Was it because of some misalignment growing out of the fact that he had "done her majestie good service" in "matters touching the benefitt of his Countrie" that his brilliant young life was snuffed out by a dagger thrust through the head in a Deptford tavern on a spring night in 1593? It would seem not. Yet there is much mystery and one of the men present in what was alleged to have been a sudden, violent quarrel over gambling was a retainer in the house of Walsingham, a man privy to many secrets. It is just possible, then, that espionage lost to the world one who might have outshone even William Shakespeare, whose contemporary he was, had he not died at twenty-eight.

In the critical years of Mary Queen of Scots's planning and again when the Armada's shadow fell across England, Walsingham had a score of top-flight agents in most sensitive spots, some sixty intelligencers and uncounted numbers of carefully chosen informers. Elizabeth once budgeted him some £2,000 at a time when a farthing would buy a fowl. But with danger over, she promptly reduced appropriations, and he was forced to spend his private fortune to keep his net in operation.

A living denial of the axiom that to get a rogue you must set a rogue upon him, Walsingham was one of the loftier characters of the centuries. He was, however, quick to utilize any

28

shrewdness detected in his enemies. Greatly puzzled by the way Mary was maintaining a line of communication between her closely guarded cell and her own agents and supporters outside, even in France, he finally bethought himself to check with the wine merchants supplying the royal cell. There was the answer: a waterproof container inserted in the bunghole of the wine casks going in and out. He instructed his agents, hungry for a kill, not to disturb the line of communication. Patience had its reward. How he must have exulted when he was delivered this one, done in Mary's penmanship:

When your preparations both in England and abroad are complete, let the six gentlemen who have undertaken to assassinate Elizabeth proceed to their work, and when she is dead, then come and set me free.

With Mary gone and the Armada the new threat, Walsingham adopted this device; his agent, Ousley, was braving the Inquisition to watch Spanish preparations in the port of Málaga; Walsingham told him to make similar use of wine casks. Wine never had sweeter bouquet for Walsingham than that spiced by his minion's reports.

Few examples of modern intelligence can boast of a more accurate forecast of the start of a major military operation than the one Walsingham received saying "The Armada will leave Lisbon about the middle of May." It did.

The tall man with the pointed beard, sickly for years, bent over his reports and alternated the reading with sniffs at an orange punched with cloves, suspended around his neck. With the intelligence, Walsingham hoped to fend off danger to his beloved country; with the orange charm he hoped to ward off the vapors. His success in the former is a matter of history. Less noted is the fact that he died miserable and penniless. His life and his funds had gone for England's secret services. The house still stands which saw it all, the house that held the secrets, the house from which his emaciated body was taken at night for burial to keep the fact of his death from creditors.

An author who can produce a book so popular that it remains on the best seller list, not for a year or even two or three, but for three hundred and fifty years, might well be considered a successful author. In the early 1700's *The Life and Strange Surprising Adventures of Robinson Crusoe* appeared in London and was an immediate success. It was purported to have been done by Robinson Crusoe himself. But soon everyone knew it was written by Daniel Defoe. What most did not know was that Defoe also authored the most comprehensive plan for English civil espionage that had emerged since Walsingham's time. They may also have been unacquainted with the fact that Defoe was an ex-convict jailed for political writings, and that because of his fertile imagination and his deviousness in daily conduct, he was thought by the authorities best suited to implement the excellent operations plan he had produced.

One of his noteworthy contributions to England was his personal reconnaissance of Scotland to acquaint London secretly with the true state of affairs in order to form policy for the union of Scotland and England. Under the pretense of doing a history of Scotland, he wrote the most fulsome reports. An enterprising man, he later published them as a history of Scotland.

In the course of a thoroughly untranquil life Defoe made and spent several fortunes. There is no reason to believe, however, that an impecunious old age was due to his having spent his last funds in behalf of espionage, as Walsingham had done. Nevertheless, he died poor and unmourned. Apparently the only note of the passing of a man who contributed much to British secret service was this: "A few days ago died Daniel Defoe, Senior, a person well-known for his numerous writings."

30

III

Modern Patterns—England

THE Turkish military guards had been charged by their *atabek* that morning to be especially alert. British naval ships were paying a goodwill visit to the Dardanelles area, that waterway coveted by many nations, for whoever controlled it controlled the Russian lifeline from her Black Sea ports to the Mediterranean. In the 1880-90's the Turks were busy modernizing the fortifications that one day would prove impregnable to a powerful British naval squadron, and Gallipoli would go down as one of the worst fiascos in England's history. The sentries were to show courtesy to the British, but they were to forbid sketching and photographs.

Suddenly one of the guards on the beaches raised a shout and pointed upwards. Against the skyline was plainly silhouetted a figure in the unmistakable posture of a man making a photograph. Other guards responded to his alarm and together they clambered up the slope.

If the figure on the ridge understood their cries to desist and remain stationary, he gave no sign. For a moment the angle cut their view of him. And then they burst upon him,

31

breathless and indignant. They surrounded him, demanding his camera. But the British seaman was as bewildered by the assault as he was incapable of understanding their shrill gibberish. He looked beseechingly in the direction of the British officers a short way off; one of them had hailed him only a few minutes ago as he was strolling about, and asked him to stand in the spot just where the officer himself had been standing when the seaman had come upon him. Surprised, he had nevertheless complied; he recognized the officer as one from his own ship.

The trio of officers approached. What was the trouble? The clamor increased. Finally it was made out that the sentries wanted to search the seaman. The bewildered man was prevailed upon by the officers for the sake of international peace to submit. The sentries found nothing.

Now the Turks joined in the bewilderment, making it universal—except for the British officer who had requested the stand-in. Under his own coat was concealed the camera he had been operating when the sentry had spotted him. He had relied upon his distance to make absolute identification impossible. The Turks had seen a figure. They would find one when they got to the top. Now in the confusion, the sentries paid the officer no heed.

Sir George Aston, one of the pioneers in modern British intelligence, thus early proved his resourcefulness in collecting valuable military information for England.

In his entertaining memoirs he recalls the uncertain beginnings of today's British military intelligence under the innocuous head of the Statistical and Topographical Battalion. There had been but a handful of personnel, bandied from pillar to post—or postilion, for the initial allotment of quarters was in a Whitehall coach house. That was just after the Crimean War. Aston was not a founder, but became associated in 1886, after the unit had undergone many vicissitudes and re-emerged, almost as uncertainly, as War Office Intelligence.

It became part of the General Staff in 1905. Aston was shifted to other duties until just before World War I. Then he founded a department, small but efficient, devoted to counterintelligence. His staff numbered only fourteen. How they trapped practically every German spy in England on the day war was declared will subsequently be told. By 1918, the organization had increased to some eight hundred persons.

Aston was a firm believer in personal reconnaissance. Most of the times it worked well for him and the country. Sometimes it didn't. Once, when he went to the Paris Exposition of 1889 to inspect military equipment on display, he outraged a gendarme when he attempted to sketch a naval artillery device. Unlike the Dardanelles situation, there was no opportunity for a stand-in. The policeman was so hostile that later Aston restrained himself from so much as touching a certain huge cannon. The unusual size and design, coupled with the rate of fire claimed for the piece, filled him with admiration and excitement. From memory he made out a detailed report. Not until it was too late did he discover what he had missed by not touching it, as had other observers. They had discovered that there was no real achievement in the impressive piece: the "gun" was made of *papier mâché*.

Another time he learned that acute as an observation might be, it could still lack a vital detail. Again he was at the Dardanelles, this time in HMS *Surprise* under Vice-Admiral Sir George Tryon. Determined to obtain an accurate and meaningful report, he studied the fortified shores inch by inch with powerful glasses. Everywhere, it seemed, Turkish engineer-sappers were busy with pick and shovel.

The Admiral, noting him intent upon his observation, asked him his opinion. Aston expressed his amazement at so much activity. Surely it was very significant from a military standpoint.

The Admiral smiled dourly. Aston, he said, had missed one point: "Only a few of those picks and shovels were bright. The

33

others all were rusty. Those men had started digging under orders just to impress us." Aston noted that the Admiral generously used the word "impress" rather than "mislead."

But the conscientious Aston would have his inning. As a result of a prolonged study of the Dardanelles fortifications made by him and another, he submitted an intelligence estimate that they could be reduced only at great cost, if at all, by an expeditionary force backed by strong naval bombardment. His estimate was to be ignored in 1915. He would take no joy from the accuracy of his conclusions after the slaughter at Gallipoli.

Yet one day more of siege might have made all the difference and tipped the scales in favor of Churchill's audacious gamble. Aston did not know it then. Nor did anyone else in London. It was one of those occasions where the absence of a good spy was as costly to England as the presence of good English spies had been costly to others in bygone days.

My own source for the following must remain anonymous. He may still be in the United States Army, where he has performed with distinction and absolute patriotism for his adopted land. But he was a Turkish intelligence soldier in the war of 1914-18. From the embattled forts he saw the dogged British and the gallant Anzacs come ashore under withering fire from the Turkish emplacements. He saw them falter, regather, advance again, then come to a trembling, bloody halt. The forts had suffered from the heavy guns of the British fleet in the Sea of Marmara, but not so badly that they could not lay down a deadly barrage on the beaches. Then the siege commenced. From April to December the ships glittered like diamonds as they threw their heavy shells shorewards. Still the forts replied. There were heavy casualties among the ships, too; violent explosions from mines or torpedoes obliterated some with awful suddenness. The British knew only of their own losses, and they were appalling. The other side of the story was not

34

known to London, for the British had no spies ashore. They could not know of the dire straits of the Turks, of whole sections wiped out by major-caliber shells, of portions of the forts gone to utter ruin, of entire units crippled by shell shock, disease, and exhaustion. They could not know of empty powder magazines and shell racks—with but one day's supply left! One day more and it might all have been over. The British could have advanced, faced only by small-arms fire from the few able-bodied defenders left, and the vital waterway could have been theirs almost for the taking.

But, in the morning, the Sea of Marmara was nearly empty! And the Dardanelles campaign went down on history's pages as a major fiasco, bloody and useless. 1461448

Like Daniel Defoe, another whose identity is familiar to every schoolboy is Sir Robert Baden-Powell, founder of the Boy Scout movement, and a contemporary of Aston's. As in the case of Defoe, it is not generally known that he was responsible for some highly productive intelligence writings and sketching. In fact, only a naturalist might have been critical of one of Baden-Powell's sketches of a butterfly which he had supposedly observed in Herzegovina in 1891. But he'd have had to have looked closely, for it was an extremely capable representation of one of the order of *Lepidoptera*, excepting for superfluous spots here and there in the wing outlines. British military intelligence analysts in London, following Baden-Powell's instructions, were able to discern a perfect plan of Herzegovina's fortifications within the general form of the butterfly, the extra spots being gun emplacements. No one had suspected the short-sighted naturalist with the butterfly net who trapped speciments near the fortress and sat himself down to sketch them. Young Baden-Powell was also an amateur theatricals enthusiast. He put his adeptness at make-up and costuming to good use and thus personified the spy in disguise, so popular in fiction. It worked, anyway, however amateurish his techniques.

Not so amateurish was the work of certain other espionage operators, this time against England, during this period and in the years prior to World War I. But the British were to prove as astute in defensive maneuvers as in positive work against others.

Frequently what is spectacular in war has its genesis in the cool green days of peace. It is in these relaxed times that "sleeper" agents are installed. It is the never-ending task of counterintelligence in cold war to detect these moles, identify them as lone operatives or members of nets, and know how they can be neutralized when hostilities commence. But not until, for a canceled agent simply means a new search for his replacement, and it may be a long one.

In 1910, Edward VII of England died. It was only natural that the related crown families of Europe should pay last respects at the state funeral ceremony. Practical London counterintelligence men, while no less respectful of the dead monarch, considered that the occasion also might be used by visiting royal mourners to cover a rash of "sleeper" preparation. Not surprising, therefore, was the discovery that the Kaiser's retinue included his acting chief of naval intelligence. Accordingly, when the officer slipped out of the rear entrance of his hotel one night, Scotland Yard Special Section agents were behind him to note whether this was simple relaxation or something more purposeful.

It was the latter. The officer made his devious way to a part of London not usually visited by a foreign dignitary. He called on a hairdresser named Karl Gustav Ernst. No harm in that, but afterwards Ernst was carefully studied by counterintelligence. One observation included the very extensive mail this obscure hairdresser was receiving from abroad.

Postal censorship was applied. Bulky envelopes to Ernst were found to contain smaller ones for different individuals in Britain and bearing proper British postage. Obviously Ernst was what is known as a spy-ring "postbox." There were twenty-two different addresses. Each one now got the detailed attention of the special branch. There were no arrests.

But on the day World War I was declared in August of 1914, every one of the twenty-two German "sleepers" was taken. Germany thus was deprived in her hour of need of every agent she had so patiently prepared in the years before.

Incredibly, the same lightning struck on the opening day of World War II. It was the more incredible because the Nazis had anticipated a repeat performance by the British, and had devised a scheme to succeed despite them. There were to be two nets. The first, not too well hidden, would be a deliberate sacrifice to London counterintelligence; the second, deeply buried, would lie concealed until the authorities were relaxed, and then go quietly into operation. All went as anticipated. The first net was swept up. But then, to Berlin's dismay, so was the second! Some thirty-five key agents and four hundred subagents were apprehended within the first forty-eight hours of war. Once more, postal censorship had provided preliminary clues. Patient, dogged exploitation of those clues and careful sifting of all leads did the rest.

The 1914 fiasco was a near-fatal blow for the efforts of the Kaiser's directors of intelligence. Germany was to succeed in getting a few other spies into England, but for the most part British counterefforts were lethal. Some alleged German intelligence successes have not stood the test of scrutiny, although a few stories, including that of the "Watchmaker Spy of Kirkwall," persisted until well after World War II, as we shall see. Meanwhile, however, England in the first quarter of the 1900's proved too tough a hunting ground, and German efforts were directed instead toward the United States, with far greater rewards.

37

And on the Continent—France ...

A HUNDRED years after Defoe in England had written his masterly operations concept, a disillusioned, disgraced field marshal of Austria who had seen his army ground to destruction by Napoleon at Ulm, shook his head bitterly and muttered, "A most plausible rogue."

Upon the ears of the crafty son of a Lutheran minister in Alsace, those words fell like sweet music. Few men would have thought them an accolade. But Karl Schulmeister was no ordinary man. In his youth he had excelled in the slick and dangerous game of smuggling. His mind had alternately dallied with schemes for hoodwinking the border police and dreams of taking dancing lessons from the most élite dancing masters in all France. His hero was himself. Next below himself, as he reached maturity, he ranked Napoleon. Schulmeister was smugly confident that one day he would be possessed of the wealth to buy many things, including dancing lessons. But only Bonaparte could satisfy his other yearning—public recognition in the form of the broad sash of the Legion of Honor. Therefore, he determined to make himself indispensable to the warrior-genius of Corsica. To Napoleon, foreknowledge of all things that concerned the enemy he proposed to annihilate was absolutely essential, and Karl Schulmeister had the brain, the cunning, the deviousness, and the sheer brashness to obtain it. And so it came that Marshal Mack met disaster and lost his army, for Karl Schulmeister, who by then was Napoleon's most gifted spy, was also Marshal Mack's chief of intelligence!

At seventeen the Alsatian had organized such a successful smuggling ring that he was at once the despair of the police and the delight of less enterprising citizens who paid well for the luxuries they could not otherwise obtain. His exploits came to the attention of one Colonel Savary, who had similar qualities in his make-up. Savary remembered the smuggler, and after he became a general under Napoleon, enlisted Schulmeister as an agent. He felt that Schulmeister was just the man for a particularly infamous piece of work that would shake Europe but prove that Savary's choice had been sound for what lay ahead. War with Austria and Russia was imminent.

Napoleon intended to give full attention to the reduction of the Austrians. Characteristically, he would tolerate no surprises on his flanks or at his rear. There had been the usual rumors of Royalist schemings. He proposed to set an example to the Royalists that would put fear in their hearts. Then he could deal with the Austrians.

Living quietly in Baden as a Royalist refugee was the youthful Duc d'Enghien. He couldn't have cared less about politics, but he deeply cared for a certain young woman of Strasbourg. D'Enghien was harmless to Napoleon and filled with tenderness for the better things of life. From Schulmeister's dark brain came a plan for luring the young man into forbidden France. Accordingly the girl was kidnaped and taken to a point so near the frontier that d'Enghien could almost have seen it. Then Schulmeister bent to another of his specialties—forgery (which was to serve him admirably later when he decided that he was of noble lineage and needed documents to prove it). He forged her name to a letter entreating the romantic nobleman to rescue her from "durance vile." The poor Quixote was not even across the border when he was set upon and dragged the rest of the way into France. His trial was farcical. He was condemned as a Bourbon who had re-entered France under penalty of death. At Vincennes, where more than a century later Mata Hari would face the firing squad, he was shot as he complied with his executioners' request to hold up a lantern so they could bring their sights to bear on his chest.

Savary is claimed to have given Schulmeister the equivalent of $30,000 for this display of ingenuity and resourcefulness, and the next year presented him to Bonaparte with a glowing "Here, Sire, is a man all brains and no heart."

The two men, both of genius in their chosen specialties, appraised each other. Neither was guilty of underestimating himself or the other. In Napoleon, Schulmeister saw his own ultimate elevation to French nobility as a just reward for services, the whole thing bound round by the coveted riband of the Legion of Honor. In Schulmeister, the Corsican saw the answer to his need for a super-spy.

In 1805 the fury of the Napoleonic campaign against Austria mounted rapidly. Throughout his military career, Napoleon had specialized in character analysis of the generals opposed to him, quite as much as in estimates of tactical strengths. After all, field strategy was merely an extension of the personality in command. Thus he knew that opposing him in Austria was a congenital believer in things royalist and one who never could bring himself to believe that the upstart Napoleon from a small island in the Mediterranean was the idol of the French people. Certainly there must be a way to bring this to advantage. Napoleon summoned Schulmeister.

In due time, Marshal Mack in Vienna was reading with kindling excitement a letter purporting to come from a young Hungarian of noble blood who had lived in France. The letter explained that he had been banished by the obnoxious Corsican upon the suspicion that he was an Austrian spy. Bitterness was evident in the lines and in the offer to serve the Austrian cause in any capacity. Promise lay in the hints of valuable information from well-placed sources in Paris, and the means of getting more data into Austria. Indeed the sources were well placed, for Napoleon himself was feeding the carefully screened information to Schulmeister to use once Mack's confidence had been gained. The smooth Alsatian was not long in achieving this. Nor is it any special reflection on Mack that he proved gullible, although there is evidence that he was not as critical as he might have been in assessing the sincerity of his advisors. In this instance he was being baited by an expert, one born to the business. There was in Schulmeister's make-up a charm peculiar to the French, expressed in his case in a finesse of mind and manner so polished it would enable him to skate with amazing success on the brittle ice of one of the proudest societies in Europe. Mack introduced him to Vienna's *haut monde,* even abetting Schulmeister's insinuations (convincingly supported by forged documents) of noble ancestry; his grandfather, he pointed out, had been a Hungarian refugee of the noble family of Biersky who had fled to Baden about 1730 and had become a schoolmaster, hence the Alsatian name. Inevitably there were stirrings of doubt in the minds of some who were genealogically inclined, but Mack was not one of them, and the others could not readily confirm their suspicions. Outwardly they accepted the intelligencer, but quietly they set about to discover what they could.

Schulmeister now "confided" to Mack that the French had not been wrong about him—he had in fact performed extensive espionage against them and he was prepared to turn over his estimates to Mack as a patriotic duty. The grateful general promptly got him a commission in the army and named him chief of military intelligence. Meanwhile the Alsatian had provided himself with two stooges who were prepared, under the stimulus of gold supplied by Napoleon, to confirm any report Schulmeister made to Mack. They were two Hungarian officers, Wend and Rulski. The conversion of Marshal Mack seemed to be complete. But Schulmeister made sure, especially playing on the old nobleman's contempt for the low-born Corsican. He showed Paris newspapers, suitably tattered and worn from their perilous journey along the underground. Mack read with growing delight of serious unrest on the French home front. His beliefs that he would be immeasurably aided by a decaying civil situation became a certainty. Only Schulmeister knew that these newspapers were specially printed for Mack's edification. They had been edited for him by Napoleon himself.

Schulmeister strode on. The record shows that his social successes attained new heights. Those who would discredit him dared not show it. For his part, he radiated euphoria. Under these conditions it is hard to account for one contemporary writer's observation that "his face was like an impenetrable mask"—unless it was the inner mask that covered the superb duplicity. Perhaps another observer of the time was more accurate in estimating that the man had a potentiality "for great things." Certainly he was the glowing exception to Napoleon's own (if highly debatable) statement that it was "rare, if not impossible to find a Frenchman whose heart was truly in spying."

Mack was convinced that the time for action was at hand. Orders to his thirty-thousand-man army streamed out of his headquarters. As they did, the flow in Schulmeister's own secret channels was reversed. Masses of military data went to Paris together with specifics of strengths, composition, lines of march, and other invaluable points in Mack's order-of-battle. But discerning studies through the years have shown that even Schulmeister's devastating deceit cannot account for the magnitude of the disaster that befell the Austrian forces at Ulm. Mack's inherent ineptitude as a field commander emerges in the mass of contradictory, ineffectual orders he issued for the defence once the true situation began to dawn upon him. Fraudulent intelligence and jittery leadership were a bad combination with which to stay such masters of the military art as Ney, Soult, Dupont, and the others who, far from having turned tail for Paris to subdue imaginary rebellion, were arrayed around Ulm in Napoleon's famous "necklace of steel" grimly awaiting the kill.

Mack's army was hacked to pieces. He barely escaped with his life and might have regretted that, too, in the bitter aftermath that was to see him stripped of rank and imprisoned in disgrace.

As Mack's star plunged, Schulmeister's soared to new

heights. Never in his fantastic career would he exceed the audacity of his next moves. First, he allowed himself to be "captured" by the French—only to "escape" and "flee" to Vienna. It could only have aroused admiration in the victorious Napoleon to see this man boldly crash the very council room of the monarchs of Austria and Russia there and prevail upon the grim heads of state to listen to him in their hour of defeat to which he had so richly contributed. Furthermore, he convinced them. It was Mack's fault, he declaimed with such eloquence and unassailable logic that far from ordering the man thrown into prison, the Russian Czar and the Austrian Emperor actually sought his advice. Austerlitz was thundering down the pages of history, and this thick-chested, broad-shouldered man who aspired to dance with mincing elegance now was enabled to set in motion a second time the same mechanism of deceit for the allies and of flawless intelligence for the Corsican. Greater than Ulm was Austerlitz for Napoleon. When it was done, it would surely seem that Schulmeister's triumph was complete. But one more neat fillip remained: those suspicious Austrians of earlier days at last were ready to strike. Their researches had showed not the slightest support for Schulmeister's claims to nobility. And they were convinced that the existence of a counterfeit in a high staff position and the disastrous defeats to the allies were no mere coincidences. They demanded to be heard. The order went out for the man's arrest. But Schulmeister had disappeared. It was a point of fine timing. He could never hope to elude the now voracious police for long, but by this time the armies of Napoleon were clamoring at the gates of Vienna. The police were scattered. The super-spy welcomed his countrymen, not so much with tears of relief and patriotic joy as with boasts of his gains through trickery and praise of his own bravery in the face of great risks. It was another curious facet of the man's complex character, and it produced unfavorable reactions. The Austrians vowed eternal revenge; the French

43

found his boasting distasteful. Napoleon showered wealth upon him, but the coveted riband seemed as remote as ever. It was an odd rejection, for the Corsican had granted that honor to his head of police, who had performed unpalatable deeds.

But Schulmeister's self-praise was not without justification. He sought and obtained a combat command. At Landshut he led a furious cavalry charge that obliterated enemy positions. At Friedland his courage earned him shrapnel fragments in the face, and De Gassicourt makes mention of the resulting deep scars. At Strasbourg he confronted a rebelling mob and brought it to heel by shooting the ringleader out of hand.

Nor was his courage only of the spectacular kind. Upon Napoleon's second occupation of Vienna, he went blandly and boldly back into the midst of those he had once so thoroughly deceived. Not only did he establish himself as an effective censor of newspapers and the stage, but he used publishers and all other media to introduce to the Viennese the treasures of French thought and literature, a strange occupation for a smuggler-*cum*-spy.

But the man who had contributed so much to the twists of history now himself was to be given a turn. The House of Hapsburg, which he had so affronted, was to provide France with a young new Empress. As Hapsburg influence in Napoleon's court mounted, Schulmeister's position deteriorated. He was forced into retirement, but not until he had been named to the highest post in his specialty, chief of Napoleon's secret service. His retirement was cushioned by tremendous wealth and fine estates.

Was it strength of character that led him to uncomplaining acceptance of his casting aside by Napoleon and refusal to join the camp of the Emperor's enemies? Or did his character contain elements of the lackey? Rowan has observed that Napoleon affably called him Karl but treated him as a lackey and suggests that since Schulmeister took his reduction without a show of remonstrance, perhaps Napoleon's treatment was based on a conviction of low caste.

Still, in that day, none could be sure and no man dared put the matter to test. Another side of Schulmeister's character emerged during this period of affluence: so generously concerned was he in the welfare of the common people about him that he won for himself a solid place in their esteem.

But Austrian memories were long and bitter. At Leipzig the French were defeated. A whole regiment of Austrian artillery was assigned to smash Schulmeister's magnificent home to bits. He fled. During the Hundred Days, he once more rallied to Napoleon's side. But with final defeat came his capture, and this time there was no French army to rescue him. He managed to extricate himself, but only upon the payment of such a huge ransom that even his great fortune could not sustain the blow. With what was left he attempted to recoup his loss by speculating on the Bourse. But he had reached the end of his inner resources, too; he was a failure as a speculator and lost what little he had.

For this man who had known so much success and wealth, forty years must have been a long time indeed to eke out a hand-to-mouth existence. Yet he appeared to accept those four decades remaining to him without rancor and to have achieved peace of mind in running a little tobacconist's stall near Strasbourg. In long waits between customers on dark winter days he may have reflected that, if his deceit had landed Mack in prison, it also had freed him: tireless friends of the disgraced Marshal finally prevailed upon the authorities to clear his name on the basis of the spy's duplicity. It would not be until much later that research would reveal the equally disastrous inefficiency of Mack's command.

In 1850 the little stall was the scene of a momentous handshaking. Napoleon III, paying his respects to the man who had done so much for his illustrious uncle, made a visit to the tobacconist's shop. Perhaps in that gesture the then old man felt the

45

stirrings of a sincerity that had been denied him to the last by that other Napoleon so grandly stamped on the pages of history. A century later another and very astute chief of intelligence, Colonel W. Nicolai, would echo the sentiments of many in the intelligence family by remarking that Schulmeister was "a very unthanked individual." This man, whose achievements as head of the German Kaiser's military intelligence in World War I marked him among the intelligence greats, has noted in a discussion of early intelligence efforts: "Espionage is of military origin. At all times and in all places accurate information supplemented by means of espionage among the enemy has been an indispensible auxiliary help in military struggles. Ignorance regarding the enemy's intentions and the conditions of the hostile camp meant the peril of surprises and with that the loss of the battle which often decided the destiny of the state and of people. In this primitive kind of intelligence service it was wise to have a couple of audacious young fellows whose dash and trustworthiness could be depended upon. The incentive generally lay in a big money reward and they were eagerly got rid of when the work was done, so that the glory of military success had not to be publicly attributed to the results of cunning and treason."

Schulmeister had been such an "audacious young fellow." The old man in the tobacconist's stall finally died in utter poverty. He was buried in the St. Urban cemetery of Strasbourg.

Germany

In two world wars the people of the United States had ample reason to be German-spy conscious—as much then as they now are Soviet-spy conscious. Every light that flashed in the night, every chimney that belched smoke intermittently, was seen to be the sinister signal of a hidden agent communicating coded information to other agents of the Fatherland.

Fanned by the nation's security agencies, in turn backed by the occasional genuine instances of detected spy activity, the imagination of the people conjured up a super-German of incredible cunning. The desired effect was achieved: a stringency in security measures that doubtless discouraged and sometimes trapped wrongdoers.

Allied counterintelligence people learned that there was indeed much capability in German military intelligence circles and occasional flashes of brilliance in political intelligence (which alone would be responsible for all the operations against the continental United States in World War II). One of the organizations our modern Counter Intelligence Corps came to respect in Europe was the *Geheimfeldpolizei,* or secret field police.

If not the actual founder of this sort of thing in the 1860's, William Steiber was at least its first important director. He infused the *Geheimfeldpolizei* with the spirit of his shrewdness, a mixture of the disarming deceit of the natural spy and the unfeeling thoroughness of the successful policeman, which he was. America's Civil War was to prove that negative and positive intelligence were synonymous. But in Steiber, Germany had found a man combining the essential characteristics of the two specialties.

Steiber studied both police methods and criminal law, as well as the concepts of the father of modern German secret service, Frederick the Great. (It was Frederick who said: "Marshal de Soubise is always followed by a hundred cooks. I am always preceded by a hundred spies. . . . the ratio of spies to cooks in my army is twenty to one.") Steiber combined his learning with an agile imagination and a wry amusement at the behavior of the human being. And so it was that, while our own Civil War raged, there appeared in Austria an itinerant peddler with a horse and cart. The cart was burdened with sacred statuettes for all to see and choose from. Not in evidence were packs of pornographic pictures. For the devout

47

he was devout. For the unimpressed there would come into his eyes a gleam of amusement. Perhaps, then, the pictures? He seldom failed to interest a considerable portion of all whom he encountered in his wanderings throughout the empire— which he knew his Prussian masters were secretly planning to eliminate in an 1860's version of the modern *blitzkrieg*. With inexhaustible patience the peddler traversed the land, selling, seeing, and compiling.

When the Prussian fury struck in 1866 with devastating precision, Austria lasted but seven weeks. Now the one-time peddler became director of the new and terrifying *Geheimfeldpolizei*.

In 1870 the lightning shifted to strike the France of Napoleon III. His generals had grandly declared the French Army to be "ready to the last gaiter button." But Steiber knew the military machine of France was, as Aston later found the huge Paris gun, *papier mâché*. French peasants on farms along the classical invasion route were astounded when German officers produced lists to show the ability of the countryside to sustain German troops down to the last egg, hock of ham, and blade of forage; innkeepers were told the precise capacity of their establishments for quartering officers, and *bistros* learned their proper inventories of wines for dusty German throats. French officers were to be informed not only what was lacking besides gaiter buttons but how many gaiter buttons there were.

Back of this demoralizing knowledge was the mastermind of William Steiber. Farm hands who had sought employment years before, hotel maids who had been added to the staffs, garçons, quartermaster clerks, ordnance specialists, Steiber had placed them, layer upon layer, over civil and military France well before 1870. Here he demonstrated an essential difference between himself and Schulmeister; Steiber was equally fertile in ideas, but excelled in organizing and tightly controlling a system for its most effective exploitation to the benefit of the Fatherland.

48

After France was defeated Steiber wrote with glee of how he tricked the French peace envoy, Jules Favre. Favre had come to the victorious Prussians at Versailles to discuss terms for the surrender of Paris. The Frenchman was amazed, then delighted, with the hospitality of his Teutonic conqueror-hosts. Everything was done for his comfort, even to the supplying of a personal valet. But that valet was a most unusual one, for it was none other than Steiber himself. Steiber, the servant, was obsequious, efficient. Favre never knew. But Bismarck did, for a copy of every important document, telegram, and memo that Favre brought with him on the subject of the all-important conference was in the Iron Chancellor's hands well in advance —thanks to his manservant's diligence in duties not concerned with shining shoes and pressing pants. At the bargaining table Favre was as a naked babe in a den of lions.

In our own time there has been public and official concern at the presence of sexual deviates in sensitive military and state positions. Unhappy experience has confirmed their vulnerability to exploitation by foreign agents. Steiber was aware of this facet of intelligence operations. His infamous "Green House" in Berlin near the close of the last century was a design for total wickedness. Here were provisions for the practice of every imaginable form of deviate indulgence. Admission was restricted to the selected few of neighboring nations who were, on one hand, the possessors of many secrets of state, and, on the other, of deviate tendencies. Indulgence at the Green House ultimately put these people quite hopelessly in Steiber's hands. Betrayal of country was preferable to betrayal of self before the world.

Steiber was to be remembered with apprehension far into our own day, for it was he who laid the pattern that for generations made the word espionage synonymous with "German spy." He began with France immediately after the victory of 1870. He rightly concluded that the French would eventually develop a sharp counterespionage to prevent repetition of the wholesale infiltration that laid France bare before 1870. Every German would be watched. Therefore, he would not use Germans. French-speaking Swiss were his favorite recruits, and these he stationed from Alsace to the Mediterranean. Then he turned his attention to the rest of the world. His concept revealed him as a master planner. Germans were generally accepted as superlative hotelkeepers wherever they set up business. Steiber pushed a national program that set them up in strategic locations all over the world. Their staffs were, of course, German. Their attentions to important travelers, particularly those of rank and diplomatic status, left nothing to be desired—either by the travelers or by Steiber, whose minions they were. This policeman become big businessman invaded the field of international banking and set his agents in key financial spots in the capital cities of the world. He fed other high-grade men into shipping lines, and he set the pattern for the import-export cover businesses. It was Teutonic thoroughness on a grand scale, and it paid off, as we shall see when we presently consider the destructive World War I work of von Rintelen in New York, of the smooth Dr. Albert, or the beautiful blonde Victorica, and others less glamorous than she but even more effective—the murderous pair, Jahnke and Witzke, for example.

Curiously, though, Steiber's efforts against the French forced them to develop the superb counterintelligence that was to make their country pre-eminent in this field. Herein, it might be observed, lay a fundamental difference in the German and French specialties and methods of operating: the Germans collected grandly on a world scale through a multiplicity of agencies, all of which led into Berlin; France depended essentially on trained attachés for outside collection, but within France developed to a fine art the *dossier* system. This catalogued every fact about persons of any consequence at all, as

50

well as about many persons of seemingly little consequence. Essentially a police job, this meticulous attention to the individual gave the government the kind of detailed information it needed for planning its defenses against all types of wrongdoers and for quickly neutralizing enemy agents. Thus offensive action was made possible through effective defence. But, the reader might ask, if this is true, how does one account for fifth column successes against France in the two World Wars? The answer is that, by and large, these were *alleged* fifth column cases; actually, the number of successful efforts against the French was negligible.

Steiber outlived Bismarck. But the Chancellor's memory lingered fondly in Steiber's mind. Unlike Napoleon, Bismarck rewarded service, and the talent for performing it, with high honors as well as the coin of the realm; Steiber had more than two dozen recognitions by the time he died at over seventy years of age.

Russia

THERE is an ancient Persian proverb which says,

Devaar moosh darad,
Moosh goosh darad

which in translation is, "The walls have mice, the mice have ears." Through centuries dark with betrayal and blood, the hunted ones of Russia, the plotters and the innocent alike, shortened the warning to "Walls have ears."

Contemporary with Walsingham and Elizabeth I was Ivan the Terrible. Simultaneous with Walsingham's launching of the forerunner of positive intelligence the Oprichniks emerged from the dark brain of Ivan as a negative intelligence agency to ferret out plots against his life. From that day to this, the

Russian has lived under the scourge of the police state, and uncounted thousands ceased to live because of the truth of the old Persian lines.

Until comparatively recent times, then, a mention of spying in Russia almost surely referred to those informants for the secret police who were charged with protecting the state against all who intended it harm. Thus, through the years, the Oprichniks gave way to the Ochrana, and that to the Cheka. Then the modern passion for alphabets came into vogue and there emerged the OGPU and the NKVD. But still, nearly four hundred years of secret police effort were punctuated with the assassinations of a third of all the czars of Russia, together with dozens of lesser officials, some royal, some of the nobility, and the heirs of both. With the emergence of the modern Russian state in 1917, the record descends into the murk of police-state secrecy and no man can say what have been the tolls under the alphabetic decendants of the Oprichniks.

Essentially, then, this was civil counterintelligence. But operating under the dictum that the best defence is an aggressive offense, agents of the Ochrana and Cheka insinuated themselves into all the capital cities of Europe during the 1800's to spy upon absentee plotters against the state, whether they were individuals or secret societies. When they struck, it was with scant regard for the feelings of the country that happened to be host to both of them. From this disregard it was but a step to consider any activity within another country morally justified on the basis of its being in the interests of protecting the home state. Thus our day has seen the continual flagrancy common to the Russian espionage effort, whether it originates with the Soviet political machine or the military.

But back in the days of Schulmeister and later, of Steiber, Russian positive intelligence work was undistinguished. Then military espionage began to be developed in Russia. By the time of World War I, the shadow of Russian cunning would lie darkly across the wreckage of men and nations.

Redl

As we shall see in the section dealing with present-day security problems at home, exploitation of the sex deviate for espionage purposes is a favorite *modus operandi*. The Russians proved in this connection that their appreciation of human frailties was second to none. Some military writers have placed as high as a quarter of a million the number of men whose lives conceivably were forfeit to the sexual aberrations of one man in modern times. The inevitable attrition of war would have claimed multitudes in any case, but because of the abnormalities of Colonel Alfred Redl, the total Austrian casualties in World War I were far greater. Redl's guilty secret was his own, until Russian intelligence got hold of it. Then they applied pressure, and Redl sold out his Austro-Hungarian homeland with a completeness and viciousness still unparalleled in our own day. Of slight compensation was the irony of his death. His own genius as an exponent of counterespionage was to trap him so hopelessly that he would have no alternative but to fire a bullet into his brain.

Of humble beginnings, Redl's rise in his chosen career of the army became rapid early in the century. So keenly analytical was his mind, so vivid his imagination, that Baron von Giesl, who then headed the intelligence service of the Dual Monarchy, put the young officer in charge of the *Kundschaftstelle,* an innocuous term meaning information service. It was, in reality, the nation's espionage arm. In five short years Redl engineered intelligence scoops of sufficient magnitude to bring about satisfaction to his chief and give formidable stature to the Austrian secret service. Some tricks of the trade practiced today originated in Redl's highly professional organization. He used concealed cameras to snap images of visitors unaware they were being catalogued. Articles almost certain to be used by visitors were coated with an invisible

53

chemical film to enable fingerprints to be reproduced later; such articles might be a cigarette lighter or the covers of a magazine in a waiting room. In the days before tape recorders, he caught confidential conversations on hidden phonographs of the old wax cylinder kind. A penetrating student of human nature, a scholar, and a linguist, he compiled the forerunner of modern technical manuals in counterintelligence. He suggested postal censorship, and at a critical period in the history of the Dual Monarchy, catalogued post offices from which trouble-making foreign controllers might transmit instructions or money to their hidden agents within the monarchy. A magnetic personality, he won the unstinted loyalty of his subordinates, and none, from his adoring disciple, Captain Ronge, to the least ranking clerk in the branch, made a move without the prompting echo in his mind: How would Redl do it? or, What would Redl think?

Socially he was just as successful, yet somehow he gracefully eluded the traps of designing mothers and eligible daughters alike. Nothing was suspected of the dark side of his life, his consuming preference for his own sex. And this took money, far more than his army salary could cover, for his appetite was insatiable. Yet never was he short of money.

About this time, in 1905 or 1906, von Giesl was promoted to the most important command in the army. He insisted that his protégé be promoted and accompany him to Prague. Accordingly Redl was made colonel and he bade farewell to the *Kundschaftstelle*.

Ronge, who succeeded him, had stepped into big shoes. Nevertheless, he was determined to make his own mark. He developed to a fine art the postal censorship Redl advocated. It promptly trapped one important agent operating in Vienna. The system was working, how well he was not to know until the shattering morning of the last of May in 1913.

For two months Ronge's counterintelligence agents had been taking turns waiting in a little room in the police station next

54

to the post office. But the alarm bell that could be actuated by the clerk attending the *poste restante* window of the post office never sounded. Whoever was supposed to call for certain letters that Ronge had examined two months ago seemed to be aware of the trap and avoided the post office. And for an excellent reason: The letters, addressed to "Opera Ball 13," had been postmarked from one of the locations Redl's own early research based on Austrian agent reports had shown to be sensitive. Accordingly the Opera Ball letters had been opened by Ronge's secret service. They had contained much money, and nothing else, an almost sure indication of underground activity. Ronge returned the letters to the post office and set the trap.

Then on the 24th of May the bell did ring. As sometimes happens, neither of the two agents on duty heard it right away, and by the time they did arrive at the post office, it was too late. The only taxi available was just disappearing with a male passenger. They were still fuming, when to their delight, the same taxi returned. They engaged it at once and demanded to be taken to the same place the former fare had gone, which proved to be the Kaiserhof Hotel.

As they were about to leave, one of the agents saw lying on the cab seat a suede sheath such as might contain a small penknife. He pocketed it, little guessing the enormity of the disclosures to which it would lead.

At the Kaiserhof the trail was cold. But the agents persisted. Nearby was a cab stand. A check of the drivers elicited the information that one cab had just taken a fare to the Klomser Hotel. It might or might not be significant. They decided to check further and themselves went to the Klomser.

There the agents came to a halt again. After all, whom were they looking for, what did he look like? They had only the vaguest of descriptions and none seemed to fit the gentlemen they observed. At this point, one agent stuck his hands in his pockets and encountered the sheath. He had an idea, a thin

55

chance but better than nothing. They went to the reception desk and turned in the little container, suggesting that perhaps one of the guests had lost it. The clerk thanked them and said he would inquire. The agents took up stations where they could observe the desk. They were prepared for a long and most probably fruitless wait. But almost immediately a well-dressed man of military bearing who had stopped at the desk registered interest in the clerk's inquiry and more in the sheath. He pocketed it, thanked the clerk courteously, and turned to leave. The two agents were nearly paralyzed with surprise.

The man was the famous Colonel Alfred Redl. Did this mean that he was the recipient of the Opera Ball letters? There was a hurried conference. One agent would follow Redl, the other would telephone Captain Ronge.

Ronge was incredulous. But he didn't let the news stun him. He directed his agent to go at once to the post office and recover the receipts that would have been signed by the suspect to enable him to withdraw his Opera Ball letters. Then he went into the secret files and came up with some of the monographs that his one-time chief had penned in his own hand. The top one was called "Advice on Espionage Detection." Impatiently he waited for the receipts. When they came he placed them side-by-side with the monograph. The handwriting was identical.

Meanwhile, out in the city, a fantastic game of hide-and-seek was in progress. Apparently sensing that something had gone wrong and that he might be the object of surveillance, Colonel Redl, the master, employed every trick of evasion he had ever known or taught. But the pupil had learned well from the master and knew the countermoves. It was only a question of who would make the first slip.

It would seem that Redl did. Apparently he committed the cardinal sin he had so often warned against, and he panicked. Some have disagreed and said that it was simply human error. In Redl's mind the need to gain time on his pursuer was uppermost. He employed a good trick, but in it was couched the elements of his destruction.

He reached into his pocket and removed papers. Apparently without carefully observing what the papers contained, he tore them into bits and at intervals scattered them on the pavement. With satisfaction he noted that a light wind dispersed them. He had especially emphasized to his pupils that they must recover every single clue. Recovering all those bits would require no small interval when time was so precious to him.

The minutes passed. He breathed easier, for no longer could he detect signs of the human bloodhound that had harassed him. The paper bits had done it. He slipped back to his hotel and prepared to pack.

The bits had indeed done it. Faithful pupil that he was, the Ronge agent had painstakingly recovered every piece and taken them to the laboratory. The counterintelligence men got their second shock of that eventful day. The reassembled papers were, incredibly, receipts for money from various European centers which Austrian counterintelligence, thanks to Redl, so well knew were hotbeds of espionage intrigue. Again the handwriting checked with Redl's.

So great was the possibility of damage to the empire if Ronge's worst fears were realized that he went straight to the commander-in-chief. In a top-level conference it was decided that even the Emperor should not be informed until, at least, the full extent of the defection was certain. Then a deputation which included Ronge called upon Redl at his hotel.

Redl was calm. But in that very calmness they read disaster. Quietly Redl informed them that the answers to all questions would be found in his flat in Prague. Meanwhile, he had some letters to write. He was asked if he had a gun. He did not, but asked that one be supplied. A Browning was obtained and Redl was left alone in the room, which they and he knew he would never leave alive.

The Redl apartment in Prague was secured by an elaborate

lock which only an expert could force. Such a man was Wagner, leftback on a local football team. Against his protests that he would let his team down if he did not play that day, he was commandeered. He forced the lock on the door and others on private cases and trunks. So shocked were the searchers at their findings that involuntary exclamations escaped them. Wagner heard them and observed their faces stiffen with anguish at the disclosures.

The next day the captain of the football team upbraided Wagner for his absence. The captain was also subeditor for a Prague newspaper. He had just seen a story about a fatal shooting that morning of the famous counterspy authority, Redl, apparently a suicide. A Browning had been found beside him, a bullet in his brain. Wagner described the scene at Redl's flat. The subeditor suddenly realized that he had a tremendous scoop, yet he dared not use it. He did the next best thing from his standpoint and published a story *denying* that security officers had found anything wrong in their preliminary investigation into the death of Colonel Redl. And now even the Emperor demanded to know the truth.

It was appalling. For ten years Redl, an Austrian, had been Russia's chief agent in Austria. Not only had he sold the Russians all his country's secrets in return for protection of his social secret and money to indulge it, but he had actually betrayed to them his *own* agents operating at *his* direction against Russia. Again, in an equally grotesque twist, when a tremendously important Russian plan for attacking Germany and Austro-Hungary was offered to Redl by a defecting Russian unaware of Redl's own treachery, Redl drew up fake plans that seemed to smack of some vague Russian treachery and showed them to his own government. Meanwhile he returned the real plans to Russia and betrayed the defector. For this he received a handsome bonus from the grateful Russians.

But all this was child's play compared with what was to follow. World War I first exploded in the Balkans. To cancel

58

military opposition in the south, Austria had years before perfected "Plan Three." Every gun, every soldier, and every movement had been planned to the last detail. It was almost a push-button affair. Now Plan Three was implemented against the Serbians. But to the surprise of the whole world, the little army of Marshal Putnik literally cut the Austrians to pieces. Everything seemed to be anticipated by Putnik and the slaughter was enormous. The surviving Austrians reeled back, their army almost gone. Re-formed through ensuing months, another army was fed into the maw and was in turn ground up. Austria itself was invaded. Although Austria, directed and supported throughout by Germany, eventually was to liquidate the Serbs, the empire ceased to exist as a military power, and the full burden of the war fell upon her ally, Germany.

Redl had sold his country's Plan Three to Russia, and Russia had given it to its ally, Putnik of Serbia. With Redl's suicide, Austria knew of the compromise of Plan Three, but time was too short to modify it greatly, for certain factors were not variables, geography, for one thing. How then would Austria try to modify whatever it could? Putnik imagined himself in Austrian shoes, thought as Austrian staff officers would. And he knew where to meet their hasty changes. Redl's treachery had done the real damage, and Putnik's assessments assured that the most would be made of it. All over the stricken empire countless women mourned the loss of their men. No woman mourned the passing of Colonel Redl.

The Russian secret service had indeed served well. But the nation was crumbling, and the Czarist rule of more than 300 years was extinguished in a roar of rifle bullets in a cellar in Ekaterinburg. A new order was born, one that would vastly extend the concept of defence through ruthless espionage offence in every country of the world. It was the octopus that would outmaneuver the devious Orient in the person of Richard Sorge before World War II. It was the octopus that would insinuate its way into every level of society in the Western democracies. And through the softening processes of its twin-in-subversion, political brainwashing of once-loyal citizens, Russian espionage would insure the betrayal of practically every important Western secret, from defence plans to the atom bomb, from order-of-battle to space travel.

IV

"Made in USA"

AND what of espionage in our own country? The official as well as the popular attitude for a considerable period of time was that spying was un-American—"reading the other gentleman's mail." This catch-phrase is expressive of a smug attitude, quite at variance not only with thousands of years of espionage reality, but with our own earlier history. Astute espionage repeatedly has served the country and even contributed to her establishment as an independent nation in the first place.

It is highly doubtful that the War of Independence could have been won by General Washington with only meager colonial resources to draw upon. The aid given by France was especially significant in determining the outcome.

Benjamin Franklin, aging as he was, sailed for France once it was obvious that war could no longer be averted. He knew the struggle would be long, bitter, and woefully draining upon the country. Never in history had a valuable colony won against a powerful and determined parent. France must help with money, men, and ships.

61

Immensely popular with the French, Franklin was also a realist. He knew that Louis XVI was himself hard-pressed; it would take more than charm to convince him of the wisdom of backing the colonies. The king reflected. What was the true depth of American revolutionary spirit? What part of the population did Franklin really represent? What were the colonial resources in men and materials?

To these questions of strategic and tactical intelligence Louis required answers. The so-called "Baron de Kalb" was sent with overt missions to the colonies. But his secret task was to satisfy Louis's requirements for a critical intelligence estimate.

Meanwhile, with winning social ways, Franklin was playing an informed, sure-handed game of his own at his headquarters in Passy. Not only the activity of the French court, but the very mind of George III of England was revealed to him. In London a remarkable woman named Patience Wright, formerly of New Jersey, operated a wax museum. So accepted was she at the Court of St. James's that she addressed the royal couple as "George" and "Charlotte." She also addressed many secret communications to Franklin.

But Louis still waited for de Kalb's estimate. When it came, the French king studied it and decided to advance the sorely needed foodstuffs and war matériel. There were some ten million *livres* in money, too, as a gift, and a total of forty millions in loans, about $200,000 and $800,000 respectively.

It is only fair to add that Franklin himself was being efficiently spied upon by one who posed as his intimate friend. As a scientist of advanced thinking, Franklin found more than mere congeniality in the person of a certain eminent British chemist named Edward Bancroft, the inventor of a dye process and an amateur philosopher of modest measure. And Dr. Bancroft was genuinely engaged with the massive intellect and winning personality of Franklin. But he was a staunch Tory, too. Perhaps he once had hopes of reconverting the great

Franklin to Tory convictions, but failing that, he sought to neutralize Franklin's efforts against King George. The two men apparently became firm friends.

In this atmosphere, it was no hard task for Bancroft to inform himself of Franklin's plans and actions. Bancroft would take his leave on occasion, giving as his reason for going to England his eagerness to act as an agent for the American delegation. He would next be seen in the Court of St. James's. Here he communicated all that he had learned to King George. Then he would return to France to resume his contact with Franklin, revealing to him documents and other data he allegedly had collected on Franklin's behalf while in London. Actually, the material Bancroft brought had been carefully collated and censored by Lords Wentworth and Suffolk, acting for the King.

Bancroft enjoyed the game. He was a born gambler and, ironically, it was to earn him the disfavor of the King. This came about when the strait-laced George learned that his agent was speculating in securities which dealt with American colonial developments. The King immediately suspected Bancroft of double spying, but essentially he was a double agent or courier only, for what he transmitted to Franklin, as has been noted, was not of his own garnering. The King dismissed him. It remained for Wentworth and Suffolk to quietly arrange an annuity in recognition of his services. If Franklin suspected that he was being tricked, evidence of it has yet to be uncovered. But in the larger scheme Franklin triumphed, and vital French aid came to America.

And now we come to Washington himself, who gave the Continental Army its first intelligence organization, rudimentary as it was. The records indicate that this was in August of 1778, and that the first director, if that is not too grand a term, was Major Benjamin Tallmadge. Tallmadge, a Connecticut cavalry commander, was instructed to recruit agents for missions back of British lines, especially in the headquarters of Generals Howe and Clinton.

General Washington himself exhibited that mixture of daring and caution which make up the successful intelligence director. He bade Tallmadge to report directly to him but on no account to bring along any of his recruited agents. That would constitute an "impropriety" which, if discovered by the enemy, would "blast the whole design." On another occasion he arranged for Tallmadge to communicate with him by means of secret ink. The chemical had been brought over by Lafayette. It was used by Tallmadge in an amateurish fashion that led to a hurried directive by the alarmed commander-in-chief. In a secret communication to Tallmadge he expressed fear that the British, too, might have the reagent for developing the ink,* and added that Tallmadge should

> ... avoid making use of the stain [ink] upon a blank sheet of paper, which is the usual way of its coming to me. This circumstance alone is enough to excite suspicion. A much better way is to write a letter in the Tory-style, with some mixture of family matters, and between the lines in the remaining part of the sheet, communicate with the stain the intended intelligence. Such a letter would pass through the hands of the enemy unsuspected and even if the agent should be unfaithful or negligent, no discovery would be made to his prejudice as these people are not to know what is concealed writing in the letter and the intelligent part of it would be an evidence in his favor.

Resourceful spies on the American side used other means of communication as well. There was Thomas Rivington, editor and printer of the *New York Gazette*. Slow to warm to the colonial cause, he nevertheless came all the way round. But there was nothing in the columns of his newspaper to

---

* Washington had cause for fear. While Lafayette's formula might have been new, the idea was not: as early as Walsingham's time there is mention by that spymaster of "... a chymical device ... which would make writing both invisible and visible again." Three bottles of the stuff were made and kept "by a corn-factor in Southwark—a person well affected."

show it. On the contrary Tory supporters in New York were delighted with his ever more fiery abuse of the Whigs and all their works. This was but a clever cover for the work he secretly was doing for Washington. With entrée everywhere in occupied New York, he enjoyed many confidences. The vital gist of them found their way to Washington via tissue paper expertly bound in the covers of school textbooks. Tallmadge rated him as a "gentleman of business, education, and honor." Ultimately the British found themselves unable to echo the lofty regard.

Tallmadge learned his business rapidly. For one thing there was always before him the bitter reality of what unsuccessful espionage could mean. Two years before, a college mate of his had died with magnificent courage at a rope's end when convicted by the British of spying. His alleged last words were to stir the hearts of his countrymen: "I regret that I have but one life to give for my country." The fact that both Nathan Hale and Benjamin Tallmadge were Yale men and both from Connecticut has prompted speculation as to whether there was organized army intelligence prior to 1778. But this is unlikely. Apparently Nathan Hale volunteered for a specific mission as a result of Washington's own directive to his commanders that they should seek such volunteers as line-crossers for single missions.

Hale's execution by the British stirred as much controversy as would that of Major John André by the American forces some years later when the treason of Benedict Arnold blew up in the astounded faces of the colonials. Cries of "murder" were angrily hurled against the British commanders when Hale died.

But unfortunately for the accusers, it would appear that Nathan Hale satisfied all the requirements of a candidate for a spy's death. True, he was a captain in a regular Connecticut unit. But when taken by the British he was not in uniform but in the garb of a Dutch schoolmaster. Furthermore, while records of the affair are very sketchy and generally unsupported by documents, it would appear that he had military information on notes secreted in his shoes.

General Washington had been in sore need of information on British dispositions and intentions applying to the New York area. He urged individual commanders to get it. Hale, who had both friends and relatives in the area north of New York, apparently believed he could penetrate the British zone.

Accounts vary, but evidently he succeeded in gathering good data and was on his way back. At an inn where he was to await a boatman to ferry him across a stream, he is believed to have been recognized by a Tory sympathizer who knew Hale for a Continental. Awaiting him at the ford was not the friendly ferryman but the redcoats.

He was hanged the next day. It is said that his request for a Bible was refused by the British commander. Washington was informed of his death by a flag-of-truce courier from Howe's headquarters.

Was it bitterness over the Hale execution that hardened the heart of General Washington four years later when appeals were made directly to him to spare the life of the handsome young Major John André? Even British writers have stated that the American commander-in-chief was too big a man for that. Was it overwhelming disillusionment over the treason of Benedict Arnold? Not likely either. Yet there was ample justification for a pardon had Washington been inclined that way, for André's case turned on a very fine point: when does a military scout become a common spy and therefore a candidate for the noose or firing squad? André was not on a spy mission when taken back of American lines. He was a scout sent by the British to meet the traitorous General Arnold, still in the American uniform he so thoroughly disgraced, and at Arnold's own request.

A vain, brilliant man who from childhood had shown a besetting impatience with anything that did not move rapidly and move in his direction, Arnold had come under severe censure for social conduct unbecoming an officer. Despite exoneration on all but two relatively trivial counts, for which Washington almost apologetically reprimanded him, he apparently nursed injured feelings. Thus when the Continental Congress passed him over for promotion to major general despite an impressive military record, he indulged himself in a full-blown persecution complex and apparently then decided that he would sell out to the highest bidder.

Washington still believed in him, even after Arnold had taken no pains to hide his displeasure at being given an active field assignment, which normally would have pleased such an able commander. Washington thereupon changed the assignment, naming Arnold to command West Point. It was a fateful decision. West Point was so strategically important that should it be lost by the Continental Army, a wedge would be driven, splitting the sorely-tried new nation north and south. It would be a blow from which Washington's forces probably could not rally and Clinton knew it as well as Washington. But he lacked the force needed to effect such a stroke. Arnold knew it, too. What would the British pay for his cooperation that would guarantee the fall of West Point and the delivery of its garrison?

Arnold sought unsuccessfully to get lists of American spies of the line-crosser type. Presumably he hoped to make use of one or more of them to open a line of communication with Clinton. A woman going to New York ostensibly on family matters and moving under a flag of truce actually was the first messenger for Arnold, knowingly or not.

Clinton then cast about for an absolutely trustworthy and suitably daring scout to make contact with Arnold. His choice fell upon a young Swiss whose parents had settled in London. The military life had not been the choice of André and, but for a maid who had not returned his affections, he might have died quietly in bed at a ripe age. Broken-hearted, André joined the British military. His excellent qualities marked him for early promotion. Once, captured by the colonials during an action, he had been stripped of everything—everything, that is, but a tiny picture of the woman who had long ceased to concern herself about him. Hiding it in his mouth, he still "esteemed himself rich" in worldly goods. But death was not yet for him, and he was exchanged.

At some time in his career he had made the acquaintance of Benedict Arnold. The schemer apparently felt on safe ground with André. Things proceeded apace. There remained the need for only one final meeting.

The British sloop *Vulture* sailed silently up the Hudson to a rendezvous six miles below Stony Point. The meeting took place on shore in the dark of midnight.

The final negotiations should have required only a couple of hours. But Arnold was effusive. Doubtless the thought of what he could do with $20,000 had some bearing on it. He made light of André's nervousness and insisted that the young man breakfast with him at the farmhouse of one Joshua Smith, an intriguer himself. Reluctantly, André agreed.

Hardly had they sat down when the air thudded with the fire of heavy guns. The Americans had surprised the *Vulture*. To André's dismay, he saw her swing about and race downstream.

Again Arnold's optimism prevailed. He would personally escort André to a point where the latter could go through the lines. But first he must change into civilian clothes. After all, an American general and a British major could not be seen strolling about.

André knew the rules of war. Yet once more he let Arnold prevail upon him. Arnold did escort him to a favorable point, then gave him a safe conduct pass under a fictitious name.

André was beginning to think he might get away with it, when he was accosted by three men in the woods. To his great relief, he noted that they wore the greatcoats of British soldiers. He said to them: "Good morning, gentlemen. I hope you belong to our party."

68

The three stared at him. "What party?" asked one.

"Why, the lower party," André replied, nodding toward the British lines.

He was invited to prove it. That was only natural. He explained that he had a pass signed by the American General Arnold. "But," he explained, "my right name is engraved in my watch."

To his astonishment, he was seized. The men were colonials who had come upon abandoned British overcoats and had gladly appropriated them for warmth.

Major Tallmadge now came upon the scene. He is credited with having suspected irregularities around West Point, although whether he had any definite information concerning Arnold is doubtful. He personally escorted André to General Washington, but the commander-in-chief refused to see him. Tried by a court-martial of ranking officers, he was sentenced to die.

General Clinton immediately wrote to Washington, appealing for André's life. As an enclosure was an astounding explanation written by *Arnold* as to how it came about that André was wearing civilian clothes.

Doubtless Washington was suffering acutely. He remained stony-faced before a deputation of British officers who appealed to him under a flag of truce. André was hanged, as Nathan Hale had been.

It is history's tribute to André that even the Americans lauded his bravery and high principles while excoriating the opposite qualities in their own general, Arnold.

Arnold escaped to the British and later led enemy troops against the colonials. He died in England, his passing ignored by the press, and in consequence unknown even to some who might have found it in their hearts to plead for mercy upon his soul.

The dismal precedents of Hale and André did not discourage Tallmadge's top deputies. Robert Townsend, for example, kept a general store in New York City and saw to it that the place was a congenial, cracker-barrel forum for all who cared to come and discuss any topic. Many did. His summaries made potent information. One man who came for supplies seldom joined in the talk. When he departed on one of the magnificent mounts for which he was well known, it might have been noted that he often rode off for Setauket, although he lived in New York. But then, riding was a passion with Austin Roe, and he went where fancy took him.

Whether he discussed horses with his friend Abraham Woodhull at Setauket is not known. But often following Roe's departure, Woodhull himself set out for the north. At a certain point on the Long Island shore, he would strain for the sight of a black petticoat and handkerchiefs. He was not a ladies' man; these bits of feminine attire were signals on a clothesline that Caleb Brewster would welcome him and his dispatches for General Washington. In due course Brewster would leave on one of his habitual trips on Long Island Sound, for he was a well-known boatman. Tallmadge would be waiting on the Connecticut shore.

It was a tight, well-found net that worked perfectly throughout the war. It is noteworthy that all of the men used operational names, Tallmadge's being Mr. John Bolton. None in the Continental service but the commander-in-chief ever knew that the cavalry commander was anything or anyone else than just that. There were others in Tallmadge's organization, of course. But he preferred quality to quantity. That might have had something to do with the fact that there never was a serious compromise in the whole seven years of the struggle. Unfortunately, it was a lesson little noted and less heeded by his successors in the business some generations later.

Venerable, stained, but proudly intact is a certain volume in the British Museum Library so slender that edge-on it can

70

hardly be seen from a few yards away. It is the record of secret correspondence concerning one of the more flagrant instances of espionage against the United States. This is not a product of recent wholesale Soviet operations, but covers the years immediately preceding the outbreak of the War of 1812.

Obviously rebound, the little volume bears on its original outer cover, done in a brown, marble pattern like the flyleaf of an old ledger, a square white space in which has been written in a black copperplate hand, *Essex*. The subtitle amplifies this: "The Essex Junto and the British Spy, or Treason Detected." The book was published in Salem, Massachusetts, in March of 1812.

The initial exhibit is a copy of a letter to the office of the *Boston Patriot,* signed by one Eben Seaver, concerning the validity of the exhibits which follow. He explains that the documents had been turned over to the Foreign Relations Committee of Congress. The chairman of the committee then called a night meeting at which he requested the presence of Secretary of State Monroe. Upon being shown letters from Lord Liverpool, Mr. Monroe asserted that he was familiar with the handwriting of Lord Liverpool, and he judged the letter to be authentic. Others sustained his opinion and also declared authentic a letter purported to be from Liverpool's secretary, Robert Peel, concerning the spy. The handwriting of Sir James Craig, ex-governor of Canada, was also authenticated, and this, considering the burden of communications under his name, was significant.

Then follows a reminder that the only condition upon which the spy, James Henry, had turned over the documents to the Americans was that his contacts in America would not be revealed since he "would never in any circumstances betray the confidence they had placed in him" and that he would not have betrayed the confidence of the British government if its top servants "had not been perfidious" to him. Apparently Peel

71

and Liverpool had not honored commitments made to the agent by previous operations personnel; otherwise the record of Henry's directive and subsequent operations against the country would never have come to light.

As it was, President Madison took a serious view of the matter. In a joint session of the House and Senate on the ninth of March, 1812, he said:

> I lay before Congress copies of certain documents which remain in the Department of State. They prove that at a recent period whilst the United States, notwithstanding the wrongs sustained by them, ceased not to observe the laws of peace and neutrality toward Great Britain, and in the midst of amicable professions and negotiations on the part of the British Government, through its public minister here, a secret agent of that Government was employed in certain States, more especially at the seat of government in Massachusetts, in fomenting disaffection to the constituted authorities of the nation, and in intrigues with the disaffected, for the purpose of bringing about resistance to the laws, and eventually, in concert with a British force, of destroying the Union and forming the eastern part thereof into a political connection with Great Britain.
>
> In addition to the effect which the discovery of such a procedure ought to have on the public councils, it will not fail to render more dear to the hearts of all good citizens that happy union of these States which, under Divine Providence, is the guaranty of their liberties, their safety, their tranquillity and their prosperity.

Chronologically arranged, the exhibits first show a letter to Mr. Henry from H. W. Ryland, secretary to Sir James Craig when he was governor-general of British North America. Dated Quebec, the 26th of January, 1809, the letter proposes that Henry go on a "secret and confidential mission to Boston . . . and there is no doubt but that your able execution . . . would give you a claim not only on the governor-general but on his Majesty's ministers which might eventually contribute to your

72

advantage [Henry was to remember this] . . . At present it is only necessary for me to add that the Governor would furnish you with a cypher for carrying on your correspondence, and that in case the leading party in any of the states wished to open a communication with this government, their views might be communicated through you."

The next letter is Henry's answer and ready acceptance.

This is followed by a "Most Secret and Confidential" letter of instructions from J. H. Craig himself. It is obvious that Sir James had confidential information which led him to believe that at least some members of the Federalist Party were sufficiently antiadministration in their views as to make them possible converts to a scheme for splitting the union and establishing a separate northern confederacy embracing the New England states. Sir James said to Henry: "The earliest information on this subject may be of great consequence to our government, as it may also be, that it should be informed how far in such an event they would look up to England for assistance or be disposed to enter into a connection with us . . . Although it would be highly inexpedient that you should in any manner appear as an avowed agent, yet if you could contrive to obtain an intimacy with any of the leading party, it may not be improper that you should insinuate, though with great caution, that if they should wish to enter into any communication with our government through me, you are authorized to receive any such and it will be safely transmitted to me." Broadly, Henry was to "obtain the most accurate information of the true state of affairs in that part of the Union, which from its wealth, number of inhabitants and the known intelligence and ability of its leading men must naturally possess a very considerable influence over, and will probably lead, the other Eastern States of America in the part that they may take in this important crisis." He was to give particular attention to the state of Vermont. He would be supplied with a letter of credential, which he was

73

strictly enjoined not to use unless he was absolutely certain that he was dealing with one who beyond all doubt wanted to come over to the British side.

As President Madison pointed out, and as Patrick Henry later outlined in a fiery speech, there was an organized political move in the northeastern United States to generate discontent and disaffection. This was, in fact, the "Essex Junto." It was Henry's mission, whether expressly stated or not, to evaluate this move and to make available to it the means of getting British aid for a full-scale secessionist movement.

There follows a series of reports from Henry to his master. These include one dated the 14th of February from Burlington, Vermont. Here he tells of remaining there "to ascertain the progress of arrangements for organizing opposition to the general government." He is obviously a man of political and economic discernment. His observations are such that had London been more inclined to follow them, not only might war have been averted, but a period of peace between England and the United States would likely have ensued. This would have enabled England to devote more of her energies and resources to prosecution of the campaigns against France.

But London pursued its own ways and Henry became uneasy. Still he worked. As indicated by Secretary of State Monroe, no names are included of those he actually contacted and worked with, and there is no statement of whether he actually did open a secret line of communication with London to serve the disaffected elements.

The situation thrived until the middle of 1811. But instead of union with New England, war seemed closer. Then came disillusionment for Henry. More uneasy than ever, he directed a letter to Lord Liverpool, then secretary for war and the colonies, calling attention to the promise of compensation made by Sir James Craig, and especially of one wherein Craig said that he would make available to him a post in Canada worth a thousand pounds a year ($5,000 in those days, when $12 would buy a fine suit of clothes). But the job had gone to someone else. Robert Peel, secretary to the unpopular Lord Liverpool in London, in an attempt to mollify the justly outraged Henry, suggested that an appointment which would entail £500 emolument would be quite enough.

Characteristically, Liverpool shrugged the matter off, allowing deputies to deal with the troublesome Henry, who by now was becoming apprehensive that he might be left without any support whatsoever. He petitioned Peel to advise him as to how he was to proceed in order to get some satisfactory post "without loss of time."

Then there is a gap in the record. The next entry is a reversal in more ways than one: Henry has turned on his lackadaisical and perfidious employers, and he has begun sending information to the opposition. His communication of the 20th of February 1812 to Mr. Monroe in Washington completely exposes the situation. ". . . I have the honor to transmit herewith Documents and Correspondence relating to an important mission in which I was employed by Sir James Craig . . ." He gives the opinion that continental powers treat the United States with contempt and do not forebear from embarrassing Washington because of a conviction that no administration ever could get the concurrence of a majority of its citizens to take a united, strong stand at risk of war. He offers himself in any capacity to influence such a unity. He believes that the publication of the papers may help, at any rate would "demonstrate a fact not less valuable than the good already proposed; it will prove that no reliance ought to be placed on the professions of good faith of an administration, which, by a series of disastrous events, has fallen into such hands as a Castlereagh, a Wellesley or a Liverpool . . ."

If hell knows no fury as the woman scorned, it has yet to know that of the spy scorned. President Madison's disclosure to Congress followed.

Cheaper by the Dozen

IT IS a curious fact that students of the history of positive intelligence activities in this country must turn to one of the more obscure of our wars to find the real precedent. True, there were spies from the first; Captain John Smith used them, or, to raise the fine distinction again, were they only scouts? But it remained for the Mexican War of 1846-47 to give us something in the nature of a definite organization to provide secret service for the military. Generals Zachary Taylor and Winfield Scott both utilized what were officially listed as "Spy Companies" for the commission of irregular operations against the Mexicans.

The essential point of this operation was that the membership was not to be of American citizenship, nor were the men recruited for the Regular Army establishment. For the most part they were itinerants, adventurers, and others whose records did not encourage scrutiny; they were Mexicans, or Indians of tribes on one or both sides of the border. In other words, they were indigenous to the land, a qualification that has become paramount in the "line-crosser" of more recent days. Money and excitement appear to have been the primary motivations of these people, as indeed they have been so often throughout the ages.

Major General Ethan Allen Hitchcock of the U.S. Army would appear to have been the organizer of this country's initial mass effort in low-level military spying. A meticulous diary-keeper, he traces the modest, and dubious, beginnings in mid-1847. His own account carries such interest that the reader is asked to forgive the length of the following quote:

Puebla, 5th June, A.M. I have taken into service a very extraordinary person—a Mexican, rather portly for one of his profession, but with a keen, active eye and evidently "bold as a lion" or an honest man. He has been a very celebrated cap-

76

tain of robbers and knows the band and the whole country. I have engaged him to carry a letter to the commanding officer at Jalapa, and if he performs the service faithfully, I shall further employ him.

Puebla, 20th June. The Mexican robber-chief Dominguez, whom I sent with a letter of General Scott's to Jalapa and Vera Cruz on the 3d, has got back here bringing a return dispatch from Colonel Childs. . . . Through this man I am anxious to make an arrangement to this effect: that, for a sum of money yet to be determined, the robbers shall let our people pass without molestation and that they shall, for extra compensation, furnish us with guides, couriers, and spies.

Puebla, 23d June. The robber Dominguez is a very curious and interesting man. When General Worth first arrived here, some person pointed out this man as a great robber and desired that he might be seized. He was living quietly with his family here, the people fearing him or the laws being powerless in regard to him. General Worth arrested him, but, after a few days, sent to him saying that he was arrested on complaint of his own people, and, giving him to understand that he had no friends among the Mexicans, offered to take him into our service. The plan took, and when General Scott arrived, he at once sent Dominguez to me.

I tried him and found him faithful. When I settled with him, paying him about $110, including his outfit, I suggested his bringing into our service the whole band of professional robbers that line the road from Mexico to Vera Cruz. He assented, but frankly spoke of the difficulty of giving security for their good faith and honesty. I told him to think the matter over and we would talk again.

The next day, Major Smith's interpreter (Mr. Spooner) recognized our Dominguez as the fellow who had robbed him on the highway: Dominguez took $5 from him and gave him a pass of protection from the robbers.

Last evening we saw Dominguez again and engaged five of his men at $2 a day, with himself at $3 a day. I told Dominguez to

77

find out how many men he can control on the road. He thinks some 300. I have ordered the five men in different directions for information.

26th June. This morning I brought twelve from the city prison into the presence of Dominguez and saw a most extraordinary meeting. Dominguez met some of his friends for the first time in years—men with whom he had doubtless been engaged in many an adventure, perhaps highway robbery. They embraced and swore eternal fidelity to each other and to the United States. I remanded them to prison, saying I would report their cases to the General and ask their release.

June 28, and I did report to the General, who ordered their release. I distributed about $50 among them and last evening I arranged with Dominguez that he should forthwith enroll about 200 of them. They are to be formed into companies and to operate under the orders of the General. We are to pay $20 a month to each man and they find everything. Each man counts, in fact, two for us, for if we did not employ them the enemy would; so that one detached from the enemy makes a difference of two in our favor. Dominguez says he will bring over the guerillas to our side or seize their chiefs and bring them prisoners to our general, etc., etc.

There is evidence of the Spy Companies' telling work in General Scott's campaign that resulted in his eventual defeat of the hard-fighting Santa Anna and the capture of Mexico City. One record credits Scott's Spy Company with having supplied him with information of such caliber that it tipped the scales of decision and primed him to launch the drive that ended the war. It was a campaign that went forward despite almost universal forecasts of disaster: Scott's lines of communication and supply were tenuous at best; now he proposed to lengthen them interminably through hostile territory, in effect to cut himself off in order to drive straight into the heart of Mexico. But if the information with which he had been provided was accurate he could substantially discount the extent of risk to his life lines. He believed it was accurate, plunged ahead, and won.

As danger diminished so did the need for the irregulars' services. Promises of payment remained promises only. Apparently President Polk had an appropriation he could utilize for such things, and it would seem that he drew on it. But either the commitments were made by irresponsible people, or the political and military machines simply were not set up to administer such unorthodox operations despite the official-sounding name of Spy Company. Some officers of high personal integrity paid out of their own pockets. When they did, it was their own decision, and their own loss, as far as the government was concerned.

With the signing of peace, even these amenities stopped. The once sought-after irregulars were bandied about, even ordered from camps. Doubtless the qualities which had been found useful to the army now posed threats or at least embarrassment, and their possessors were classed as undesirable. Some were ordered to get out of the country. Others still in the United States were advised that the best that could be done for them was an offer of transportation to the border and freedom to cross into Mexico, the one area on the face of the globe where they could not live, at least not for long. General Hitchcock's last entry is a curious mixture of compliment, rough affection, and relief:

Orizaba, Mexico, June 5, 1848. Left Mexico [City?] last Monday at 3 P.M., and got here this (Monday) morning at 10:30, under the escort of the Spy Company . . . The Spy Company I am to discharge, with their own consent, by paying them $20 per man at Vera Cruz—except the chief, Dominguez, who will go to New Orleans. He says he would be killed like a dog if he remained here. The remainder of the company expect to go to Campeachy on an expedition proposed by General Lane "on his own hook!" . . .

V

Civil War Spies—"Rebel Rose"

THE day of August 23, 1861, was saturated with heat
and humidity as it can be in few places besides the city of
Washington. But on Sixteenth Street a slender, striking woman
in crinolines seemed indifferent to it. She strolled leisurely, a
delicate parasol shading her face, small-boned and smooth.
If her expression in repose inclined to pensiveness there was
reason for it: she, of all the women in the United States that
day, was probably in the best position to know the desperate-
ness of the struggle her beloved South must win if its way of
life was to survive. But this pensiveness was remarked only by
those few who shared "the other side" of her life—a side taut
with danger and of vital service to the South. For Rose Greenhow was one of the most dangerous women to the Union government that ever lived.

Already a field of battle was littered with the débris of a
major Union defeat. What was to have been a gala outing so
that Washingtonians could witness the trouncing of the Rebels
in the vicinity of Manassas had been converted into a ghastly
Union rout. Across the fields from Bull Run that July day had

80

streamed horses without riders, wagons without drivers, frightened soldiers in blue without canteens, rifles, or cartridges. Confederate batteries that the Union commanders had believed to be far away had blasted swaths in the blue ranks. Confederate muskets by the tens of thousands, when there should have been only a fraction of that number, had performed bloody execution. What had gone wrong?

That night a railway train pounded along in the night from New York to Washington. In one of the coaches, lighted only by uncertain oil lamps swinging from gimbals, sat a woman with a slender face and dark hair parted severely in the middle. She knew what had happened and why. For her, things had not gone wrong, but right!

Her secret couriers all had got through to General Beauregard. In consequence of that, the Southern commander on the eve of Bull Run had known three things for certain: The Union forces would leave Washington on July 16th for advances into Virginia and "on to Richmond"; second, there would be approximately 55,000 men in the advance by way of Arlington Heights and Alexandria, thence to Manassas via Fairfax Courthouse and on to Centreville; third, the Federals were going to cut the Winchester Railroad and intercept General Johnston in order to prevent him from rushing to Beauregard's assistance at Manassas. In his hands Beauregard held an actual copy of McDowell's orders to the Union troops.

What more could a commander in a desperate defensive situation wish for? Beauregard subsequently stated that he was "almost as well advised of the strength of the hostile army in my front as its commander." His own masterly shifts put two Southern armies where there had been one before and a score of field guns to cover the lines of Union approach where there had been few, or none.

And now a month later the woman who strolled along Sixteenth Street knew how well she had served. Among her secret papers was a message acknowledging hers. It said: "Let them

81

come: we are ready for them. We rely on you for precise information. Be particular as to descriptions and destinations of forces, quantity of artillery, etc." A later message had filled her with exultation: "Our President and Our General direct me to thank you. The Confederacy owes you a debt."

If ever a defeat in modern warfare could be laid at the door of successful secret service by the opposition, it was the First Battle of Bull Run.

Rose Greenhow was not alone as she strolled toward her little house on Sixteenth Street. She had been joined by a prominent member of the Washington diplomatic corps. Neighbors who might have been peering from behind lace curtains, as they often did when the comely widow sallied forth, would not have been surprised. She was waited upon continually by men. And not ordinary men, but individuals of consequence. One who perhaps used to call oftener and remain later than any other had been a President of the United States. That was before the advent in the White House of the man Rose Greenhow despised even more thoroughly than she had admired James Buchanan. Other callers at her home would one day be members of the cabinet of the hated Lincoln. High-ranking Northern officers of the Army and Navy alike, resplendent in gold braids, sashes, and epaulets, paused for admittance to her drawing room as did congressmen, diplomats, and bankers. Maryland-born Rose Greenhow moved in the best of circles.

Her flattering attentiveness took in every significant word; her analytical brain retained and evaluated what she heard.

The extent and distribution of her favors for coveted information will likely never be known. Opinions depended upon political sympathies: to Southerners she epitomized one whose nobility ranked her with Caesar's wife; to some of her neighbors and most women Unionists she was one who worked long hours in indiscriminate bartering of her charms to exploit her helpless "male properties."

The fact remains that despite the most stringent counteres-

82

pionage measures the North could establish against her, she repeatedly succeeded in passing vital information to the South. Heaping audacity on cleverness, she smuggled petitions to top politicians in the North to cease the persecution which was shortly to come upon her.

As she strolled, she apparently was giving her entire attention to her diplomatic friend; one of the secrets of her success was the impression she gave of favored and exclusive attention. But now her brain was alert to a sense of danger.

Those men standing near her doorway she had seen before, and her lip may have curled with the contempt she openly expressed for Abraham Lincoln's "detectives."

Her friend was about to take his leave. She played for a moment's time. Then she heard the reassuring steps of another stroller behind her. That should be one of her own confederates, and there should be another in the neighborhood.

The diplomat bowed good-by; the stroller sauntered past. There was no sign of recognition. Only a whispered word: those men were going to arrest her.

Mrs. Greenhow paused as if debating whether to visit a neighbor or terminate her outing and go to her own house. In that moment she touched her lips with her handkerchief. It was a natural enough gesture on such a hot day. But the cambric had masked something inside it. In another moment she had chewed and swallowed the little paper that contained cipher characters.

Again she heard unhurried footsteps. Her second collaborator. As he passed she whispered to him: "They may try to arrest me. If they do, I'll signal you with my handkerchief. You know what to do."

She turned toward her doorway, ignoring the waiting men, who now moved purposefully toward her.

"Are you Mrs. Greenhow?"

She stared disdainfully at the short man with the beard that hid his lips. She suspected those lips would be cold and unfeeling, like the pale eyes. In her published account, Mrs. Greenhow accuses Allan Pinkerton of fidgeting at that critical moment. It isn't very likely. The stocky Scotsman had been commissioned by President Lincoln to give the North a complete intelligence service, positive and counter. The decision was based on Pinkerton's record as a tough, tenacious investigator. The detective organization he founded then, even if it was not to serve as an intelligence unit for very long, was sound enough to endure under the same name for generations. He was a hard, able man in any man's book and his name was to become a synonym for sleuth. Had her instinct warned her against him? Was her virulent contempt really born of fear?

She acknowledged her name and he ordered her into the house. She fixed him with a look of hatred. Had she been armed, she informed him coldly, she would have shot him like a dog. Perhaps she would have, for she claimed one notch on her pistol grip because a man had accosted her and died as a result.

For a moment she stood, defiantly. As if in distaste for him, she flicked her handkerchief over her lips and turned. A man a dozen yards away walked down the street. He would spread the alarm. Any of Rose's accomplices who came near the house would know to behave as the personification of discretion and innocence.

Now began the ordeal. She would write of it in detail one day: how the house suddenly was filled with men of a stamp much different from what she had known; how under Pinkerton's direction they began to turn the place inside out with scant regard for her heirlooms and most personal possessions. Every instinct in her urged her to resist with all her strength but she remained utterly aloof, icily calm. This was to be her weapon, then and for as long as she was destined to face her enemies.

The heat was even more oppressive inside the house than out. Now she seemed to feel it. Of Pinkerton she presumed that even a Yankee would not deny a lady permission to go to her room and change into something more endurable.

But he was not taken in; he put a guard over her and went to supervise some of the searchers.

Time was running out. Any moment now they might search her. And there were tremendously important papers on her person and in her room. Furthermore, she must get a warning out and across the Potomac, couriers from Richmond and Beauregard in the field must be diverted, held in suspension, until she could devise means.

It would not be the last time Rose Greenhow shifted the center of her attack to win ends. She sensed that the guard might not be indifferent to her sufferings. Her great dark eyes implored him. They had brought down men far better trained than he in the warfare of the social jungle. He was hesitant but nevertheless agreed. In her room she quickly removed from her bodice an incriminating paper. The luck that attends the bold was hers. Only minutes later Pinkerton sent a woman operative to search her until, as she said, "I stood in my linen." But not quite. Later she would recall that her shoes and stockings had not been removed, to her immense benefit.

Now she heard visitors arrive. She heard the sentries challenging and a frightened woman's voice replying. Rose Greenhow held her breath. But her closest friend and most devoted collaborator had been warned. Lillie MacKall came in, the picture of bewildered innocence. Yet these rough men really had terrified her. The two women were permitted to talk and their eyes said as much as did whispered phrases slipped into less guarded comments on the "outrage" being perpetrated by Pinkerton.

The papers: how were they to be gotten out of the house? Lillie might take them, but she would most likely be examined when she left. From the next room came sounds of furniture being pulled apart. The house search was obviously no perfunctory gesture.

85

Then Rose remembered and smiled in spite of herself at the silly sanctity of shoes and stockings. Fortunately for her and Lillie the styles for the women of the 1860's were far indeed from the revealing fashions of a century later. If Lillie's feet hurt from the pinch of the papers in her shoes as she departed in front of the door guards, and if her gait was a little stiff from the other documents wrapped around her calves, she gave no perceptible sign. Like Rose she had been thoroughly, but not too thoroughly, searched before being allowed to go.

In the introduction to her book published in England two years later, Mrs. Greenhow stated that she told all, only "avoiding disclosures which might compromise the safety of certain Federal officers whom I induced without scruple . . . to furnish me with information, even in my captivity, which information I at once communicated with pride and pleasure to General Beauregard." But actually she leaves to insinuation and imagination many details of her methods of keeping her line of communication operating despite rigid supervision.

As the days went into weeks, her house became one of the most closely guarded areas in the Union, which makes it the more astonishing that at no time was there a really serious interruption to her vital lines of contact with the Confederates. Doubtless Lillie's shoes and hose served often and well. But this frail woman was suspected too thoroughly to allow her to operate for long. There came the dark day for Rose when she was informed that Miss MacKall would not be permitted to enter the house again. It was a severe blow but worse was to come. Lillie MacKall had pushed herself far beyond her limits for weeks. Now the strain told on her, and word came to "Greenhow Prison" that she was seriously ill. Rose asked for a pass to visit her dedicated friend but it was refused. This, alone, broke her composure. She stormed, threatened, even pleaded. She sent word to the Capitol itself and was again refused. Then she sank down, whipped and beaten for once in her life, for word came that Lillie MacKall was dead.

86

It was a bleak period for Rose Greenhow. But out of her despair was born a hatred so bitter that it would sustain her to the end of her battle with the North, indeed, to the end of her life.

To this day speculation continues as to how she did it. Other couriers she certainly had, as we shall see. And although every day saw further curtailment of the visitors permitted even a few moments with her under scrutiny by sentries, nevertheless, until near the end of her confinement on Sixteenth Street, she *was* permitted callers. True, they were of the class and stamp surely beyond suspicion of treason, certainly of a level in society that would permit no bodily searches. Yet, who was truly immune to this woman's personality which had so many brilliant facets? She was permitted to write letters, too, though they were censored. Pinkerton himself scrutinized some of them. There was the series addressed to "Dear Aunt Sally." Inanities were hardly characteristic of the knife-edged Greenhow brain, yet trashy trivia constituted whole passages of most of these letters. But there seems not to have been even such a basic security precaution as checking on the identity of some of Aunt Sally's alleged friends and acquaintances alluded to in the letters. She wrote poems, too, and riddles. There is no question but that some of her directives to couriers were concealed in this gobbledygook, and soon another Rebel-bound messenger would bribe, steal, or deceive his or her way across the Potomac.

Why, the reader might reasonably ask, was this dangerous, treasonable woman not put before a wall and shot out of hand? The answer is that the administration did not dare risk the consequence of such an act. The upheaval would have been nearly as disastrous in the North as it would have been violent in the South. It is necessary to keep in mind the social standing and political strength this woman possessed. True, Rose Greenhow was of humble enough origin, but her rise was meteoric; she had "made Washington her cup of tea," to use her own words. Possessing innate charm and grace, she early won social position through her marriage to the serious-minded scholar Robert Greenhow of the noted Richmond family. Linguist, author, researcher, and friend of Lord Byron, Greenhow was respected and accepted everywhere. Then Rose's sister married James Madison Cutts, a nephew of Dolly Madison. At the time of her arrest, her brother-in-law was actually second comptroller of the U.S. Treasury, appointed to the post by Rose's admirer, Buchanan, and retained there by Lincoln. True, Robert, her husband, had died following a fall in San Francisco some years before that, but already the Greenhow name had become solidly established on the national scene and already his widow was known as a political force and confidante of such influence that she was listed as "the leading hostess of the powerful Democratic administration." Many a man, political and military, owed his appointment to her. She was also on close terms with every leading name in the international diplomatic circle, and no Northerner could afford to ignore the fact that her voice in receptive ears would quickly produce repercussions in Europe. To deny her access to those ears could have even greater repercussions.

One who had cause to know referred to her as "the most persuasive woman ever known in Washington" and "a woman of almost irresistible seductive powers." All this, too, despite the fact that she was then in her middle forties and the mother of four daughters. Her "wild freshness" had given way to a "softened loveliness, a great elegance."

One of those whose station precluded interference by the minions of the provost marshal, or of Pinkerton's office, was Colonel E. D. Keyes, who had been General Scott's military secretary. The striking pair often had been observed together, and more than once the inquisitive neighbors had grown too sleepy to keep watch any longer in order to note the hour of Keyes's departure. The looks that flashed between them in public were charged and meaningful. At one time it was rumored that they were to wed. In subsequent writings, Keyes sought to give the impression that the relationship was a mere peccadillo. But a more eloquent evaluation of La Rose's powers would seem to be included in his recommendation that "beautiful women should be considered as contraband of war and captured whenever found and detained until after the fight under the guard of old persons of their own sex."

Surely it could only have been through her importunities to gallant and once-favored admirers like Keyes that she was able to smuggle out and send to Richmond such reports as verbatim transcriptions of Lincoln's cabinet meetings. And surely the same human factors explain her ability to obtain them in the first place. Yet to accuse any one of her intimates in that day would have involved great courage or great foolhardiness. Nor has time revealed much more; what Rose Greenhow knew, she took with her to her grave.

She hints in her notes that at one time she made use of color codes in tapestries. She had developed a sudden interest in weaving tapestries. The provost marshal's office, doubtless relieved that she was occupying herself for once with domestic pursuits, itself supplied the yarns she needed for her creations. If Pinkerton had been as excellent an espionage expert as he was a detective, he might have suspected this sudden interest in aesthetics. Codes based on the sequence of colors in woven goods have been used in various periods of history, though flexibility of expression by this means is very limited, and such systems are too prone to error to justify their use in important matters.

Mrs. Greenhow hints that her little daughter, Rose, was of considerable help in smuggling messages past the indulgent sentries. Her mother appears to have sewn them between the soles of the child's shoes. But eventually even this channel was denied her when the little girl was placed under severe restrictions.

At times other women suspected of disloyalty to the North

were placed in "Greenhow Prison." Rose always risked the possibility that any newcomer was actually a Pinkerton "plant" charged with discovering Rose's *modus operandi*. But she sensed these *agents provocateurs* unerringly and froze them out. Just as surely she sensed loyalty and doubtless used such temporary prisoners as Mrs. Eleanor Lowe, an English woman whose son served in the Confederate Army, to take out messages upon their release.

With each success she scored, the security measures at her house were tightened another turn. Wherever she went now, a detective followed. "If I desired to change my dress, or anything else, it was obliged to be done with open doors and a man peering in at me. That every delicate sense recoiled from this indecent exposure may be imagined."

Had she ever slipped? Probably, but she confesses to only one bit of carelessness in the early days that caused her and Miss MacKall a moment of real terror. During one of the endless rounds of searches when furniture would be pulled apart, beds upturned, and clothing ripped open, the two women spotted an exposed piece of blotting paper that so far had escaped even their sharp eyes. On it was reproduced the cipher that had contained "the whole of my dispatch to Manassas on July 16th." The women were able to dispose of the incriminating piece just before the searchers ordered them to another room.

Still, she did not destroy everything of value. For instance, various researchers have commented upon the batch of love letters which, either by accident or design, she allowed to fall into Pinkerton's hands. These apparently were written by one of her most devoted admirers, Senator Henry Wilson of Massachusetts and chairman of the U.S. Senate Military Affairs Committee. That an intimacy existed between the two for some time there appears to be little doubt. Her "handler," Lieutenant Colonel Thomas Jordan, of Confederate Army intelligence, knew of this and urged her to make the most of her association

90

with Wilson. It would appear that she did. And doubtless there were many uneasy Union heads on sleepless pillows when it became known that Pinkerton's heavy-handed sleuths had uncovered a large volume of her correspondence. Another who had succumbed to the charms of Mrs. Greenhow was Senator Joseph Lane. There were terms of endearment and protestations of love in notes that came to light. The mystery concerning the source of her unerring information was at least partially solved.

Spymasters throughout the ages have seldom relied upon their own assessment of their female operatives but have sought opinions of other women. From women spy contemporaries of Rose's, came few terms of endearment. Mrs. Augusta Morris, for instance, who had been arrested on the personal orders of General McClellan said that Rose "enjoys herself immensely."

Pinkerton himself had cause to recall ruefully one of the first episodes that convinced him, well before her actual arrest, that Mrs. Greenhow was a most dangerous foe of the Union.

The night had been black and a spitting wind drove rain before it over Washington. Pinkerton and two others hunched their backs to the weather across the street from Mrs. Greenhow's house and kept watch. Slits of light appeared under the window shutters.

The men slipped across the street. Pinkerton kicked off his shoes. His assistants formed a scaffold of themselves for him, and he mounted to their shoulders. He peered. But before his eyes could accustom themselves to the light, there was a warning hiss from one of his men. He was spilled onto the wet ground with barely enough time to scramble into bushes before a man, head bent to the storm, came out of the night and after a brief, expectant wait was let into the house.

Pinkerton's eyes blinked. He had recognized the Union infantry captain in charge of the nearby provost marshal's office. That surprised him, but he received a greater shock when he was able to clamber up the backs of his assistants and peer in again. Mrs. Greenhow and the officer, congenial and obviously on the best of terms, were bent over a detailed map of the fortifications of Washington. For a considerable time they talked earnestly, the captain's finger tracing salient points of the plan. Then they straightened up. The woman fixed glowing eyes upon the Union officer. She placed her hands in his. They embraced. The captain held her tightly as they left the room. It was a long, wet wait for Pinkerton and his companions until once more the widow and her admirer reappeared, relaxed and happy.

When, at last, the officer took his leave, Pinkerton "tailed him," leaving his shoes behind in the hurry. The quarry turned in at the provost's office.

Pinkerton paused, wondering what would happen next. He did not have long to wait. Figures burst out of the office. Rough hands seized the master detective and he was thrown into a wet, cold cell. He had to concede that the captain had retained some sense of reality. Pinkerton refused to answer questions and was left to his own outraged thoughts. Only later in the night, when he was able to bribe a guard, did he get a message out.

Morning came and the situation was reversed. On Pinkerton's information, the captain was imprisoned. He languished there longer than had Pinkerton, a year, to be exact. However, he admitted nothing and nothing was ever proved against him. But his career was ruined; he dropped from sight and it is thought that he finally committed suicide.

Pinkerton's ruthless pursuit of the Greenhow case might have been delayed or ended by that smarting incident, but he was cunning, he was patient and indefatigable. As bits of Mrs. Greenhow's correspondence came to him, he studied them with painstaking minuteness, and bit by bit he drew a chart of a theoretical net. Then one by one he replaced theoretical names with real ones: Van Camp, a Washington dentist who was also

92

a courier; a powerful banker named Smithson; a Colonel "Empty" who in reality was Colonel Michael Thompson. But Pinkerton was not ready to spring his trap.

In counterintelligence, waiting to catch still bigger game is always a calculated risk. Eventually Pinkerton would win, but meanwhile Mrs. Greenhow scored triumphs of evasion. The days of the "Great Armada" arrived, to use her term. Actually she was deceived and deceived herself about the value of this information that came to her "by a little bird." Apparently history was about to repeat itself, and now a great fleet was being made ready by the North to smash Southern ports and strangle the life lines of the Confederacy to Europe and England.

Mrs. Greenhow knew that the information was a confidential revelation by Secretary Seward to a friend he had every reason to trust. She valued it highly. At all costs she had to get it to Richmond. She coyly states that the "little bird" slipped out with a message prepared in the cipher for which the North was offering huge rewards. Once, she says, the little bird in the course of the flight to the southland actually had to take refuge in "the dovecot of the enemy" for protection. The identity of this individual has eluded the most persistent researchers. Some think it was little Rose, others that it was a more glamorous messenger disguised as a charwoman.

The federal Navy had been too weak initially to effect more than a token blockade of Southern ports. True, it was to be reinforced to a point where it would seriously hamper Southern commerce in contraband. But only in Mrs. Greenhow's mind was it deserving of the term Great Armada. Her real and only triumph in this instance lay in the masterful evasion required to get the message through. Was it some presentiment that conjured up the terrifying proportions of an armada in the mind of this woman upon whom the bitter imprisonment was beginning to tell? For Rose Greenhow the "Armada" would indeed prove a grim reality.

93

In the spring of 1862 the Union government felt obliged to transfer Mrs. Greenhow to Old Capitol Prison, where even stricter security could be imposed upon her. But even from here she was able to transmit messages to the South as well as to cabinet members and congressmen, alternately berating and appealing. There was apparently no way of stifling her line of communication, although by this time the implacable Pinkerton had all but smashed the heart of her ring.

Late in May, 1862, the government decided to send her, and other female prisoners suspected or convicted of espionage, to the Confederacy. A pale, thin Rose Greenhow went, hailed by Northerners and Southerners alike for her unquenchable spirit of patriotism and service.

In the summer, President Davis sent her to England on a secret mission. Her luck at smuggling messages now applied to her own person. The Confederate blockade-runner carrying her evaded Union gunboats near Wilmington, North Carolina, guarding against this very possibility.

In France and England she was a public figure. Queen Victoria received her. She wrote a book which became a sensation. Not appreciating the strength of her position with Northern admirers in high position, Englishmen marveled that she had been able to do such damage to the Union cause. She became the toast of London. But, witty, brilliantly social as always, she never ceased to work for her beloved Confederacy.

Then came the time to return to America. Her passage was booked in a fast, specially constructed blockade-runner, the *Condor*. The ocean spanned, the blockaded waters off Wilmington lay ahead. The night was dark and gales had made the sea a frenzy, but the lookout aboard the Union gunboat was alert. At his cry, the gunboat veered, her sails bellied, and her funnel belched smoke.

For three hours the chase went on. Closer and closer to the river mouth raced the *Condor*. She appeared to be winning, her three funnels further darkening the night. Another shadow appeared dead ahead and the *Condor's* captain brought his ship sharply around to avoid a drifting hulk. But the next moment his vessel staggered and heeled. She had come hard aground on New Inlet Bar.

The Union gunboat closed in. Mrs. Greenhow stared at the wild, black water. It was her only chance. She demanded that she be put ashore in a small boat. The captain, horrified, declared that no small boat could live in that sea. But she had prevailed upon men against their better judgment before, and she prevailed upon this one now.

This time it cost the lives of the men who tried to row the boat away from the stricken *Condor,* and it cost her own life. Her corpse was recovered from the surf. The funeral cortège passed through a hushed and mourning Wilmington on the first of October, 1864. A military salute crashed out over her grave, for indeed she had proved one of the greatest soldiers of them all.

Some may reject the Greenhow chronicle as too exceptional to deserve treatment at such length in a survey of espionage. It might be argued that this was no secret service in the sense of an officially constituted organization. Rather it was an open defiance of authority made possible through the flagrant treason of United States military and civil servants on all levels. These were men sworn to protect the integrity of the country. They stumbled over each other to betray it. Rose Greenhow was merely the instrument of their betrayal, whether by force of personality, the hypnosis of extreme femininity, sex, or a combination of all. Certainly she could not have continued her work through weeks of tightest surveillance without outrageous collusion. But, with or without such assistance, she remains a study in resourcefulness, shrewd psychology, and perfect timing. These are tools of the successful operative in any land or age.

How did she enlist those who had no contact with her devastating personality? Couriers like the faithful Lillie might give their all for her at the Sixteenth Street house. But then there was the rest of Washington, and beyond that the Potomac, and often miles of territory patrolled by hostile Union troopers with scant or no knowledge of Rose Greenhow and her works.

How she got her vital reports to Beauregard on the eve of Manassas is a matter of record. Her prime instrument was a woman, like herself. Quiet, youthful Betty Duvall appears to have been very attractive with her luminous eyes, fine features, and raven black hair.

On this day in July she reported to Rose Greenhow. From the widow she took a small square of black silk sewn so as to make a very flat pocket. Inside was a paper closely inscribed with cipher characters. Miss Duvall knew what to do. Manipulating the heavy, ropy coils of her black hair, she slid the rectangle into one of the whorls until none of it showed. Rose Greenhow looked over her habit of rough grey homespun. She resembled the marketman's daughter she was supposed to be, and no one took notice of her as she climbed aboard a light farm wagon in the street. The horses trotted down along the Union side of the Potomac.

One account says that Miss Duvall was in no hurry, that her dusty wagon rumbled along until dusk, then turned into the yard of a Commodore Jones, a Confederate sympathizer related to her. Overnight the tradesman's daughter disappeared and in the morning was replaced by a young woman smartly attired for riding her spirited mount. In the company of a cousin she dashed off for the vicinity of Dumfries. Here they crossed the Potomac. Rose Greenhow herself wrote, "At 12 o'clock in the morning of 16 July, I dispatched a messenger to Manassas, who arrived there at 8 o'clock in the night. She got back on midday the 17th," which does not suggest leisurely travel.

In any event, as Miss Duvall neared the Confederate field headquarters at Fairfax Courthouse, a sentry in grey barred further advance. She spoke of her urgent need to see General Beauregard. But the man's hands did not relax their grip on the long musket with its glistening bayonet. His orders were adamant: no women were to pass; too many of them pretended to be friends of the South and were anything else but that.

Precious minutes were being lost. Betty Duvall's usually placid eyes flashed. She demanded to know whose orders these were. The sentry replied that they came from General M. K. Bonham, the provost marshal. Betty Duvall demanded to be taken to him, and the sentry, after hesitating, complied.

General Bonham was a Southern gentleman. He was not a man to be tricked, but neither was he blind to feminine charm and beauty. Years later the picture of this striking woman would still be vivid in his mind as he wrote of her. Her glossy black hair specially caught his attention. Well it might, for now she shook it out. To his amazement she took from it a black rectangle of silk. It was, she said, a "vastly important matter" for General Beauregard. Bonham was happy to forward it with the utmost dispatch.

The second phase of Mrs. Greenhow's vital enlightenment of Beauregard was through the aid of a courier sent by Rose's "control officer," Beauregard's chief of secret service, Lieutenant Colonel Jordan. No one paid attention to the stolid Donellan as he made his way through Washington to Sixteenth Street. It was all very familiar to him. For years he had been a clerk in the Department of the Interior. But one day he had not reported for work nor would he again. He simply faded from the Union scene. At Fairfax Courthouse he offered himself to Jordan in any service useful to the South. A shrewd appraiser of men, Jordan was convinced that he had here a dogged, thoroughly unobtrusive courier and one who knew Washington as his own hand.

Directed to Rose Greenhow's home, he met her penetrating gaze without a tremor. Here was one man who didn't seem to be concerned with Rose Greenhow's opinion. He thrust a small paper into her hand. Its cipher message informed her that the bearer was to be trusted.

Thankfully, she sat him down and got ready the last precious data for Beauregard. As unspeaking as when he had arrived, Donellan departed. He was not one to concern anybody, and no one was concerned with him as he rode in a leisurely manner along the Potomac. But his eyes were alert and penetrating. There was the horseman just where Jordan said to expect him. Passwords were exchanged and the cipher message changed hands. Sparks shot from the hooves of one horse as he was spurred to Fairfax Courthouse. The other turned and ambled back toward Washington.

There were other trips such as this. Not just one person, one incident, or a single line of communication makes the Greenhow story. It was not just Rose Greenhow, who in the years before had done many a favor for Union officers still truly grateful to her. It was not just one man who sold out, either because of honest political conviction, or adoration of a woman. It was not just one raven-haired girl whose heart lay with the opposition. Not any of these, singly, constitutes the story. Many factors, many people, all the emotions, the entire galaxy of human complexes: these are the things that defy any "typical" classification for secret service. The total Rose Greenhow epic is the stuff from which selfless secret service is made.

Civil War Spies—Kerbey

THERE were countless incidents of secret service in the War Between the States. Some like the Greenhow case are famous and fairly well documented. The vast majority died with those who performed them. There is no record of their commission and no measure of their contribution. Nearly all were the work of amateurs, likely the more zealous for that fact.

98

Even the so-called professional was a specialist in the art of detection only. Pinkerton had no training for positive work, nor was he a military man. The result was disastrous for the North.

It is no secret that Union General "Bob" McClellan generated more hostile regiments in his imagination than Jefferson Davis was able to create in all his recruiting. McClellan's apprehension of these illusory legions sparked his constant pleas for more Union strength and formed the basis of his reluctance to move. Doubtless he communicated something of this to the man whom he appointed chief of secret service for the Northern armies. Pinkerton's untrained eyes in turn saw strength where none existed; not so much because of outright distortion as inability to discern significant factors in what he and his assistants did observe.

He thus epitomized, in the breach, a basic truth in military espionage: not only must the eyes be there to see, and the communication lines exist to carry back the data of that sighting, but those eyes must also be servants of a trained and discerning mind. For those who argue against adequate budgets in peacetime to enable the proper training and employment of our agents, it can be set against their demands for economy that there is nothing more costly than expediency in espionage. It will never be known how much it has cost this government to rely on tyros for this vital service, whether they were in directorial positions or had roles as line-crossers. But if they find it expedient to be at all candid, those who have been associated with some of our amateur efforts in the recent past will admit to the rubbish supplied them as "information" from almost wholly untrained agents. Too often they were recruited from the homeless, the cold, the hungry—the flotsam of war whose patriotism was proportional to the prospect of a hot meal and the likelihood of being paid good money or, even more valuable, barter goods for any kind of a job. Even those agents with a streak of honesty and determination could

99

hardly know what they were looking for, if indeed they crossed the lines at all. Little wonder that field commanders distrusted reports from such sources.

But McClellan believed Pinkerton, and before him, McDowell, with no formal intelligence organization at all, had little choice but to believe the stories of panicky observers after Bull Run. Better had McDowell taken stock in the report from a mere boy, a Union-sympathizer, who not only had worked his way into the Confederacy but was in a uniquely advantageous position to gain valuable information.

Young J. O. Kerbey had acquired proficiency as a railroad telegrapher. Convinced of the rightness of the Union cause before the outbreak of open warfare, he proposed to influential friends in Washington that he go south "to see what he could see and hear what he could hear." It was to be considerable. But his first experience illustrates the axiom: It is not enough to be merely accredited as an agent; if one is to be useful, he must be attested as reliable. But, if he is untraind, such assurance is impossible.

In the fateful hours before Bull Run, the youth from Maryland was behind Rebel lines—Johnston's. It was a most auspicious position for a Union spy to offset some of the mischief of Rose Greenhow.

To his surprise Kerbey saw the unmistakable signs of a Confederate withdrawal from under the watchful eyes of the Union's General Patterson. It was stealthy and effective. But why didn't Patterson move to check it, or move against Johnston at all for that matter? Kerbey discovered the reason: dreaded "masked batteries" that in reality were dummy cannon made of logs, fence rails, and brambles. Here was news of the first magnitude and it had to be gotten to Patterson.

In the process of trying to get it there, he was captured by Patterson's own troops. Instead of seeing the general, he saw the inside of a stockade for many precious hours while the wily Johnston slipped cleanly away and made his rendezvous with Beauregard, anxious but now fully informed. At last prevailing upon a young federal officer, Kerbey was led to General Fitz-John Porter, Patterson's chief of staff. Porter, brave but conservative, heard the young man through politely enough, then dismissed him. Did the general believe him? No, frankly, he did not.

So there was the other side of the coin. The untrained agent had observed accurately a movement upon which hinged victory or defeat, but his unprepossessing appearance and undecipherable credentials had defeated him. Frantic with frustration, he could only quit the camp. The result was Bull Run and Johnston's surprise reinforcement of Beauregard.

Once more Kerbey was off, determined to make his weight felt. Fortunately he had left his credentials behind—fortunately, because he was next to find himself obliged to offer his services to no less than General Beauregard himself. He had been captured again, this time by an officious Confederate colonel of militia. The Rebel officer insisted upon delivering him up to the Southern field commander in person. The Creole, who reminded Kerbey of a "polite Jew," accepted Kerbey's offer to be of use as a railroader. He was sent to the Rebel rear. To Kerbey's delight, he found himself at a wayside station and telegraph office. By lazing under the open window, he could hear and interpret the code traffic on the wires. One line handled business to and from Richmond.

The strain of concentrating on the chattering instruments through the hubbub of soldiers coming and going, coupled with the Virginia heat one day, was beginning to tell on him, and he almost dozed. Then suddenly he was alert. The Richmond relay instrument was clicking at high speed. It was a report from Manassas to Jefferson Davis stating that more than twenty-five per cent of the total Rebel strength was prostrated by dysentery and diarrhea.

A quarter of the Rebel strength fully immobilized! What

welcome news that would be to McDowell! The rout of Bull Run could be redeemed with one smashing drive into the disease-ridden ranks of the Rebels. That night Kerbey slipped away with a complete copy of the medical statistics.

Through a country swarming with Rebel troops he made his perilous way. Despite darkness he barely escaped capture twice. When at last he saw the lights of Georgetown itself he knew he was near the end of his journey. Then came a cry to halt, not from the Union lines ahead of him, but from behind. He was taken again and his story that he had lost his way after visiting a sick friend and blundered toward the Union side did not seem to convince his captors.

He prayed that they might not search him. But if they started to, he would try to drop his hat. It would only prolong his life a few minutes at best, for in the hatband was fateful copy. The Rebels preferred to take him to the rear rather than shoot him then and there. Carefully guarded, he lay down to rest on the porch of an old house. Compelled for his life to dispose of the incriminating paper, he looked around him. A brief ray of moonlight, the only one that night, disclosed a small hole in the porch floor. The momentary inattention of his guards was all he needed, and the job was done.

Far south the next day he made his second escape. Southern chivalry, as mounted guards stopped to converse with a Southern belle, gave him the chance. He knew the whole country would be swarming with hunters now, but if it was hopeless to go north, he would go south. It was the roughest kind of going. Like a weary fox with the pack in full cry, he went, pausing only when complete exhaustion stopped him. He decided it would be better at night.

He was traveling through woodland when in the darkness ahead he saw a pair of glowing eyes. His nostrils caught an odor that he had first encountered after Bull Run where the fields were drenched with it. At that time the eyes belonged to some beast of carrion. Trying to detour, he felt his way to

102

the top of a log. His foot slipped and he stumbled into a soft mess that exuded a miasmic stench. His mucles went tight. Both hands were buried in the ooze of a corpse's decaying head.

Kerbey's mind nearly left him in that moment of horror. He ran crashing and sobbing through the black woods, utterly unmindful of capture. It would have been welcome if only to deliver him from that grisly token of battle.

Eventually he did reach Richmond. But not before his nerves and body gave way in a period of severe sickness. During this time he was attended by a Negro boy. Later he found that his secret had been penetrated.

"You-all say *down* south . . ." the boy observed one day, smiling. A Northerner would say it that way. But Kerbey was not betrayed.

In Richmond he managed to get his delayed message north. He had learned of secret lines of communication out of the Confederate capital for Washington, just as they existed in Washington for secret traffic bound to Richmond. Kerbey's cipher was simple, to a telegrapher, and he sent it to an opposite number in the North. What appeared to be careless scratches of the pen on the long, prosaic letter would really be the Morse characters for "five" and for "word": every *fifth word*. Reading every fifth word gave the reader on the other end this message:

> Been all through Southern Army, again obliged delay here account sickness impossible Confederate advance are exhausted half army sick balance are demoralized look under front portion Blanks house situated on hill road Manassas to Washington black roll of papers official proofs wish friend Covode secure them officers are there night students Georgetown signal South from dormitory will be home soon as I can.

In addition to the critical information concerning the acute debility of the Rebel forces at Manassas, Kerbey had made

103

the discovery that the lights of Georgetown contained a sinister secret: messages were being flashed nightly from the dormitory windows to Confederates waiting on the opposite heights. It was onto one of these recipient units, with courier horses saddled and ready, that he had stumbled the night he had been captured.

McClellan had been named to take over from McDowell. McDowell had been unable to rid himself of the spectre of Southern strength. McClellan was to have Pinkerton to help him prove it. When Lincoln relieved McClellan for his inaction, Pinkerton's organization faded from the scene as an intelligence organization.

Young Kerbey went on to perform efficiently in Richmond. His messages continued to stream northward via blockade-runners that rivaled some of Rose Greenhow's for efficiency. His cover story was that he was a Southern-sympathizing Marylander only awaiting the formation of the proper Rebel unit for such people. He was one day called to substantiate this story and was obliged to sign his name on Confederate rolls. In Washington, Edwin Stanton had succeeded Cameron as Secretary of War. Kerbey assumed that Stanton knew of his services to the Union while a Rebel soldier. It didn't seem to worry Mr. Stanton amid his multitude of other concerns. It didn't worry Kerbey, either, although it would.

The youthful adventurer-telegrapher mixed courage and daring with an appropriate seasoning of judgment; he seemed to sense when the game had gone as far as luck could take it. And he knew it was time to leave Richmond. Besides, he was homesick.

Eventually he arrived in territory controlled by the North. There he worked as a Union telegrapher. There also he met romance, and a requirement to sign an oath of allegiance. He accepted both. But though the former went smoothly, the other did not. His attention was called to fine print in the oath, to the effect that he had never borne arms against the Washington government. He considered and felt that in conscience he could not sign. Stanton surely would understand if he scratched out his name. But Stanton didn't. Through some inexplicable twist the harassed War Secretary ignored Kerbey's services. And when the matter of the scratched-out name was brought to his attention, he personally ordered the telegrapher tossed into Old Capitol prison in Washington. There is a possibility that the wily Stanton was actually paying the highest tribute to Kerbey by making him an unwitting *agent provocateur*.

Kerbey, however, was stunned, bitter, sullen, and stubborn. He shunned everyone. The prison grapevine soon circulated that he was a dangerous man to the North. The Rebel political prisoners and sympathizers, thronging the lice-infested jail that lately had housed Rose Greenhow, sought him out as one of them.

It would have been understandable under the circumstances had Kerbey defected. His actual behavior supports the point that spies motivated by idealism are hard to swerve in their loyalties. Again, it is possible that Stanton was banking on this. There was much about Old Capitol's prisoners that he wanted to know.

Despite the depths of Kerbey's bitterness, he realized that this was an opportunity to penetrate an entirely different Rebel objective from any he had attempted. He committed himself to nothing, but he grew more approachable.

Then one day he looked up from his bunk to see what seemed to be a vision. Incongruously framed in the doorway of his mouldering cell stood Belle Boyd, the famous *femme fatale* spy for the South. She was smiling down at him. As with most woman spies through the years, Belle Boyd has taken on attributes which make her seem a paragon of feminine beauty. Kerbey conservatively found her ". . . of light, rather fair complexion, hair inclined to be strawberry blonde. While she was not strictly a handsome woman, there was something in her manner that was very attractive." She was, he said, "lithe and graceful of figure," which might confirm another report that she possessed the best-looking pair of ankles in the Confederacy. She was not loath to display them in "pretty confusion" should it serve her purpose. Belle Boyd passionately loved the South, and she had served it as well in her dashing, far-ranging way as Rose Greenhow had in hers.

On this day, she "stepped forward smiling and, with hands outstretched, took mine in hers, as she said: 'I was anxious to see who it was that was here by Stanton's express orders.'" She then assured Kerbey that he now was "among friends."

Thus sprang up an apparent alliance between the accredited, yet apparently unfrocked personal spy of the Secretary of War and the "Cleopatra of the Secession." Before she was twenty-one, Belle had been reported as a spy numberless times, had been arrested seven times, and had been twice imprisoned.

Gaily, as was her nature, she schemed with Kerbey to smuggle him out of the prison disguised as the Negro boy who brought them their meals. She fabricated a suitable duplicate of the boy's ragged clothing and, with another prisoner, she applied burnt cork to Kerbey's features. Then Kerbey in disguise mingled with the Rebel inmates. He took their banter and occasional ill-natured cuffing as befitted a "nigger" and got away with the deception.

Belle Boyd proceeded to drill him on the escape route, the southward line of communication, and the list of forwarding agents that began in high places in Washington itself and went down into the heart of the Confederacy. Kerbey obediently memorized all the names and places. He knew only too well what excellent use the Union could make of such a rich supply of positive intelligence. Spies going south could benefit from it, so could counterintelligence in Washington, which was charged with neutralizing the South's espionage apparatus. The problem was to get out of Old Capitol prison!

The time approached when he was to substitute for the unwitting tray-bearer. But the day before the switch a prison

106

guard marched to his door and halted. Kerbey held his breath. Then the guard announced, "You are wanted at the commandant's office. Bring your things. Come on."

There was no time for anything. In near despair he obeyed the guard. In the office of the commandant, Colonel Wood, were his brother and a federal official bearing an order for his release from prison. It was signed by Stanton himself.

Civil War Spies—Belle Boyd

KERBEY went on to more adventures, but as a second lieutenant in the Union forces, bearing a commission signed by Abraham Lincoln. Belle Boyd was exchanged as a prisoner and went on to more dazzling achievements for her beloved Southland. Eventually she became, as Rose Greenhow before her, the toast of Europe and England, all the more hailed for her amazing exploit in getting there at all.

Just east of the scene of Rose Greenhow's last, fatal encounter with the federal gunboat and the sea, Belle Boyd's homeward-bound blockade cruiser, in turn, suddenly changed course and ran for her life, a Union warship in hot pursuit.

The Southern captain threw overboard valuable cotton and a keg of money. But shells dropped closer and closer. Belle Boyd sat atop the highest bale, the better to see the chase. If she was worried about the outcome, she did not show it. When the Union boarding crew finally took over, she received the handsome Yankee prize officer with a radiant smile. She and the Confederate captain were made prisoners. But Belle Boyd had, on other occasions, shown that her heart responded to male gallantry regardless of the color of the uniform. There was even the possibility of a convert, and the present officer, Hardinge, was good-looking.

The Union gunboat began escorting the Rebel vessel back to port, Hardinge aboard the Confederate. And Belle began the job of converting Hardinge. She did not have much time, but she was no amateur. Strangely enough, this time her heart was in her work, for she had instantly fallen in love with Hardinge and he with her. Together, they plotted to effect the release of the Confederate captain who had done his best in Belle's behalf.

Ashore in New York, news of the identity of the sensational Rebel captive leaked out. As could be expected, the newspapers made the most of it. Meanwhile, the Confederate captain escaped. There was an inquiry and Hardinge was court-martialed and dishonorably discharged. Belle was deported to Canada. Like Rose Greenhow, she had proved too popular for prosecuting.

She went to England and Hardinge joined her. On August 25th, 1864, they were married amid great display at St. James's church in Piccadilly. Belle's star was at its zenith with but one thing to mar her happiness: she dared not leave the security of English soil, for Washington was determined to lay hands on Hardinge. In marrying Belle, he had renounced his allegiance to the Union and now would work for the South. Why she eventually agreed to a plan that he smuggle himself back is hard to understand. He lacked the advantages of her personality and beauty. In the event of capture he could expect no leniency.

As it developed, he was captured and while he languished in Northern prisons, Belle Boyd in London was forced to sell jewelry and take loans to try to effect his release. But eventually even money could not help, for his health failed. He grew steadily weaker and died. Belle Boyd was a widow at the age of twenty-one. After the war she did return to this country. She became a success on the stage. Ironically, she died in Yankee territory in 1901 and lies buried there, in Wisconsin.

It would be appropriate to mention here that, strictly speaking, military counterintelligence in the United States originated

108

with the abortive Pinkerton organization which was formed primarily for information gathering. Technically more deserving of the credit, however, is the organization of Lafayette C. Baker. He established a headquarters in Baltimore for the apprehension and detection of Confederate spies. He was as singularly successful as his methods were dubious. Despite this he enjoyed the friendship of men on the highest levels. But postwar years saw this originator of true military counterintelligence in our country disgraced. Baker became involved in the robbery of a district attorney's office, with the connivance of the district attorney himself. Congress was unable to stomach any more and withdrew all budgetary support. There was no re-establishment of formal counterespionage on a large scale until the outbreak of World War I, although, as will soon be shown, foundation stones were put down within a generation.

VI

War with Spain—and a Beginning

THERE was little in the suave and buttery manner of the Secretary of War that spring day of 1898 to betray his seething feelings. He beckoned almost nonchalantly to the colonel who had just read a report before the special meeting at the White House. The meeting was to determine upon a plan of campaign to drive the new war with Spain to a swift, conclusive victory. Now the tall, slender Secretary of War was summoning America's first director of its first formally organized peacetime military intelligence unit to hear sentence of his own professional doom.

Secretary Alger's dark eyes flashed. "Colonel Wagner," he said, "you have just made it impossible for my plan of campaign to be carried out. I will see to it that you do not receive any promotion in the Army in the future."

Colonel Arthur L. Wagner of the United States Army became the first modern intelligence director to lose his job because he failed to find in favor of a predirected intelligence report. He would not be the last. Since then directors of military intelligence in the United States have had notoriously short professional lives in "G2" assignments. The pitfalls are

110

many and varied. It is an unpopular job. Those who are made directors of military intelligence sometimes wonder why they have been thus singled out.

What had led to Wagner's collision with Alger, and who was he?

In 1885 the Secretary of War had asked the Adjutant General for information on the armed forces of a certain power— it may have been Russia, against whom Germany's Bismarck was busy aligning allies to effect a balance of power. To the Secretary's surprise, he learned that no such information was readily available in Washington. Furthermore, no government agency existed for collecting and compiling such information. From this frustration was born what would become the Military Information Division of the Adjutant General's office. The grandiose name did not originally apply to the one officer and clerk detailed to "gather and file information concerning the military organizations of foreign countries in which, for one reason or another, the United States might become interested."

Four years later the military attaché system was authorized by Congress. It has functioned ever since, although sometimes with hardly more than a flicker, *overtly* to gather and forward to the War Department military information on the countries to which attachés were assigned. It became a function of the Military Information Division to select attachés, to pass them their instructions from the War Department, and to receive their reports for the Army.

By 1898 the United States had become restive at an unbroken continuance of peace and prosperity. Why not extract further satisfaction from Spain that had met, then over-met, every United States demand? The information bureau now occupied three rooms on Seventeenth Street across from the old State, War, and Navy Building adjoining the White House. A colonel headed the small staff. Unfortunately for himself, the colonel was Arthur Wagner. President McKinley had called an urgent meeting of cabinet members and service chiefs

111

to consider Secretary Alger's plans for investing Cuba's capital city at the earliest possible time. The President wanted all the information he could get about the feasibility of the proposal. One prime concern was the ever-present threat of disease in the humid, storm-drenched areas around Havana. Colonel Wagner was asked what information he had on the subject.

He had a great deal. He had consulted, among others, with Surgeon General Sternberg. That eminent researcher into the causes of yellow fever had spent much time in Cuba. He spoke vehemently against any proposal to send in troops during the rainy season, if they were to be sent at all. Wagner and his little staff sought further, but the findings all sustained Sternberg: Wagner's intelligence estimate was totally unfavorable. At the meeting he took a long breath and presented it, avoiding the eye of the stately, unpredictable Alger. The President considered. Ever a humanitarian, McKinley made his decision, and Alger made his.

As long as he was Secretary of War, he blocked any consideration of Wagner's name on the promotion lists. But he could not last forever. Unfortunately, neither could Wagner. His promotion to brigadier general was voted by Congress while the one-time director of the information bureau lay on his deathbed.

From that day some thoughtful men have held that directors of military intelligence should never be professional army officers. They have felt it would be preferable to have professional intelligence specialists, whose names never appear on officer promotion lists, men who would not have an orthodox army career to jeopardize by telling the truth.

These were considerations of moment. They still are. But policy still calls for directors of military intelligence to be Regular Army officers, whether trained for the job or not. And ever are their apprehensive eyes on their records. In recent times only one director let the chips fall where they might in the interests of better intelligence. He was the incomparable Lieu-

112

tenant General Arthur G. Trudeau, idol of every man who ever wore the sphynx insignia of military intelligence. And he was dismissed, too, for taking issue with Allan Dulles of Central Intelligence Agency. He proved tougher than those who had discharged him and went on to solid achievements in other departments of the Army before seeking early retirement to go with big business. The loss to U.S. intelligence was immeasurable.

Back in 1898, however, the nation was not ready for an intelligence service at all. Certainly the Army, which would seem to have had the greatest need for it, was not.

The War Department, perhaps as an expression of Alger's annoyance, drained officers and men alike from the Information Division until eventually only one was on duty. Similarly the military attaché system approached the vanishing point. Now only two officers remained on foreign observation posts; the others were recalled to routine duties, mostly in the fever-infested camps in the south. Yet the attaché idea was good enough to be imitated by England, hardly noted for that form of flattery.

Message from Garcia

EVEN SO, not in our history was an intelligence effort to have positive results so far out of proportion to the persons involved as had that of the Information Division. One of the most famous literary pieces of the day reflects this; Elbert Hubbard's "A Message to Garcia" swept the country. It was vivid, if somewhat inaccurate, even as to the title. There was in fact no message for Garcia.

In a curious and momentary reversal of attitude the War Department wanted information about the leader of the Cuban insurgents and the forces under him. If war came, those shadowy, shifting, and elusive guerrilla forces might be of real

113

value to the American cause. But co-ordination would be essential. On April 13th, 1898, Colonel Wagner summoned one of his subordinates in the Information office. First Lieutenant Arthur Summers Rowan was a West Point graduate assigned to the Ninth Infantry. He was also the author of a book on Cuba. He had never actually been there, but the fact could elude a reader. Whether it eluded Wagner is not known. It did seem, however, that Rowan was the man for the secret mission of penetrating the dark waters and darker jungle to locate General Calixto Garcia Iniguez, assess him as a possible ally, and evaluate his followers. If Rowan was impressed favorably, he should determine Garcia's most urgent needs. Second in priority was to determine Spanish strengths and dispositions. It would be no child's play. Capture by the Spanish would be as bad for the already taut relationships between Madrid and Washington as it would be for the scout.

What were Rowan's inner thoughts as he took off his uniform and got into civilian clothes for an espionage mission? Did he recall Nathan Hale, John André? Doubtless he did, but he went anyway. On British Jamaica he made contact with Cuban exiles. It was fixed for him to be hidden away between decks of a fisherman heading for Cuba. The Spanish gunboat that stopped the boat during the thirty-six hour trip did not discover him. On the day war was declared, twelve days after the session with Wagner in the Information office, Rowan slipped from his hiding place and disappeared among the fetid verdure of Oriente Bay.

As a penetration operation, the thing was rather better organized than many following it in subsequent wars. Rowan hardly made cover when he was challenged. Luckily for him the challengers were insurgent forwarding agents.

For six days and nights the party insinuated itself deeper into the humid Cuban hinterland. Rowan knew he never could have made it unassisted. His first impression of the *insurrectos* was a deep one and wholly favorable.

114

Then General Garcia, the tough, black-eyed leader fixed him with a hard, searching look. Where were his credentials? Was this a Spanish trick? Garcia fingered the hilt of a wicked looking bolo knife. Rowan wished that he had some written message for Garcia. He spoke the names of Jamaican collaborators. Garcia's hand dropped from the knife-hilt.

What did Garcia need? He needed everything and needed it immediately. He was so emphatic that Rowan, almost tottering with fatigue, decided to start back after the shortest rest.

If the trek in had been rough, the return was doubly hard. For now tough Spanish patrols searched the trails and frightened natives into giving information. Finally the party could move only after dark. The jungle at night was sinewy with treacherous vines, alive with millions of unseen animals and stinging insects. Rowan and his party reached the coast only to find that the hidden boat was too small to take the whole company. It had only gunny sacks for sails. Hostile patrol boats and hostile weather together failed to stop Rowan. He and a few others made Nassau and subsequently Key West. Rowan, threatened with yellow fever, managed to avoid contracting it. And he did get a captaincy for his brilliant work. Intelligence missions apparently could pay off for everyone: Rowan got his double bars, Garcia got his supplies, and Washington got military co-operation.

Wagner's little office, despised as it might have been by Alger, received another call. Unlauded in literature, the mission of Lieutenant Harry Whitney to Puerto Rico nevertheless proved of great value in the planning for the invasion of that island. But a typically impatient United States had by now dissipated its earlier enthusiasm for war, and General Miles's well-planned and executed military investment there got only indifferent shrugs. Our forces took Puerto Rico, but Whitney's secret reconnaissance, which compared favorably with Rowan's, received scant attention from the public.

Many still live who remember the epidemic of spy scares

115

that swept the country just before and during the early phases of the Spanish-American War. Actually, spy activity was limited to a few incidents generated, in the main, by a rabidly nationalistic minor Spanish diplomat operating from Canada. But this was not determined until President McKinley, urgently seeking some agency experienced in undercover work, turned to the Secretary of the Treasury's United States Secret Service. That time-honored organization had been founded primarily to perform two functions—protection of the person of the President and protection of the country's currency system against counterfeiters. Couldn't it add spy chasing to its duties? In the absence of any formal counterespionage outfit in the country, a department was created, and its staff went to work. The Canadian government cooperated fully. We shall see that the precedent would not be overlooked by another harassed President a generation later.

This country's irresponsible intervention in Cuba had set off chain reactions it was totally unprepared to cope with. (It would still be smarting under them more than half a century later.)

The Horizon Widens—the Philippines

ADMIRAL DEWEY's spectacular smashing of the Spanish squadron off Cavite in Manila Bay created a political as well as military sensation. Washington awakened one day to discover a foundling on its doorstep in the form of the Philippines. President McKinley hastily went to the big globe in his study in the White House. He later confessed he couldn't for the life of him have located the Philippine Islands within two thousand miles of their actual position in the Pacific.

Americans may have felt that the abdication of Spain from the Pacific archipelago of more than seven hundred main islands had left it a helpless foundling, but many Filipinos

116

did not. Rebellious elements had long been fighting Spain to bring about independence, and they did not now propose to simply trade masters and remain in vassalage, however benign it might appear. Spain's defeat seemed a glorious opportunity to realize their dreams. They banded together to resist American incursions even more resolutely than they had resisted the Spanish. Whether in the precipitous mountains of the interior or the swampy mangrove littorals, they proved exceedingly hard to flush out. They were fiercely proud and savagely effective under a phantom leader who personified their refusal to be adopted, the wily, hate-filled Emilio Aguinaldo.

Sixty years later, a march-past of thousands of American and Filipino veterans of World War II was held on Bataan Day in Manila. One section of the parade was composed of a single jeep. In it sat a white-haired man so shriveled by age as to be diminutive under his wide straw hat. But the black eyes, unaided by glasses, were piercingly sharp. They missed nothing. From the reviewing stands and the massed troops came a roar of applause. The parchment-like face crinkled even more. Those who knew him best stated that there was a gleam of happiness in the black eyes, a gleam that belied his never-altered assertion: "I hate *Americanos*." It was a last-word defiance becoming Aguinaldo, the old warrior who, at the turn of the century, had successfully led a rebellion against ten American generals and forty American regiments.

Possibly Aguinaldo would not have been there in the parade that day, and history since 1900 for both the United States and the Philippines could have worked out differently, had it not been for one person who was at least briefly associated with Wagner's old Information Bureau in Washington.

Frederick Funston had red hair and the disposition to go with it. He loved adventure, and there was in his stocky frame the drive and endurance to hold him to it once he had embarked on one. He had needed these qualities in Cuba, where, not so lucky as Rowan, he had run afoul of the Spanish while

117

serving as a volunteer officer in the Cuban insurrectionist forces. He had been tossed into a stockade, and there he stayed while Washington parleyed with Madrid for his release. Finally it was achieved, on the promise by the United States that he would not set foot in Cuba again. He came back to the States and was attached to Wagner's office for a thorough "debriefing." His information was seen as the product of an alert eye and a discerning mind, a natural for the little intelligence unit. But he was too active for bureau work, and when war was declared, he announced his intention of getting to the Philippines. He was commissioned in the reserves and soon he sailed for Manila. In fighting at Calumpit, northwest of the capital city, he distinguished himself and won a reserve brigadier generalship.

But as the weeks wore on, it became apparent that even General Arthur MacArthur, father of the man who would go down in Philippine annals as incomparable among white men, was having no luck in quelling the Aguinaldo rebellion. The United States had some 70,000 troops in the islands, but Aguinaldo remained at large. The balance still was frustratingly in favor of the little insurgent leader. It became mandatory for the prestige of the United States that Aguinaldo be brought to heel.

But where was he? Troops wore themselves out in the wet, steamy heat pursuing the elusive guerrilla. Rumor and counterrumor chased after them. Bandit forces melted into the jungle fastness, only to reappear momentarily with deadly bursts of gunfire from another quarter.

So it went until the 8th of February, 1901. On that day Funston in his camp at San Isidro on Luzon received a message from Lieutenant J. D. Taylor of the Twenty-second Infantry Detachment at Pantabañgan. At first it looked like just another one of those incident reports—a detachment of *insurrectos* had run into a patrol of infantry, and in the exchange of fire, some of the Filipinos had been killed. The leader had

118

escaped, but turned up later in company with the town mayor, who had induced him to surrender. Funston yawned and almost lost interest when suddenly he sat up as if touched by a live wire. He read it again. The leader was a courier from Emilio Aguinaldo with cipher messages for other insurrectionist chiefs in lower Luzon. Aguinaldo himself, it appeared, was located in the village of Palanan in northern Luzon. There he was known even to his bodyguard as only a minor rebel leader, one "Captain Emilio."

Funston's mind went into action. He knew it would be impossible to take Aguinaldo by conventional military methods —any movement of that kind would be telegraphed far ahead by means only the keen-eyed Tagalog guerrillas knew. He studied the map. Palanan lay inland from the east coast at the northern end of Luzon. A plan began to form in his head. A chosen band of Filipinos loyal to the United States and led by only a cadre of Americans, who would have to be disguised somehow, might be taken by sea to the north, then disembarked at night for quick penetration of the hinterland. By one ruse or another, Aguinaldo's stronghold would have to be breached without a fight, or the slippery rebel chief would disappear into nothingness as he had so often done before.

Funston requested more detail from Taylor. The reply said that Segismundo, the messenger, believed the messages asked for reinforcements from rebel chiefs in Nueva Ecija. Excellent! Funston would deliver those reinforcements himself! But they would be his own men. Long, hard work on the cipher messages finally broke them. They proved to be in a Malayan dialect and confirmed what Segismundo said.

Funston proposed to recruit a hundred Macabebes, fine little fighters who took their name from their home village; they had been loyal to Spain and now were loyal to the Americans. They would be the "reinforcements." He solved the difficult problem of explaining the presence of Americans with the group by providing that he and his subordinate offi-

119

cers should pose as prisoners-of-war taken by the Filipinos in an ambush in recent fighting. But the problem remained as to how to certify the genuineness of the "reinforcements" so that Aguinaldo would not detect their true identity before the Americans could spring the trap and take him alive.

An inspiration occurred to Funston. One of the messages had been addressed to the leader, Lacuna. Only a short time before, Funston's men had surprised a band of insurgents and had captured documents and personal correspondence of General Lacuna. He ransacked the captured loot. Not only were there letters signed by Lacuna, but some blank sheets headed Brigada Lacuna. Forgery was not one of Funston's accomplishments, so he sought out a competent Filipino. The reply to Aguinaldo's message of felicitation and help was a masterpiece of deception and in later years Aguinaldo acknowledged that it was this which really took him in.

General MacArthur approved the broad plan. Then trouble arose. A message from Washington informed MacArthur that Brigadier General Funston of the reserves was now to embark for the United States for demobilization and return to civil life. The cables hummed with message and countermessage. At the last moment Washington agreed to a temporary extension, and Funston's plan went into effect.

The Macabebes wore their own campaign-stained clothing, but their American Krag rifles were replaced by rebel Mausers and Remingtons. The gunboat *Vicksburg* carried the party northward. Then the Macabebes were told their real mission. Brown eyes gleamed and wide grins showed white teeth. Now cover stories were practiced endlessly. But that was not all— they had to learn the Tagalog dialect, for Aguinaldo's men knew that no Macabebes were on their side. Thus the Macabebes completed their disguise as pro-Aguinaldo fighters by linguistic cramming.

Originally they had planned to make the beach in native *bancas* and thereby give the gunboat time to get over the

120

horizon by daylight. But one of the sudden storms of the Philippines boiled up, and the *bancas* were swamped. A perilous surf landing was made in ship's boats, which then returned to the *Vicksburg*. The party immediately went inland. Now commanders became prisoners and soldiers became captors. The "prisoners" looked scrubby enough. Curious inhabitants along the trail regarded them half-fearfully, half-sympathetically. But in one key town, insurgent sympathizers would have been quite glad to cut the throats of Funston and his officers, had not the Macabebes managed the delicate moment by knocking the white officers about some and then suggesting that everyone in the town celebrate the victory.

Apprehensively Funston waited through the festivities, fearful that the potent rice wine would loosen tongues. But it did not. He was greatly relieved when a whispered word informed him that the bogus letter for Aguinaldo, along with others similarly prepared, had already gone forward by a special messenger supplied by the insurgent mayor of the town. Now Aguinaldo would have two days' reassurance—or warning, depending upon how well Funston and his interpreters and scribes had done their work.

The march inland began. The country was wildly rugged; there was nothing but dried corn to eat. And now Funston belatedly realized that lack of physical conditioning might ruin the whole business. In the strength-sapping heat the white men quickly lost their stamina and it could not be replaced by the meager fare of dried corn. They tried to catch fish with their bare hands but it was no use. The "prisoners" no longer had to simulate wretchedness. Even the Filipinos suffered. Day after day they went inland. Sometimes they scraped limpets from the rocks and ate them. They had landed on the fourteenth of February; it was now the twenty-second and there was still a distance to go. But every mile was like ten. The white men were done in.

Then came crisis. Word reached back along the column that

they were under observation. Funston told his Macabebe chief to capture the observer. To their intense relief he proved to be a messenger from Aguinaldo, who had received the letters and was welcoming the reinforcement column. But, wrote Aguinaldo, under no circumstances were the American prisoners to be brought closer than ten miles of Palanan. Aguinaldo the fox.

What could Funston do? What he did was eventually to bring down on his head charges from America of poor sportsmanship. But there was a question as to whether he was really guilty. The whole column was suffering now from malnutrition and exhaustion and a letter was sent asking Aguinaldo to send food to the "reinforcements." They would wait at Dinundungan, where as Aguinaldo had directed, the Americans were to be detained. It was this food that reinvigorated them all.

Now the main column went on forward. There was contact with Aguinaldo's outposts. Challenges were satisfactorily answered. After a tense moment, the head of the column went across a stream and into the town. The Americans lay concealed.

A double line of fifty insurgents formed a sort of guard of honor. The Macabebe officers forced their smiles and marched between the armed ranks to Aguinaldo's headquarters. Behind them the main body of the Macabebes now landed and began the same march.

But at a signal, they suddenly raised their rifles and began to fire.

In the house, Aguinaldo thought the noise merely a welcoming gesture and he stepped to a window to admonish his men not to waste ammunition.

At this moment one of Funston's Macabebe lieutenants, a paunchy Filipino named Hilario, seized the little rebel chieftain, whirled him to the floor and sat on him. Thus he felt that he was observing Funston's order that Aguinaldo be held but not harmed.

Now Aguinaldo's staff officers realized that the whole thing was a *ruse de guerre*. They drew their pistols. Shots rang out. One of Aguinaldo's principals fell, badly wounded. Others were wounded as they leaped out of windows. Aguinaldo was informed that he was a prisoner of the *Americanos*.

In a short time Funston and his officers had gotten across the stream and entered the demoralized town. They now assumed their true roles and took command. Amazingly, only two insurgents lost their lives in the fray. A number were wounded.

Word of the American success spread across wild northern Luzon with the rapidity that always has astounded those accustomed only to the electric marvels of civilization. Funston turned his force about, prepared for the worst. He knew that if the trip inland had been rough, the return could be all but impossible if the country remained hostile. To his immeasurable relief, it did not; Aguinaldo in captivity seemed to paralyze the people. The trip to the coast was made almost without incident and thence by ship to Manila. The back of the insurrection was broken.

Now Funston said he was ready to surrender his rank as well as his prisoner and be demobilized. Instead, Washington granted him the rank of permanent brigadier general in the Regular Army as a reward for breaking the insurrection.

General Funston was to go on from one achievement to another. He died in 1917. But Aguinaldo the fox seemed imperishable. He rode in that Bataan Day parade in 1959, and in some parades after that! * Although he never said so, he had presumably long since found it in his heart to forgive the red-headed man who had tricked him out of an insurrection.

* Aguinaldo's great moral victory came in 1962, when President Macapagal of the Philippines ruled that henceforth Independence Day would date from 1898 when Aguinaldo originally proclaimed freedom from Spain rather than July 4th, 1946, as set by international agreement with Washington: the new Independence Day falls on June 12.

A Prophet Emerges

BY AN unplanned cast of the line the United States had snagged itself, for better or worse, deep in Pacific waters. For nearly half a century we were to encounter Asian heritage, culture, politics, and ways of living so different from our own as to keep us strangers to one another; not so much in the Philippines, it is true, but in almost all the rest of the Orient. Our introduction to the East had been the thunder of Dewey's guns at Manila Bay. The period was to end with the thunder of Japanese bombs on our fleet at Pearl Harbor. It would be the end of an era, but not the end of our involvement. On the contrary, it would mark the initiation of a period of far more intense involvement.

That Sunday morning at Pearl Harbor represented, too, the culmination of this country's policy of deliberate blindness from the standpoint of organized intelligence. Because of it, Pearl Harbor was inevitable. Conversely, we shall see that the devastating triumph for the Japanese was based upon excellent intelligence studies, spot reports by a trained observer and their nearly flawless intelligence estimates.

It is pertinent to note here that the first unmistakable sign of Tokyo's dedication to intelligence occurred almost as soon as we became installed on Luzon as a military power at the turn of the century. Ironically, at the same time in our own intelligence circles there occurred an incident that seemed trivial enough but was actually heavy with implication and contained a near-fatal blow for American military intelligence.

In January, 1901 a lean, hatchet-faced captain reported to Lieutenant General MacArthur for duty at the Manila headquarters in the Walled City. The commander observed that Captain Ralph H. Van Deman was a West Pointer and that he had at least a bowing acquaintance with Colonel Wagner's

124

military information unit in Washington. Van Deman had a genuine pride in West Point but at mention of the intelligence office, his pale eyes kindled. MacArthur observed the flash of interest and probed it. The captain soon betrayed his convictions of the danger of inadequate intelligence organization in the Army and his abiding interest in seeing the deficiency remedied.

A few days later Van Deman was delighted to receive an assignment to organize a Philippines Military Information Bureau. By his action MacArthur had opened a door to a man fitted by temperament, desire, and dedication to bring permanent military intelligence into the service picture. The way was to be rough and, we shall see, at times in danger of obliteration due to prejudice, indifference, and persistent stupidity. Sixty years later students in the Army's Intelligence School were to think of Van Deman as the father of the Counter Intelligence Corps and of all intelligence in our senior service, for that matter.

Van Deman patterned his division on that of the unit on Seventeenth Street. Despite identical names, however, no official connection between them existed. There was one difference: Van Deman enlisted the aid of *undercover* operatives, all Filipinos except for one American. It was these undercover men who one day reported a plot by insurgents to perform what today would be termed a commando raid to assassinate General MacArthur, together with ranking members of the headquarters staff. By prompt, swift counteraction, the plotters were isolated, then scattered a dozen ways. (Counter Intelligence Corps was to smash a similar plot against General Douglas MacArthur in devastated Manila in 1945.)

It was at about this same time that Van Deman was interested to see sitting stiffly in the anteroom of the commanding general a Japanese naval officer in full uniform, sword and all. A ranking visitor from a Japanese warship, perhaps? Van Deman blinked at "credentials" the officer produced as military attaché to Manila. But such attachés were accredited on a legation or embassy level; in Manila, Japan was represented only by a consul. Van Deman's long nose detected a fishy odor. Three days later Captain Tanaka departed from Manila upon the official announcement that there would be no impediments placed in his way should he desire to do so. It had been ascertained that under these spurious credentials the officer had planned to travel extensively on Luzon. It was concluded that he was under orders to perform espionage and possibly to make contact with insurgents. At MacArthur's *Intramuros* headquarters came a dawning realization: Japan was vitally interested in the Philippines, and now that the United States was there, in Americans and all American affairs. Still, confirmation would be needed.

A few days later one of Van Deman's undercover men sent word that he wanted to see him. The counterintelligence man spoke in soft Tagalog of a Japanese who said he represented a boat-building firm, but who was singularly evasive when it came to details. Furthermore, his only credentials seemed to be blueprints for a type of craft of little interest to Filipinos. In short, the agent considered the Japanese to be a military officer doing espionage.

The Japanese was invited to the *Intramuros*. The interrogation was not in his favor. It was suggested that he follow Captain Tanaka homeward, and he seemed relieved to be able to do it. Headquarters had its confirmation.

Some years later the tables were turned on Van Deman, and he was given cause to respect the thoroughness of Japanese counterespionage. Following the Boxer Rebellion in China, Washington believed it expedient to survey the country paralleling the railroad escape routes from the interior to the coast. Could Van Deman's unit do the job without stirring up a hornet's nest? The well-equipped information division in the Philippines quietly sent out a survey party. Van Deman operated in the Tientsin area. He lived at a British pension in the

British concession. There was nothing about him, he thought, unless it was his military bearing, that might betray his identity. His plain civilian name was followed by a plain address, the American consulate at Tientsin.

The job was nearing completion. All had gone well and apparently no one suspected that this was really a military intelligence operation. Then one evening he returned from a three-week field trip. While washing up he was surprised to receive a visit from the Japanese postmaster of Tientsin. The man had a letter for him.

Van Deman was cautiously curious: Why was he honored by this special service when the letter was addressed to him at the consulate? The postmaster explained blandly that the "Captain" had been away so long, three weeks to be exact, he was sure to want his mail as soon as he returned, and so, here it was. Captain! This time the American's expression betrayed his interest. "You have Japanese cook," smiled the postmaster, bowing. Van Deman's opinion of himself as an intelligence operative underwent a downward revision. In big things and little, Americans would have to improve if they were going to match these people in intelligence craft.

What Van Deman did not then know was that his very zeal in intelligence matters already had set in motion certain official resistances that would work for the destruction of intelligence in the U.S. Army.

For the story it is necessary to go back to Aguinaldo and to realize that he was a foe of the Spanish in the Philippines before he was foe of the Americans. The Spanish had, in fact, banished him and his adherents from the archipelago in 1895 for insurgent activity. They took refuge in Hong Kong. One of the most active, known as Robinson, went on to Tokyo to enlist the aid of the Japanese. The Manila information division scoured the records and came up with something pertinent: the man was *persona grata* with certain high officials of the Japanese government organization that had most likely been

127

responsible for the activities of Captain Tanaka and others in the Philippines with similar missions. Van Deman's interest quickened at an application by Robinson to return to the islands, now that Aguinaldo was in custody and the rebellion crumbling. The application was curious in that Robinson apparently felt it necessary to give proof of his new amiableness to American authority: he included an impressive bundle of documents concerning personalities and other data of the insurgents, as well as mention of his own doings in international circles. It was a real windfall of intelligence information and Van Deman proposed to retain it for his files.

Surprisingly, there was opposition by General Franklin Bell, then provost marshal of the Philippines command. Bell was a man of substantial character, of positive convictions and at least an average distaste for being crossed. In the Robinson case he proposed to the commander-in-chief that the papers be returned to the applicant and that the man be admitted without further ado. MacArthur was, to use the modern phrase, an "intelligence-conscious" individual. He decided to refer the file back to Van Deman for comment. The junior Captain of the Philippines information division respectfully but firmly disagreed with General Bell and suggested, instead, that certain originals of the Robinson collection be retained permanently and others returned only after copies had been made. MacArthur's antithesis in intelligence consciousness, Bell irritably demanded to know what on earth for. The file came back to the commander-in-chief for decision. MacArthur decided in favor of the lean Captain and against his Provost Marshal.

Bell clamped his teeth on hot words that might have prejudiced his career; he was determined to go up, and he would, but he would not forget Van Deman, or his Military Information Division.

In 1903 the United States Army underwent a major organizational change. The General Staff system was introduced. In the main it has prevailed ever since. To the great joy of that small group dedicated to giving the Army an intelligence service, the Military Information Division of the Adjutant General's office in Washington became the Second Section of the General Staff. The Philippines office had only a short time before been made a branch of the Second Section. This was surely a major step, a belated but solid recognition of intelligence as a needed member of the military family. Such a conclusion and the elation attending it were premature.

General Bell became Chief of Staff of the Army. Meanwhile, the new Army War College in Washington which comprised the Third Section of the General Staff had burgeoned until it was housed in its own building instead of the private dwelling on Jackson Square. There had been only one convenience about the old location: it was close to the Military Information Division. The Information staff could easily toss books and pamphlets wanted by the War College into a pushcart and wheel the data straight over to the house on Jackson Square. It was done every morning; the college was one of the division's best customers, but now several miles separated the two institutions.

The president of the War College called upon the Chief of Staff. He suggested to Bell that the Military Information Division be moved bodily into the new War College building. The division was promptly moved. Whether anyone else's opinions on the matter were consulted is not readily apparent in the records.

A very short time later the president of the War College called again. He explained that the physical move had been accomplished, but that there should be two separate establishments under one roof seemed needlessly cumbersome.

A question arises whether this represented an honest confusion in the niceties of function versus organization, or reflected the Chief of Staff's dislike of the information unit.

In any case, Bell's reaction was prompt and decisive. The Second Section of the General Staff ceased to exist as such.

It became instead merely a branch of the War College; the Third Section was renumbered the Second Section. There would be an information committee, overwhelmingly composed of War College personnel with no knowledge of the intelligence unit's aims and functions and no interest in learning them. Thus the hopeful young infant not only found itself banished from its new home in the General Staff system, but even bereft of its identity as an intelligence organization.

That was in 1908. Military intelligence in the Army had suffered a catastrophic setback at a time when Japanese interest in the United States had burst its confines in the Far East and was sounding purposefully on the Pacific coast of North America, a time when the whole of Europe was seething with the political intrigue that in 1914 would erupt in World War I.

Coming Events and Espionage Shadows

JAPAN was still stimulated by its victory over the Chinese giant in 1895 and was openly resentful of the American attitude against Japanese immigration into California. Tokyo's image loomed over the Pacific horizon in ever-enlarging proportions in the minds of western Americans. Neither Japan's hostility nor American apprehension of it was lost upon Kaiser Wilhelm II of Germany. The erratic monarch could gloat one day over his China Coast naval base snatched from Japan's spoils of war, and chuckle the next over a plan to unite that same Japan with Mexico in a scheme against the United States. The Kaiser could hardly have chosen more fruitful ground for sowing his seeds of mischief. For Californians, with 60,000 Japanese immigrants within state borders, the back-slapping between Japanese diplomatic missionaries and Mexican military politicians just across the border did little to lessen "Yellow Peril" jitters.

Rumors were rife. Many of them were nonsense or were

130

mountains of fiction erected from molehills of fact. Yet time would show that some were too solidly founded to be explained away, and attempts to do so only made Washington the more convinced of danger. For instance, there were the clumsily concealed negotiations by the Kaiser with Mexico for the acquisition of a German naval base site on the Pacific coast. This was between 1905 and 1910 and led to immediate repercussions in Washington, so severe that Berlin apparently dropped the matter. Actually there had merely been a shift of pieces on the international chessboard, and now persistent reports came in that it was Japan who was making offers for the same site. The tension was maintained during the next five years, and the Grand Admiral of the Japanese fleet paid a visit to Mexico, expounding a blood-brother theme. There were sightings of Japanese fleet units off the coast of Lower California. Washington's nervousness increased; Japanese warships had shown the world at Tsushima that they were formidable. Yet oddly enough, the crack *Asama* now proved so badly officered that she went aground in Turtle Bay in the Gulf of Lower California. That was incredible enough, but still more, was the ineptitude of the normally facile Japanese in refloating her. The ship was there interminably while the bumbling efforts went on, and while her officers thoroughly familiarized themselves with the coastal waters and the surrounding terrain.

This situation reminds the author of an account which he did not hear until the mid-part of World War II in Australia. The story was told by one of the better intelligence officers the U.S. Army has had, Colonel Sidney Mashbir of General Douglas MacArthur's famed Allied Translator and Interpreter Section. Mashbir related a startling story of his personal uncovering of what, to him, were unquestionable proofs that whole companies of Japanese soldiers had traversed a part of southern Arizona in 1916 during secret exercises, proceedings that could only have been associated with the *Asama's* wallowing in the mud the previous year. None of us connected with

131

Mashbir were inclined to question either his veracity or his intelligence sense.

As an intelligence officer in 1916 with the First Arizona Infantry he had been detailed by that General Funston of Aguinaldo fame on a mission to seek the truth of rumors among Indians of Japanese columns present in northern Sonora in Mexico. Mashbir, who later acted as a spy for America in Manchuria, tramped across the desert (which he knew well enough to make the first map of it our Army ever had). His knowledge of the desert told him that even the Japanese, incredible marchers that they are, could not have made the trip without violating Arizona territory to the north for water. He made his estimate and headed for the area he believed they would have to touch. There he discovered Japanese ideographs written in charcoal upon the rock walls of passes of the Tinajas Atlas Mountains. They were, he estimated, the notes of column commanders who had gone before to those who would follow. His own Indian scouts told him that parties of fifty came ashore at intervals and made the killing march.

Mashbir hastened to send a detailed report to Washington. But in 1916, a General Staff that had no intelligence section for receiving and assessing information, appended a comment to the report that the ideographs "had no military value." Even in retrospect, as he was telling the story, Mashbir's mustachios bristled. The point completely missed by that commentator was, of course, that any indication of Japanese presence in Arizona or northern Mexico at that time had the highest military implication. One can imagine how a similar bit of information indicating the presence of Americans on Hokkaido would have been treated by Tokyo intelligence analysts at that time.

But the intelligence nonbelievers in the U.S. Army then still predominated. True, General Bell had gone on to other assignments after an impressive performance in the Chief of

132

Staff's office, but some who came after shared his views to the full. It would be Van Deman's fate to encounter one.

Returning from Asian duty in 1915, Major Van Deman, as he was now, was assigned to the War College staff in May, to the information branch. He was delighted but soon found reason to be appalled. He discovered that reports had been coming in from all over a warring world, gathered by conscientious military attachés and from intelligence organizations of belligerents on both sides, a treasure trove of information. But these priceless documents had never left the War College building. Van Deman found them in tall, dusty piles. In other piles were telegrams marked urgent filed by an information officer especially assigned to General Pershing, then engaged on the Villa punitive expedition in the same regions of northern Mexico that were giving so much concern to Washington. These had never left the room where they had been filed.

Van Deman went into action. He pressed the War College president with a recommendation that the Military Information Division be re-established to insure proper processing and distribution of pertinent data. The president listened, wavered, then sent the proposal forward with a favorable endorsement. Chief of Staff Major General Hugh Scott ignored the correspondence. Van Deman changed front. Since the president of the War College was chairman of the Information Committee, could he not on his own authorize some form of distribution? He could, but demurred on the ground that there was no staff for processing the accumulation, mounting daily. Then perhaps the Command and General Staff School at Fort Leavenworth might be prevailed upon? Leavenworth agreed.

Curiously enough, at this juncture Van Deman seems to have lost contact momentarily. The next thing he knew was that the plan had gone over, but too well. Someone at the War College, he said later he did not know who, had sent to Leavenworth an initial report. It was a most unfortunate selec-

133

tion. Given to our attaché in London under pledge of secrecy, its open publication shook the British government and in turn, our own. The resulting blast from Scott's office disintegrated Van Deman's new plan and almost did the same for Van Deman's job. Scott would regret that the action had not been complete.

Once more intelligence reports relating to a war rapidly becoming critical for the Allies were dutifully buried in the little room at the War College. Van Deman was in despair. It seemed that his star had truly set, and with it all hope of an enlightened intelligence program for the United States.

He was wrong, even though things got worse before they got better. But they did get better, and his fortunes with them. Before that can be told, however, we must examine other events in which intelligence had a vital bearing on our history from without.

VII

World War I—Intelligence Genius

DURING this critical period in United States affairs, others were doing the seeing and hearing for Washington—the Central Powers headed by Germany on the one hand, as well as the Allies with France and England in the lead on the other. But the Allies were doing uncommonly well, and the period marked a zenith for British naval intelligence.

This fact was not fully appreciated by Germany, and the underestimation was to prove fatal in her forthcoming decision to gamble all, in preparation for which she had greatly intensified her secret efforts to embroil the United States in a struggle with Mexico and Japan while at the same time affecting to support the peace ideals of President Wilson.

How was Woodrow Wilson informed of this? As we shall see, although our positive intelligence program had declined until it scarcely existed, good counterintelligence results were achieved by once more pressing the United States Secret Service into action. Washington was thereby made painfully aware of gross violations of America's neutrality by all of the belligerents. But despite the degree of knowledge, the full extent of Germany's intentions remained hidden.

One man knew that Berlin was striving to the utmost to bring about not only American disinclination to help the Allies, but America's downfall as well. Admiral Sir Reginald Hall, Britain's beetle-browed, peppery director of naval intelligence, had absolute proof of it in his safe at the Admiralty in London. The thing was so potent that even Hall, noted for explosive impatience, determined to keep it there until he was sure that his own government would use it to the utmost. This man, a near-genius in intelligence affairs, easily one of the best produced by any country in any day, was convinced that his evidence would mean salvation for an England so exhausted that she could not long survive what Germany was preparing next: the revival of unrestricted submarine warfare. He knew, too, that Germany was equally bled, equally exhausted, but for this one weapon. She had to use it or perish.

Yet Germany hesitated. Such a move could well break the back of the pacifistic camel in Washington. And sober thinkers in Berlin did not believe that Germany could sustain the weight of a new, fresh enemy, unless that enemy could be kept preoccupied by the eruption of a Japanese-Mexican threat on her southern border. It was true that Japan was still in the war *against* Germany, but she was no longer a serious inconvenience. Japan was, however, as we have seen, a silent, inscrutable worry to America and the Allies alike. Mexico was now openly hostile to Washington due to President Wilson's missionary zeal in giving Mexico democracy whether anyone in Mexico wanted it or not.

The White House crusader was equally determined to negotiate a peace for Europe. "Peace among equals" he clarioned to nations equal only in their determination not to have an indecisive peace, after draining themselves of youth and wealth alike.

It was to Germany's advantage that the discussions of peace

possibilities be strung out until two hundred submarines were ready to foray in a "sink without warning" offensive against all ships, neutral as well as belligerent. So convinced was Wilson that there was still a chance for peace that he grossly maligned the laws of neutrality himself: To facilitate communications between the German representatives in Washington and Berlin he allowed them the use of American-owned cable and wireless facilities for the transmission of encoded messages. Apparently it never occurred to his honor-bound mind that the German government was betraying his Christian altruism and using the channels for anything but peace discussion.

Admiral Hall knew that Wilson was being betrayed. And he knew that time was running out for England. If he could convince his own government that what he had in the safe was authentic, and that in turn it could be brought to Wilson's eyes in such a way that he would be convinced immediately and beyond reversal that it was not simply a British invention for tricking America into the war on the Allied side, only then could he confront his own Foreign Secretary with it. How Hall had come into possession of this documentary bombshell comprises one of the most fascinating stories of modern intelligence.

"40 O.B."

ON THE August day in 1914 when German armies in gleaming helmets and polished jackboots streamed across Belgium in the first *blitzkrieg* of modern times, a solitary little British ship tossed in the North Sea off the coast near the Dutch border. She had slipped across the English Channel during the dark hours after the declaration of war in response to secret orders. She was small and inconspicuous, but on her decks were steam winches of a weight and power out of all proportion to her size. Stout steel lines had been paid out fathom by fathom into the sea as the little ship inched forward. She was for all the world like an oversize troller out to lure a breakfast of fish. She was trolling all right, but her catch was far more important.

Now there were shouts from the wheelhouse. The maps supplied by the Admiralty, together with the almost forgotten secret plans for severing marine telegraphic cables connecting Germany with the rest of the world in case of war, said that another of the big lead-encased lines should lie at just this point. The ship moved slowly, rising and falling on the North Sea swell. Then the steel troll lines tautened and the vessel shuddered.

The crew, sodden and dirty from the work of grappling the encrusted coils from the deep, prepared to seize the loop of heavy cable as soon as the snorting winches had hauled enough of it alongside. Surely these few sweating Britons were in sharp contrast to the spanking, precision-drilled hordes of German troops in the brilliant, terrifying spectacle to the south. But history would show one effort to be as fateful as the other.

The cutting apparatus ground through the cable, snipping in mid-word the encoded telegraph messages it had been carrying. The winches hauled in more and the dripping stuff was coiled in drums. Another cut, and the severed ends fell back into the sea with a dull splash.

It would be a hard, time-consuming job under the best of conditions for any nation to locate the cut ends, bring them to the surface and splice in missing sections, and then to re-establish communications. England with her mastery of the seas did not propose that such conditions ever would be realized by German technical crews. Thus Berlin would be cut off from her far-flung colonies, naval and coaling stations, and from the rest of the world, just when the demands of war would make such communication the more vital.

Of course Berlin could take to the air, for the new marvel, wireless, was quite capable of sending signals across seas and

138

continents. But the burden of traffic would be enormous to serve both the needs of diplomacy and the military machine. More important from the counterintelligence standpoint, anyone with proper equipment could listen in on wireless traffic. England had the proper equipment in several coastal monitor stations, manned day and night. An intercepted message would be sent to a special laboratory designed to decipher the combinations of otherwise unintelligible letters and numbers. Because of this, England, and Admiral Hall, would know about the Zimmermann messages. The Zimmermann messages were to tip the scales of American neutrality and send the United States into the war against Germany.

So unostentatious, then, was the beginning of the end: the little ship with its wet, dirty crew tossing off the Dutch coast while the spotless legions marched. Some history commentators have seen in the contrast that day in 1914 a manifestation of British understatement, whether in casual conversation, in intelligence operations, or the conduct of a war.

The unit in London to which the coastal monitor stations fed the grist of their listenings was designated by British naval intelligence simply "40 O.B." Intelligence analysts of more flamboyant nations, and writers who mixed fiction with fact, read all degrees of sinisterness into this group of figures and letters. It became a symbol of cloak-and-dagger work. But to the little circle of mathematicians and other cipher experts pressed into wartime service by the Admiralty to try to crack the gibberish included in German transmissions, 40 O.B. simply meant Room Number 40, Old Building. Whatever in the world else? Number 40 was a dingy, soot-blackened, almost unnoticed wing of the old section of the Admiralty structures on Whitehall.* In it was included space for Admiral Hall

* On May 5th, 1960, as I stood at the entrance of the Admiralty Building gate leading to the one-time 40 O.B., chatting with an old uniformed guard who had personally known Admiral Sir Reginald Hall "and them eyes o' his that'd look straight through a man," the tall sooty wireless aerials atop the roof that had caught so much of history in those times caught another

139

(originally for his predecessor Admiral Oliver), for furniture, and a safe.

In the beginning there was not much need for the safe. The bright-eyed Scotsman named Alfred Ewing, who had a yen for acrostic puzzles and mathematics when he was a youngster, had been summoned by the nation from his professor's post in Scotland to set up a cipher-breaking bureau. Ewing had called upon some university colleagues of his and together they had waded into the jumble. Gradually it became apparent that the Germans were using codes that in turn were wrapped up in cipher. A code is merely an arbitrary substitution of words to mean other whole words or phrases. To say that between ourselves the word cauliflower will mean loaded transports and whalebone will mean New York City constitutes a code. Each party must have the list of equivalents, or code book. On the other hand, a cipher system works with letters of the alphabet as they appear in words or are combined to make words. There are many methods of encipherment. A simple system can be demonstrated on one's own typewriter. Suppose it is agreed to give each letter of the alphabet a number, with a being 1, z being 26, and all the intervening letters being numbered serially. In that case the letter n would be 14 and the letter d would be 4. The word and then would be typed 1 14 4. To complicate it, agree further that instead of using the simple numbers we will press the capital-letter key of the typewriter, and thus get L L$ $ instead of 1 14 4 for the word and. That is a cipher. Now supposing a code agreement provides for the word and always to be represented by one or a number of other words, such as sugar or mint or rain. "Rain," already a code word, in turn enciphered in this most simple system would be 18 1 9 14. In the more complicated system, it would come out L' L (L$. They'd both mean "and" to the recipient who

historic message, and it was relayed down to us by a messenger with excitement in his voice. "He's gone up—an' he's come back down, by gum!" He was speaking of America's first spaceman, Alan Shepard.

140

had the code book of word substitutions and a copy of the cipher system. Cipher systems, of course, can become fantastically complicated. But what one mathematican can concoct, another may be able to unravel, laws of mathematics being what they are, provided there is ample material to work on. This is true even though encipherment may be protected by a key word that is changed daily. On the other hand, endless tomes of material must be available to reconstruct a code.

That is why, clever and patient as they were, Ewing and his devoted group were making only modest progress. Then a number of events in widely separated parts of the war zone occurred. In one a ship ran upon fog-shrouded rocks in the Baltic. In another a young man with a relative in England was found by the Germans at a defunct wireless station in Brussels, and in Persia a man lost some personal baggage. These, together with the sinking of certain German submarines in relatively shallow water combined to give Ewing what he had to have to eventually become a facile reader of the ceaseless traffic from Nauen, Berlin's high-powered transmitting station.

The Baltic was a relatively unimportant zone of naval activity in 1914. Mostly third-rate German and Russian vessels were involved, both Germany and Britain engaging their powerful units for control of the North Sea. Lesser German ships were occupied in destroying lighthouses on Baltic shores and sowing mines, when on August 26th their light cruiser *Magdeburg,* feeling through fog, grounded heavily on the rocks. Her plating went like cardboard and the sea poured into her. She went fast. From all over the stricken hull sailors plunged into the sea. Out of the wall of fog came the reassuring calls of their comrades in the German destroyer *V26.* She put out boats to make rescues. The boats became dangerously overloaded.

Then the fog curtain jumped with flashes and reverberations. The sea leaped as shells from the Russian light cruisers *Bogatyr* and *Pallada* threw up cascades. The *V26* gathered her boats and sped off. Now Russian small boats combed the area. They took in swimmers and floating bodies. One of the latter, in his death throes, still clasped a book. It was weighted and would have sunk except for the seaman's dying embrace.

The Russian commanders knew they had the *Magdeburg*'s naval code book. Unbelievable to us today, the Russian high command decided it should go to England's director of naval intelligence, who might know what to do with it. Ewing had his first great "assist." Much of what Nauen was handling for the German Navy now began to make sense.

But at this juncture another powerful station came on the air. Direction finders located it in the German-occupied city of Brussels. Ewing could do little with its snarl of numbers and letters. Obviously another code, possibly one used by the German diplomatic corps. It seemed hopeless.

Then Allied espionage agent H523 in Europe discovered the young technician at the wireless station and learned that he now was a code clerk for the Germans and that he had a blood relative in England where he had been born; he actually possessed British citizenship as well as Austrian! Using techniques so popular with the Soviets in another generation of espionage, Allied contact men isolated the relative and persuaded her to write a letter imploring the young man to secretly serve England. The devious channels were again resorted to and the letter was given special delivery by the Allied agent. He was months persuading the code clerk to agree to copy pages of the German code book bit by bit and turn them over to him. At last, with the final pages in his fist and panic in his heart, he slipped away from the code room and was never seen alive again. But his copies reached 40 O.B., and Ewing had his second great assist.

It is perhaps natural that on the Allied side the story of Lawrence of Arabia should have achieved such popularity,

142

and just as natural that his quite as legendary opposite number on the German side should not be at all so well known. But to Persians in 1914, Wilhelm Wassmuss was entirely well known as the German vice-consul at Bushire in the Persian Gulf. British intelligence knew him as one of the most dangerous operatives they had to face. He was as dedicated to winning over the oil-rich Persians for the Kaiser's Berlin-to-Bagdad dream as Lawrence was in becoming the phenomenal leader of the Arabs that he became. Daring, imaginative, inspired at times they both were, tremendously destructive as their tribesmen swept after them in their flowing white robes. The depredations of Wassmuss caused the British the utmost concern, nor were all Persians pleased either. Time after time the British would swoop down on what appeared to be a sure dissolution of their guest. But their quarry was so elusive that they never took him and even in the midst of their disappointment they were moved to admiration.

At Bebehen where the Khan actually had trapped the clever German for the express purpose of earning British gratitude and gold, particularly the latter, all the hard-riding British raiding party got for its efforts was the sight of Wassmuss' dust in the distance. If it was any satisfaction, they knew they had been close—Wassmuss had been compelled to abandon personal baggage and quantities of propaganda material.

Months later in London Admiral Hall was reviewing the situation. There were grimly amusing reports of Wassmuss' inordinate annoyance at the loss of his baggage. Hall's steeltrap mind closed on the point: The German's whole mission was fully known to the British; why then his deep concern? Word went out to locate the gear. Surprisingly, it was stored a stone's throw away from 40 O.B.

Hidden in it, when they unstrapped it, was Ewing's third big assist, Wassmuss' code and cipher books.

A submarine fatally attacked has slight if any opportunity to dispose of code books. The nation owning the craft can only hope that she sinks in water too deep to permit enemy diving operations. The German mine-laying submarine *UC-44* went to her grave in shallow coastal water. A British diver got into her black depths crowded with drowned machinery and peopled by corpses swaying grotesquely in the slow currents. During his search he had to prod aside one that seemed determined to enfold him in some blind act of obstruction. But the diver found the signal book, still fruitlessly weighted. Ewing welcomed it. Together with one or two others from similar ships, it helped fill in hitherto indecipherable groups.

Now by the end of 1916 and early 1917, Hall knew much; among other things, that while German minister Count von Bernstorff in Washington was denying any knowledge of alleged unfriendly acts by Germany against the United States, he was using Wilson's own naïvely loaned cables for the transmission of messages to report the progress of both the sabotage and the deceptions.

But Hall knew that to reveal this in America would generate a derisive, even angry chorus of "British trick!" Furthermore, it would surely reveal to the Germans the efficiency of British interception and cryptanalysis. (The Germans at Neumünster were doing the same thing but with much less effect.) So it was that when Ewing presented him with the biggest disclosure, Hall was sorely perplexed to know how to avoid American rejection.

Employing its total resources, 40 O.B. had cracked a long diplomatic message from German foreign affairs secretary Arthur Zimmermann to the German minister in Mexico, von Eckhardt. This message was included in a still longer one to von Bernstorff with instructions to see that von Eckhardt got it "by a safe route." Von Bernstorff lifted the part for von Eckhardt and sent it, still in the same code, via Western Union out of Washington on January 19th, 1918.

The original came to von Bernstorff by courtesy of President
144

Wilson over the State Department cable. (To be triply sure, Zimmermann also had sent it via two other slower routes, one from Nauen to the big commercial wireless station at Sayville, N.Y.)

As finally broken by 40 O.B., the von Eckhardt message read:

> We intend to begin unrestricted submarine warfare the first of February. We shall endeavor in spite of this to keep the United States neutral. In the event of this not succeeding, we make Mexico a proposal of alliance on the following bases: make war together, make peace together, generous financial support, and an understanding on our part that Mexico is to reconquer the lost territory in Texas, New Mexico and Arizona. The settlement in detail is left to you.
>
> You will inform the President [of Mexico] of the above most secretly as soon as the outbreak of war with the United States is certain and the suggestion that he should on his own initiative invite Japan to immediate adherence and at the same time mediate between Japan and ourselves.
>
> Please call the President's attention to the fact that the unrestricted employment of our submarines now offers the prospect of compelling England to make peace within a few months. Acknowledge receipt.
>
> Zimmermann

Even without the dynamite of the still secret Zimmermann message, would Wilson finally give up hope of peace if Germany renewed unrestricted submarine warfare? Indignation over the *Lusitania* still was high in the United States.

Wilson was in truth badly shaken by Germany's public announcement at the end of January that she was resuming all-out submarine warfare. That meant that American ships and American lives would be endangered. World tension became taut. Then came the United States pronouncement: There was

145

to be no declaration of war, only severed diplomatic relations with Germany.

It was time for Hall to act. To his delight, Foreign Secretary Balfour eagerly seized upon the Zimmermann document. Both then concentrated on how best to approach Washington. American Ambassador Page in London was known to be pro-British, so much so that Wilson distrusted him. Therefore it was concluded that a favorable reaction by him alone might generate in them a false optimism. Perhaps it should be tried on someone more neutral in his attitudes. On Page's staff was Mr. Edward Bell, the intelligence liaison officer with whom Hall's office normally would deal. He was assessed as cool and discriminating, and an approach to him would be no breach of protocol. It was decided to try the precious document on Bell.

They studied his face intently as he read. Their excitement, and hopes, mounted as it became obvious that Bell was strongly affected. But Bell's final reaction was still disbelief. Hall stiffened with disappointment. He had cast the die and would have to go on. Together, Balfour and Hall confronted Ambassador Page. The senior American was sufficiently moved to enter into what now became a common problem: how to prove the document authentic, but Hall knew with certainty that if he failed with Bell, he would fail with Wilson.

Then was evolved the solution to the whole problem of authenticity. Let Page forward the Zimmermann decipherment as an official document to Washington. At the same time Page would point out that if the British naval intelligence claim was authentic, Washington should be able to locate the Zimmermann message to von Eckhardt in the Western Union files. Then these cipher groups could be in turn wired back to the American embassy in London. Here Hall would permit the use of his precious code books by American decoders working in their own embassy. If these men produced the text Hall

146

claimed for the Zimmermann message, absolute proof of validity would exist.

It was done. A stunned but still tight-lipped Washington wired back the groups. Bell himself was assigned to do most of the decoding, and his word-for-word confirmation of Hall's claims went back to Washington. Wilson's pacifist soul was shaken to the depths. Now he knew, and expressed full bitterness. War was declared in April, 1917.

Wide Open America—von Rintelen

CONTROVERSIAL figure that he was and still remains, Wilson amazed many that he could cling so long to his illusion of neutrality in the face of staggering proof of sabotage against the United States by German agents of high and low degree. That he was at least moved prior to the overwhelming Zimmermann incident is shown by his agreement that something had to be done to ascertain the true state of affairs regarding the activities in America of both sides in the European war. He reacted favorably to the precedent that the United States Secret Service be given the added mission of spy-chasing. Very high time it was, too. Already the country had been powerfully infiltrated by Berlin's proctors, and the effects of their underground work was literally converting the nation into an extended battlefield.

Audacity was piled upon audacity. Paramount in the initial offenses were those of the self-styled "Dark Invader," suave, brilliant, superbly educated, and wealthy Franz Rintelen von Kleist, better known simply as von Rintelen.

The April day in 1916 that he landed in New York saw immigration officials favorably stamp a passport made out to one Emil V. Gaeshe. Since this was no police state, and in any case, America was neutral, there was no examination beyond the usual customs probe. "Gaeshe" knew there wouldn't be and he was patient and self-assured despite the fact that concealed on his person was the latest German secret naval cipher system which Berlin felt sure neither London nor Washington would be able to crack. Von Rintelen was to deliver it to the German attachés in the United States, Captains von Boy-Ed for the Imperial Navy and von Papen for the Army. But all went smoothly at the docks and he smiled urbanely as he stepped through the barriers, free to enter this country, which had been described as the arsenal of Europe. It would be his job to see that its arms production was diverted into proper channels. He smiled, but Franz von Rintelen would have cause to recall bitterly that cipher system in his pocket.

Perhaps it was a significant straw in the wind that his arrival at the German Club in New York was not accompanied by the paean of welcome that one might associate with the uniting of three men dedicated to victory for the Fatherland. Von Boy-Ed and von Papen were plainly annoyed that Berlin had seen fit to send out another operative in a field they considered eminently their own. Von Rintelen tried to pacify them. Apparently he succeeded in getting some acceptance of the idea that he would operate solely to sabotage American supply of munitions to the Allies "by any means." Morally von Rintelen was not troubled. All was fair in war, and in any case, something had to be done to redress the imbalance: England controlled the seas and therefore could insure the flow of munitions, while Berlin could not; if America suffered in the process, that was fair, too.

In the records of the Commercial Register of New York for the year 1916 is to be found the entry for a new import-export firm of E.V. Gibbons, Inc. It is one of a long list of companies hurriedly formed in the "gold rush" of war contracts, for now money was no object to any of the warring principals; the cry was ever for more and more supplies of every description. Von Rintelen was patient in developing the company and scrupulous in his observance of laws. It gave him a perfectly legal base of operations. He actually did a certain limited business, but mostly he was careful to avoid involvement, until one day an official of a New York bank carrying the Gibbons account suggested that his credit could be greatly expanded if he were to present bona fide contracts now and then.

Von Rintelen, who allowed himself to be called Mr. Gibbons, thought the idea good. Meanwhile he had an appointment in an odd place for such a man of business. In the company of a mild-mannered individual the German agent was inspecting a small cigar-shaped tube in the shelter of a deserted little wood near the edge of a town not far from New York City. He handled it gingerly. The lead tube was sealed at both ends. Inside were two chambers separated by a thin copper disk. In one chamber was sulphuric acid, in the other, picric acid. The unobtrusive little man was Dr. Schlee, a German chemist. He had devised the pencil-like object and for this test had made the copper disk so thin that the sulphuric acid soon would eat through it. If the disk were thick, several days might be required. Suddenly von Rintelen jumped back as an intense white flame shot out from the end of the pencil, momentarily blinding him. This was a Thermit pencil, a savage incendiary device.

While Allied guards patrolled the decks of the ship *Phoebus* with their carbines at the ready to discourage pro-German rashness, anti-British Irish stevedores dropped at least six pencils in hard-to-see crevices in the holds now piled tier upon tier with artillery shells for Russia. From nearby, "Mr. Gibbons" observed loading operations with the casual professional air of an exporter.

The disks in these pencils were thick. Nothing would happen until the *Phoebus* was well out of neutral waters. There were niceties to be observed in this business.

149

Von Rintelen and his associates then avidly scanned the pages of the *Shipping News*. One day, this appeared:

Accidents. S.S. Phoebus from New York—destination Archangel—caught fire at sea. Brought into port of Liverpool by H.M.S. *Ajax.*

It was the first but far from the last such notice in *Shipping News*. British postwar reports are inclined to discount the extent of the success, one source referring to it as "trifling." Von Rintelen himself always claimed that several dozen ships were either so seriously damaged by the devices that their valuable cargoes were more or less total losses or that the ships were gutted by fire and explosion and went to the bottom. Somewhere between doubtless lies the truth, but exactly where will never be known. History so far inclines favorably to von Rintelen's claims. (The Kaiser thought him sufficiently important so that upon capture, he offered the British any ten Englishmen King George might name in exchange.)

World War II would see the development of the frogman type of commando and his magnetic "limpet" mine timed to shatter the hulls of anchored vessels after the saboteur had put a safe distance between himself and his target. Attempts of this kind were not new even in 1917—it was done in our own Civil War—but it may be surprising to some that von Rintelen's activities included successful sabotage of this type in New York harbor itself.

Again a meeting occurred outside the city. A tall, thin fin had been erected in an isolated spot screened by trees. The fin could be made to flap slowly around a vertical axis. It was slowly flapping now under hand power supplied by a young German engineer named Fay. At a distance von Rintelen and some of his associates waited for something to happen. When it did, it blew the model of the ship's rudder to bits, sent Fay flying through the smoke-filled air, and set fire to the trees. Fay was unhurt and he had proved that his new sabotage

150

device could cripple a munitions ship at sea, if not actually sink it, through a heavy explosion at the stern. It remained for him, well financed now by von Rintelen, to attach the gadget to a loaded transport ready to sail for an Allied port. The ordinary working of the rudder eventually would do the rest.

A short time later a lone man in a motorboat in New York harbor appeared to be having engine trouble. He drifted closer to a ship so heavily loaded with munitions that her Plimsoll mark was just awash. Lookouts aboard watched him drift under the counter, hammering on his engine the while. They lost interest. If they recalled the incident later, when far at sea a powerful explosion ripped the rudder and nearly lost them their ship, there is nothing to show it. A subsequent victim of Fay's delayed explosive device was so badly damaged that she was abandoned and became a huge floating mine. The vigilance of guards in harbor was increased now. Fay could no longer resort to the drifting motorboat subterfuge. Instead, he placed his gear aboard a small raft and actually dog-paddled the thing silently into position, then swam away in the night. Of course he could not win the war single-handed, nor could von Rintelen. But if reports of marine casualties in *Shipping News* and the *New York Times* of those days are to be interpreted as von Rintelen insisted that they must, then his assistance was not small.

The successes won him acclaim from high places in the Fatherland. These messages passed through the German embassy in Washington. The old animosities of von Boy-Ed and von Papen were fanned anew. Worse, for now von Rintelen was to be used by Berlin for much bigger game: he would become a principal in Germany's efforts to bring Mexico into the war against the United States. In later years von Rintelen spoke bitterly of his conviction that the corrosion of jealousy really set in at this point, although he was never able to prove it. He maintained that the intriguing attachés deliberately

151

hatched a scheme for exposing him to American counter-intelligence during this most critical stage of his secret contacts with Huerta, the renegade Mexican general, then in New York.

Until then, von Rintelen never had cause to fear annoyance from counterintelligence, for the cogent reason that it had hardly existed. But, as we have seen, President Wilson had called upon the Secret Service. Von Rintelen got early proof that counterespionage had gone into action. As he left a New York hotel where he had had a carefully guarded meeting with Huerta concerning German submarines supposed to land money and weapons in the Gulf of Mexico, he saw two men detach themselves from the shadows and follow him. From then on wherever he went he was followed. Twist and turn as he might, he could not shake his pursuers.

Now it was a matter of time. He must do what was needed to complete arrangements with Huerta and clear out. Already E. V. Gibbons, Inc. had folded its tents and was no more. He settled large sums for industrial sabotage on subagents, including his key agent in Baltimore, a man named Hinsch, and tried to be inconspicuous.

But now another of those factors inconsistent with iron-bound directives was asserting itself. Romance had entered the life of a minor clerk at the German embassy. Being minor, his pay was not impressive, certainly not for romancing in an expensive American city. But the object of his desire was as resourceful as she was entrancing. The lady was in fact one of those fixtures in the game so often the object of ridicule by cynical journalists—the *femme fatale* spy, as old as Delilah, as recent as the blonde siren credited with the downfall of Irvin C. Scarbeck at the American embassy in Warsaw. She prevailed upon the impecunious clerk to augment his salary with British gold. At any rate, von Rintelen learned with dismay that the top secret cipher system he had so carefully shepherded through the British sea blockade and put into the hands of von Boy-Ed and von Papen had been stolen. His scalp crawled at the news, for details of his own operations had gone out to Berlin in that system, and he had received instructions in it. Now he guessed why counterintelligence was informed of his carefully guarded moves.

Envy and jealousy were to assert themselves as well. The German agent, riding so high for so long, received his second jolt in the form of a letter through his New York bank plainly addressed to him with his full German naval military title. The banker who had been so hopeful about credits was greatly upset. Von Rintelen was enraged when he saw that it had come from von Papen at the embassy. Von Rintelen always maintained that it was a cold-blooded and deliberate betrayal. There has been little to show him wrong. Almost immediately the next set-back came. At the New York Yacht Club where he had been living and was planning how to close up and get out, he received a telephone call. Over the open wire von Boy-Ed, the naval attaché, informed him that Berlin desired the immediate recall of "Captain von Rintelen."

It was too late for rage. It was too late for everything except disappearance, and he hoped devoutly that a margin of safety still remained to him in that quarter. His hopes rose, yet there lurked a nagging question: Surely the American government had enough on him to clap him in irons. Why didn't they do it? He was even more surprised when he boarded a ship for home unmolested. There were still the British blockade cruisers to negotiate. Was it some sort of cat-and-mouse game?

It was, but neither Washington nor London was ready to pounce yet. The blockaders proved no menace, on secret orders from the Admiralty. The truth was that Washington did not want to be burdened with von Rintelen at that time. Since the principal sufferer so far seemed to have been London, let London have him. Hawk-nosed Admiral Hall proposed to allow the prey to come to him. The ship was due to call at Southampton en route to the continent. A picked man boarded the vessel and knocked at the cabin of Emil V. Gaeshe. It could have been an embarrassing moment, for the gentleman traveling under that name was comfortably ensconced with an actress of his fancy. But he was again the self-assured, patient individual who had done so well for himself and the Fatherland. Preliminary interrogation of him elicited little except a well-phrased lecture on England's foolishness in choosing the Allied side.

An excuse was found for detaining the man known to have caused heavy damage to Allied shipping. Von Rintelen blandly denied any connection, even that he had German naval connections, although, of course, he held a commission in the Imperial Navy. In a subsequent interview in London he maintained his story until a resourceful interrogator suddenly shouted in German, "Salute!" Habit clicked and so did von Rintelen's heels. He was imprisoned but escaped. When news of it reached Hall, that fiery autocrat of naval intelligence reacted with characteristic energy, an energy that would have been largely if not totally frustrated in peacetime: He had every train halted for searching, canceled the sailing of every nonmilitary vessel from every port in England and Scotland, and blocked every main road leading to the ports. The fleeing von Rintelen was taken in Leicester. Two days later a wail came down to London from Scapa Flow, far to the north: When would the ban be lifted? The port was literally overflowing. For once in the life of this martinet, Hall had forgotten. "Let 'em go!" was his crisp reply. He didn't bother to explain, nor was he obliged to. Such can be the edged tools of a democracy, too, when circumstances demand it.

Von Rintelen was so bitter about what he considered deliberate betrayal by his own countrymen that he abandoned all attempts at deception and co-operated with the British by unfolding details of the operation of the German secret service.

154

He never offered to undertake missions against Germany, however, nor was he asked to. Eventually he was extradited and served a term in the Atlanta penitentiary. Afterwards, he returned to England and stayed there during World War II. He was of further service against the Nazi intelligence machine.

Black Tom Erupts

VON RINTELEN was gone from America, but his evil lingered on, then festered and grew, and at 2:08 A.M. on the night of Sunday, July 30th, 1916, erupted in one of the greatest of military explosions prior to the holocaust of Hiroshima nearly four decades later. New York harbor on that warm July night was rocked by a series of blasts whose shock waves were distinctly felt in Philadelphia, roughly a hundred miles away. On the nearby Jersey coast hardly a window survived and in Manhattan, broad sheets of plate glass crashed to the streets as tall structures swayed in the series of blasts that sent great lurid pulses into the night sky. Dazed people were jolted from their beds and ran about the streets trying to find an explanation for the sudden chaos.

One of these was a lovely young woman, whose face and figure graced nearly every piece of publicity produced by the Eastman Kodak Company. But she was terrified on another score, for she believed that she knew what it meant—German sabotage—and felt that she might have unwittingly participated in its advent. She was to tell something of that during inquiries that followed the explosion. Years later, when America attempted to prove sabotage and collect from Germany more than $150,000,000 for this explosion and other fires and explosions allegedly chargeable to her agents, the young woman, Mena Edwards, gave testimony in greater detail. For the moment, however, we will present others who had some

155

bearing on the New Jersey eruption in order that the complicated skein of guilt be made easier to trace.

Black Tom is a promontory which juts out from Bayonne, New Jersey, for about a mile into the Upper Bay. It was veined by Lehigh Valley Railroad sidings crowded with cars discharging their loads into warehouses or into barges alongside. These cargoes were destined for ocean freighters serving the seaports of the world. Most of the facilities there were engaged by Russia, and other Allied governments at war with Germany, for the shipment of munitions. That Saturday evening as work was stopped for the weekend, there were nearly three dozen freight cars and several barges laden with raw high explosives, with shells, detonators, and other highly irritable commodities. In all, there were more than two million pounds of the stuff. The only people left on duty in the area were the night watchmen.

The job of the watchmen was made especially difficult by the fact that only rudimentary security checks existed. There was little to prevent ill-intentioned persons from secreting themselves in the complex of cars, buildings, and barges, from depositing time bombs, or setting fires; nor was there anything to prevent entrance or egress from the harbor side.

Midnight came and went. There was a soft breeze blowing which made the night comfortable. Across the bay, ladders of light in the tall buildings of Manhattan showed that the army of chars was at work. In the harbor, the red and green side lights of vessels became fewer. A discerning eye aided by good night glasses, however, might have detected one unlighted craft so small that its very presence in those waters seemed an impertinence. Such a craft could hardly constitute a menace to Black Tom. Still just such a craft rowed by two men apparently was out in the harbor, and it was headed toward Black Tom, where evidently another man had hidden himself to await their coming. Those in the boat feared for their lives, for the waves were rougher than they had expected, and at times they were nearly swamped. To their vast relief they made the Jersey shore and set off to rendezvous with the man who waited.

Shortly after a quarter to two in the morning, a guard suddenly froze in his leisurely pacing. In the fascination of disbelief, he saw a yellow glare under a boxcar loaded with munitions. As he watched, it enlarged and grew bright. Then he raced into action. He pulled the nearest fire alarm and ran from the flames that could erupt any moment into a heavy explosion. With the alarm dinning, a second fire was seen, this one some hundreds of feet away on a barge.

Seventeen minutes later the heavily laden boxcar disappeared in a mighty geyser of flame and smoke. Instantly the concussion set off new blasts. But all were dwarfed by the enormous explosion of the barge.

Now the whole Black Tom terminal area was a mass of flame shot through with the lightning of exploding shells. On nearby Ellis Island the famous immigration buildings were so shaken that they were abandoned at once. Shells fell as far away as Fort Jay on Governor's Island. Only the air cushion separating the Jersey shore from Manhattan Island saved the great structures of the financial district. And in all this, only three adults and a child lost their lives.

In the days that followed, the railroad company sought to explain the blast in terms of spontaneous combustion. Yet there were the two external fires seen by the guards. Foreign governments sued, claiming lack of care. The various American companies involved fought back. Eventually the whole tangled business went before a Mixed Claims Commission. Seldom has so persistent an inquiry been recorded in modern times. It was headed by Amos J. Peaslee, formerly a major involved in confidential work on General Pershing's staff, but at the time of the inquiry, a member of a New York law firm retained to plead before the Commission. Peaslee, however, was not to be involved for a decade or more after the events we are now concerned with.

Meanwhile, one clue developed early in the affair that pointed to more than spontaneous combustion. On the day after the great blast a woman who had been a long-time friend of police officials in Bayonne came to visit them. She was worried, she said, about her lodger, a foreign-looking fellow named Michael Kristoff. He had been out until 4 A.M., which alone might not have been so noteworthy on that night of terror, but in his room afterwards he had paced endlessly, and she could hear him moaning, "What shall I do? What shall I do?" Even that need not have been too significant, for he could have meant that his job at an oil company near the terminal was now gone. But the landlady was convinced that Kristoff was associated with the explosion, for two reasons. He had recently made numerous journeys by train to different cities, and she had come to realize that following every one of his trips there had been newspaper reports of big fires and explosions in those cities. Then, one day she had seen a letter he had carelessly left exposed. In it he demanded large sums of money from a man whose name was Graentnor, or something of the sort.

The police got together with secret service, with Department of Justice agents, and with the New York Bomb Squad officials. They put a "tail" on the swarthy Kristoff, who, it was learned, had migrated from the northern region of Hungary that one day would become Czechoslovakia. The surveillance man gained Kristoff's confidence by posing as an anarchist. He claimed that Kristoff in a confidential moment said he had been responsible for the Black Tom explosion. Then Kristoff disappeared. He was not found until after the war, in prison, where he had been committed for a civil offense. At that time he reverted to an older story to account for the journeys the landlady had mentioned by saying that he had been hired by a man with a name like Graentnor to carry suitcases on trips

158

which the man said he was making in connection with engineering works. The suitcases had contained blueprints and town plans and the like. Yes, there had been fires and explosions but he didn't know anything about that. Then he disappeared again.

No more progress was made until some years later, when Peaslee began his rooting. Meanwhile, much had gone on, and one blue-eyed, mild-mannered German apparently high in international business circles was described by an investigating senator in Washington as "the Machiavelli of the whole thing." This might have been an exaggeration, but at least that individual was the banker for the whole undertaking—until he lost his briefcase. After that things got difficult, although he still managed some payments, including one to a man who had some accounts to settle in connection with a huge explosion in New Jersey.

The Hot Briefcase

TREASURY SECRETARY McAdoo's secret service men as well as agents of the Department of Justice had taken to counterintelligence work with joy. The enthusiasm was not shared by their quarry. Among them was Dr. Heinrich F. Albert, tall, solidly built at 180 pounds, and bearing the badge of the German blueblood, a dueling scar on his cheek.

On July 24, 1915, he had unobtrusively entered the building at 45 Broadway, headquarters of the Hamburg-American Line. Had he emerged as unobtrusively, he might have escaped the attention of secret service man W. H. Houghton. It was Houghton's job to shadow George Sylvester Viereck, an American of strong pro-German sympathies. This was important inasmuch as Viereck edited a periodical aimed at German-Americans called *The Fatherland*. While circulation was considerable, it was not enough to defray the cost of publication.

159

Therefore, reasoned McAdoo's men, it must be financed from Berlin; hence, the surveillance. Houghton had seen Viereck go into the building earlier. Anxious not to lose him, he telephoned a fellow-operative, agent Frank Burke, for help. Burke was one of the most able men in the service and Houghton hoped he would agree to come even though it was his afternoon off. Burke shrugged off his lost chance for relaxation and came downtown.

He had only arrived when Houghton gave him a sign. Viereck was leaving. But he was accompanied by a man of German appearance who was carrying a bulging briefcase. It struck both agents that the editor was showing deference to the latter as the two made their way to the old Rector Street elevated depot and took a Harlem uptown train. Viereck and his companion occupied a cross-seat in the center of the car. Houghton took the one just opposite for a front view, Burke sat behind. Above the clatter of the train he could hear talk, but it was German, a language he did not understand. He concentrated on Viereck's companion, fitting his physical features into the compartments of his mind where so much of that information was filed. Something was beginning to click. The man's features were tallying with a description given to Burke some weeks ago by George Lamb, a customs agent, concerning an important and dangerous German. Then he saw the saber scars and he knew the man for Dr. Albert. Here at last was a close, high-level connection between Viereck and Berlin.

At the Twenty-third Street station the obsequious Viereck took his leave. Without a word Houghton got up, too. Burke paid no attenion. At that moment, a young lady boarded the car and sat down beside the German, who now interested himself in a book. The briefcase was beside Albert, next to the car window.

The train clattered on uptown. It neared the stop at Fiftieth Street, a transfer point for cross-town traffic. The

160

German Club was located in the area. Burke guessed Albert might be bound there. If so, he would have to change to the shuttle train. But apparently Burke had misguessed because as the train slowed down, Albert went on reading.

Burke was reviewing other possible destinations for his quarry when suddenly Dr. Albert jumped to his feet and in some confusion made for the door. Obviously he had become engrossed in his reading and realized belatedly that he was at Fiftieth Street, his transfer point.

Fearful of losing Albert, Burke jumped up too. Now Albert was at the door and Burke was conscious of something different in his appearance. Albert no longer had his briefcase. At the same moment he heard the girl call out to Albert. In one of those instantaneous decisions that characterize the good counterintelligence agent, Burke pivoted on his toe, mumbled a word of apology, and scooped up the heavy satchel.

He had a momentary glimpse of her puzzled expression and then another glance made him suddenly change his course toward the rear door: Albert, red-faced and angry, was trying to get back into the car through the front door. Burke inwardly blessed the fat lady who just as indignantly declined to be brushed aside by Albert. He thought it was like a well-rehearsed play designed for drama and laughs. He reversed and dashed out of the car.

He reached the platform, thankful that the interchange crowd was still considerable. But as he started rearward for the stairway leading to the street, he saw a commotion. Dr. Albert erupted from the train, looking wildly about him. Doubtless the girl had told him someone had taken his case.

Burke shouldered close to a wall, covering the briefcase as well as he could with his coat and one arm. He struck one match after another in an effort to light a refractory cigar while Albert swept the thinning crowd for a sign of the thief. The train banged away, the crowd melted. Albert clumped down the stairs. Burke, not wanting to be trapped if he should return,

161

and needing the greater room to maneuver which the street would supply, went down too.

Too late Burke realized that Albert was something of a tactician himself. In spite of his panic, he had stationed himself on the street to command a view in both directions and of the elevated stairs. Burke saw his staring eyes spot the briefcase. The German lunged forward.

Burke abandoned his own dignity. Sprinting like a track star he jumped aboard the rear platform of a Sixth Avenue streetcar just passing. Albert put on speed and Burke put on an act. To the conductor he explained that the wild-looking Albert was a lunatic who had just staged a violent scene on the elevated train. Burke looked all right to the conductor but Albert did not. He gave the bellcord a jerk signaling the motorman to go by the next stop. Burke felt a surge of power and the car gathered speed. It was too much for Albert, who, still shouting, dropped farther and farther behind and finally gave up the chase.

What Burke and his chief, William J. Flynn, were able to show Mr. McAdoo from the briefcase constituted one of the most spectacular proofs of subversion yet to come to light. Among other activities, such as fomentation of strikes, there was documentary proof of Berlin's work to corner the supply of liquid chlorine used in gas shells; to acquire indirectly the Wright Airplane Company in order to deny its facilities to the Allies, even the United States if necessary, to buy control of a huge munitions plant which would take Allied orders but never fill them, and to get control of the cotton export facilities of the entire south so that only the Entente could be supplied.

But if Dr. Albert knew that his loaded briefcase had fallen into government hands, what evasive steps would he take? Could anything be proved if he covered all tracks? To Washington's relief it now developed that Albert obviously did not know; it might have been just a snatch-thief. A forlorn advertisement appeared in the *New York Telegram* of Monday the

26th: A brown leather bag containing documents had been lost aboard a Harlem train at Fiftieth Street on July 24th; if the finder would return it to a Mr. Hoffman at the address given, he would receive $20.

Years later Viereck writing in retrospect compared the loss of Albert's crammed briefcase to Burke with the loss of the Battle of the Marne to Joffre. After the war, too, Frank Burke and another agent were at first startled, then secretly amused, by a story told them by a man who claimed affiliation with the British secret service. He said he had been the key figure in the purloining of the famous Albert briefcase. To his statement that the papers were of enormous importance the two counterintelligence men agreed without reserve. As for the rest, Burke said: "I don't know what his qualifications were as a detective, but he certainly was a fine liar."

At this point I should like to interject a personal experience.

During my days as an intelligence trainee, my youthful associates and I held Dr. Albert's lack of security consciousness to be as inexcusable as it was deplorable. Deplorable it certainly was. And there can be no attitude of tolerance in counterintelligence security work. But age and experience provide a new dimension: understanding. Years later I would have cause to ponder bitterly that names and dates change, but human fallibility goes on forever.

It was during World War II in the Pacific. Plain Australian men with the blood of Walsingham, of Sir Francis Drake, or of Guy Fawkes in their veins moved with cunning and stealth far behind Japanese lines in the Solomon Islands to report every important move of land, sea, and air forces to hard-pressed Allied strike units. The Coast Watchers were exponents of hit-and-run techniques *par excellence*. Their whispers would come over the hidden miles by shortwave radio, and then before the enemy could get a fix on their transmitters, they would vanish into the shadowy silence of the jungle. The

163

most stringent practices in signal security were one of their few safeguards. Frequent changes in call signs and alterations of frequencies on highly flexible schedules were imperative. To co-ordinate this meant numerous courier trips between Brisbane and Melbourne. An extensive table for two weeks had been figured out and plotted at Brisbane. Case Control officers at Melbourne would have to have it. I left on a night train, already tired and weary but sourly aware that I would have to be up before dawn to change trains at the Victoria boundary. My precious briefcase with the signal plan in double envelopes, the outer sealed in wax, was in the sleeper bunk with me, next to the car wall. At least the briefcase was easier to sleep with than the two huge roll maps of secret airfields on Java that I had had for bunkmates during four nights aboard ship prior to the outbreak of war.

I slept badly and was up before being called for the change. I was moved to a day seat for the last few miles. My foot was on the briefcase.

Suddenly I was aware of a heavy hand on my shoulder. A train attendant was dinning in my ear. I would miss my train if I didn't hurry. I must have slept again.

And I almost did miss it. Breathing heavily I found a seat on the Victoria train and we were off. It was a nonstop train, a streamliner. But it did slow down fifty miles later to throw off a message about a briefcase left aboard the night train from Brisbane. It was to be taken in charge by the railroad police and held for instructions, if it was found at all, of course. . . .

Something of Dr. Albert's agony of mind communicated itself over the years to me. Incredible and deplorable. But it had happened in that uncoordinated moment between sleep and startled wakefulness. The lives of every Coast Watcher in the Solomons could be forfeit to my lapse if that briefcase fell into hostile hands. In any case, if it was not recovered, we should have to assume complete compromise and make the most extraordinary efforts to withdraw these men, if that was possible at all.

Two years of war later and I still held my tightly kept secret of how the briefcase had been recovered—by a railroad policeman almost as soon as the streamliner left the station. It was then rushed to me at Melbourne by police courier. Careful laboratory tests of the seal and envelope showed them to be intact. And so, long after, I did tell about it.

The occasion was a council of officers at a forward intelligence operation base to deal with a breach of security by an Australian soldier, a military agent. Seven officers sat outside my tent on coral outcrops above the Celebes Sea. Each was an experienced intelligence operations man, and several had been on dangerous missions. All had survived to reach field-grade rank. Their judgments were severe. Somehow I was moved to plead. The accused had been exhausted to the dropping point by a prolonged and most dangerous mission into enemy-held Borneo. His record was otherwise flawless. The others were thoughtful. Then I had an inspiration: how many of the seven would be sitting where he was if some breach of security he harbored in his breast had been revealed? We would have a confessional and I would lead off. It was a risky business but to my intense relief first one and then another outlined some grim misadventure that had turned out all right, just as my own had. That is, all but one, a barrel-chested Australian captain.

Would he line up and confess? His grey eyes stared at his field boots. Then he looked at me and we both grinned. He knew that I knew his story would be one of the most fantastic of the lot.

Again the matter concerned locations and signal plans, this time of American, British, Australian, and Dutch agents far out to the north and northwest. He had been on a rigorous trip by air to collect data and give hidden base stations their new plans. The old ones he folded and secreted in soiled

165

clothes at the bottom of a regular army rucksack that he kept belted around his shoulder day and night—until the last fatal moment aboard a Brisbane tramcar coming from the airfield. Stupid with weariness he had not called the motor-pool car but clambered on the town-bound tram at the edge of the field, just at midnight. The rhythmical pounding of the wheels on the joints drove home to his weary brain the fact of an almost sickening sleepiness. And he apparently did sleep.

He was occupying a seat on the open drop-center portion of the tram when he suddenly realized he had gone past his stop at operations headquarters. It must have been the clatter of a tram passing in the opposite direction that wakened him. In a totally unplanned action, the captain hurled his rucksack into the night, balanced himself, then jumped off. Miraculously, he kept his feet as the tram sped on.

He turned to recover his rucksack, suddenly realizing what a silly move it had been, a conviction that mounted with each second of his inability to locate the precious pack in the street. Nearby an Australian soldier leaned against a pole. The officer breathed a grateful sigh. The man must have seen it. He had indeed. In fact, he thought it had fallen from the tram going the other way and had pitched it aboard. Between one and six o'clock in the morning, the two of them searched more than fifty trams in Brisbane carbarns. They never found it.

It was necessary to draw up a complete new plan and to move every net control station in the whole New Guinea zone, or take other protective action. Headquarters came to believe that the old plan did not fall into hostile hands. Probably some loyal Australian citizen with a thin ration book, had been only too glad to have come into possession of clothing, even though soiled, to care a black crow about a lot of papers under it, stuff he may have burned at the first chance.

But still another briefcase incident resulted in severe discipline for the offender, a Dutch operations planner. He had been a member of one of the most secret outfits in the intelli-

166

gence community of the Pacific theater. Bit by bit and man by man, the resources for establishing a secret observation station in enemy-controlled waters north of Australia had been going forward. The most rigid compartmentation had been observed, no man knowing the whole story, so that capture of one could not compromise others. The precaution had been doubly enforced since a series of betrayals had cost lives and nearly a submarine as well. One of the most rigid rules of all that governed this grim, dark house in the Toorak section of Melbourne called for strictest accounting for every paper that had been withdrawn for study or work during the day.

The D-Day approached. A great amount of detail remained to be completed. There were not enough hours in the working day. The hard-working and loyal Dutch officer figured out a way to add more, by beating the rule about checking in documents. He put several in a briefcase and telephoned for a taxicab; he would not entrust himself to blacked-out streets with his perilous burden.

At his flat, requisitioned by the Dutch government in exile, he paid off the cab and went to his private study to put the briefcase on the desk, a briefcase he realized with staggering suddenness that he no longer had. He had left it in the cab.

It was never recovered. In view of the previous compromises, there could be no further gamble. The whole operation was canceled and men scattered to the seven seas. The Dutch officer was court-martialed and stripped of rank.

Beauty Treatment

SHE was tall, stately, graceful of movement, and gracious of manner, a member of the German aristocracy. Her sister was a famous author of political works. Her father was Baron Hans von Kretschman, himself a writer of military treatises. The family moved in the exclusive circle of the

167

nobility and in that circle was Prince von Bülow, German minister for foreign affairs.

The Prince was farsighted. One day this lovely woman with her academic degrees, with her social poise, her linguistic abilities, might be of great service to the Fatherland in other countries. His tactful suggestion found such ready acceptance that he realized the idea was not original with him. There ensued talks behind closed doors with the head of the Kaiser's clandestine intelligence, Colonel Walter Nicolai.

Ten years later an emaciated woman lay dying in New York State following prolonged detention in the prison ward of Bellevue Hospital. Her agonized face bore only a shadow of her one-time beauty, and her thin form was convulsed with the torture of drug addiction. The American authorities who had shown such shrewdness, such doggedness in tracking down what they considered an exceptionally dangerous spy, now showed every consideration for her sad plight. Before their eyes she seemed to disintegrate and on August 12, 1920, she died.

It would be too much to say that she died because a man had committed the mistake of addressing two envelopes, then inadvertently placing in each the letter intended for the other. But it would be entirely correct to say that this inadvertency, one of those miscalculations which upset the best-laid plans of the most resourceful governments, contributed in a vital way to the denouement. The case of "The Beautiful Blonde Woman of Antwerp" as it is called, perhaps erroneously, in Army Corps of Intelligence Police records, is technically a good example of how an unpredictable mishap can occur in even the best operational planning. Certainly it demonstrates the formidableness of the democracies when they combine talents and facilities.

On a cold November day in 1917, Washington received a code message from London. Through continental contacts it had been learned that an agent of the German government had slipped out of Madrid for New York for the purpose of delivering ten thousand American dollars to someone on Long Island. Two addresses were stated. Either could be the recipient of the money. The reason was not known but presumably subversion or espionage against the United States was involved.

Federal agents got into their overcoats and began a careful investigation. To their disappointment, both addressees had left for parts unknown. Nothing remained but to arrange a "stake-out" and hope one or both would return. The checking would include interception of mail addressed to either man. It looked like a long, cold winter.

From the time of Alexander the Great postal censorship has been one of the most profitable weapons in the counter-espionage armory. Now it would serve the patient men of the stake-out, but not until January. Then a letter for one of the men was snared. To their disappointment, though, there was nothing useful. One hope remained: the secret-ink laboratory in New York City. Swabs impregnated with all known developing reagents were wiped across the page. Nothing emerged. But hardly had they settled down for another wait when the postman came again.

This time there was an odd circumstance: the envelope was plainly addressed to one of the men, but the enclosed letter was intended for a woman and bore her married name in the greeting. It likewise was signed by a woman. If the counter-intelligence people were inclined, they could have read espionage double-talk in the text of the letter. But still there was no real lead. Again it went to the secret-ink laboratory, while other agents were assigned to tracing the return address on the envelope. Both inquiries bore fruit.

When technicians applied the reagent for a new, highly classified German ink they called the "F" type, they were excited by the appearance of tracings hitherto invisible—unmistakably German script.

Meanwhile federal men had ascertained that while the re-

169

turn address was that of a bona fide boardinghouse, no such person as indicated on the envelope lived there. Careful study of the guests suggested one lead, a steward from a vessel that only recently had arrived from Europe on its latest voyage. The man habitually roomed there during the ship's wait in port. In one of those flashes which good counterintelligence agents have, call it intuition if you like, one of the investigators felt that the man was a courier, either knowingly or otherwise. They located him and after hours of questioning designed to give the distinct impression that they knew of his connection with certain letters, the man surprisingly admitted to exactly what they had surmised. He claimed that just prior to the ship's departure from Europe he had been given two letters for posting in New York City, so that they would bear American postmarks. He professed ignorance of the contents. Why, then, had he switched them? His face betrayed genuine bewilderment. It could only have happened when he made out new envelopes, he explained—he had carried the originals in his shoes and they had become soiled and worn. Letters carried in shoes likely were not ordinary ones, but they could get little more useful data from him.

There was further excitement at the secret ink laboratory. The concealed writing now revealed specific directives relating to the blowing up of munition centers in the United States, the destruction of shipping areas, and the wrecking of mines producing minerals vital to war industries. Obviously the addressee was a woman of importance to Berlin, and consequently to Washington. But who was she?

The steward had the name and address. It seemed easy. But to the amazement of the investigators, their quarry was the complete opposite of a *femme fatale*. The old lady in obviously straitened circumstances who greeted them was no more a spy than she was Colonel Nicolai himself. Yet, she had news for them. Someone else had mistaken her for another, too, because she had received several mysterious letters during the past year, although none for some months. They bore her name and she had opened a few, until she realized they were not for her but for someone else of the same name, so she had destroyed them. Concealing their disappointment, the men patiently queried her, trying to stimulate her memory of what she had read. But it seemed a lost game, except on one point. She did recall the name Victorica.

Seizing upon the forlorn crumb, Washington cabled Allied secret service to see if the name meant anything to them. It did, in both London and Paris. Ever since 1914, London had been trying to catch up with an attractive blonde of excellent German family who had been active in political espionage, and now they wondered if she might not be involved in something more dangerous. They would investigate.

Paris was about to pounce upon a man with an Argentine passport whom they suspected was engaged in espionage. He was thought to be married but his wife was missing. This woman was believed to have had assignments of a dubious nature in both Russia and South America before the war. Her name was Victorica.

Now London reported again. A woman of the description of their Victorica was known to have passed through immigration late in 1916 or very early in 1917 with an Argentine passport on her way to New York. Her name was Madame Maria de Victorica.

The democracies had cooperated as had the technical labs. Now it was a case of dogged trailing. All agencies were called upon: Naval Intelligence, the Corps of Intelligence Police, the Justice Department, the Secret Service, and the New York City police.

Every fashionable hotel, every high-grade apartment house in the city would have to be checked. The teams went out. First blood was drawn at the Knickerbocker Hotel. The woman was known to have registered there early in January, 1917, then left. She had registered again at the Waldorf Astoria but

171

she had departed from there very soon after paying in advance for months. The same baffling performance was repeated at the Spencer Arms. And from there her trail simply faded out.

This might have ended it, had it not been for fresh leads from London. The name of a German firm in New York was mentioned as being one from which there was reason to believe Victorica had collected a large sum of money. This proved true, some $35,000. Where was the lady, described at the firm as "a stunning blonde about thirty-five years of age"? She had disappeared but they had one temporary address, a foreign mission in New York City. And here the agents hit the jackpot.

A number of old letters, uncollected by Victorica, were recovered and taken to the ink laboratory for analysis. It was revealed that not only was she involved in plans for widespread sabotage and the landing of submarines in the Gulf of Mexico, but in the importation of Germany's newest explosive of great power, tetra. This tied her up with some of the most dangerous men in the business of destruction, one of whom was known to the Corps of Intelligence Police as "Dynamite Charlie" Wunnenberg for his adroitness in carrying out wholesale wreckage. It appears doubtful, however, that she knew the archteam of Lothar Witzke and Kurt Jahnke.

Now Victorica was seen in her true dimensions. Nor would she stop at using even the church. She applied her winning personality to unsuspecting Catholic priests for aid in obtaining religious statues from manufacturers in Zurich, Switzerland. They helped her with the technical language of ordering the images, then offered to send the orders out themselves in their names. Victorica accepted. Certainly no censor would suspect anything in that. But the hollow spaces within the statues would be plugged with quantities of tetra now awaited by the saboteurs.

As the need for finding her became more acute, the possibilities of it seemed to drop to the vanishing point. It was

172

decided to place under close surveillance every person mentioned in any communication intercepted to date. This included a few New Yorkers. But the days went by and the American war machine began to roll. There was a steady bridge of ships, carrying munitions, troops, and supplies out of New York, past Sandy Hook, past Long Beach, Long Island, to the North Atlantic.

Of tangible clues there was still nothing. All that had been remarked was that the schoolgirl cousin of one of the persons under surveillance was a devout churchgoer. So reported one of the agents, possibly out of sheer boredom. But in that innocuous observation lay the solution to the whole affair, the total undoing of the accomplished Madame de Victorica.

Not simply piety seemed to dominate the girl, but a rigid programing of it as well. At first curious, then interested, the agent noted that she arrived promptly at the same time on the same day each week for her devotions at St. Patrick's Cathedral on Fifth Avenue. He could set his watch by her as she scurried through the traffic at dusk and entered the church between Fiftieth and Fifty-first Streets exactly as the clock chimed the quarter hour.

This time the agent followed her in. He noted that she carried a newspaper as she entered the pew halfway down the great nave. She kneeled, her head on her hand supported by the pew ahead. The agent knelt too, but not in devotion. He kept his eyes on the girl and noticed that she did not take the newspaper with her as she arose. Genuflecting, she crossed herself and left the church.

He determined to get the newspaper but he was too late. She passed without any outward sign a well-dressed elderly gentleman coming up the aisle, also carrying a newspaper. The agent knew he was going to see the old "switch technique." The man went into the same pew, knelt at the identical spot, and after some moments apparently spent in meditation, he

173

left. He still had a newspaper under his arm, but not the same one.

Here, at last, was something concrete. The agent trailed him closely as he took a taxi to Pennsylvania Station and later as he boarded a Long Island train. At Long Beach he left the train and engaged another taxi. The agent was still close behind when he got out at the fashionable Nassau Hotel on the sea front.

For some time the gentleman sat in the lounge, smoking contentedly. People were moving about in a leisurely fashion. Suddenly the quarry arose and turned toward the main entrance again. The federal man prepared to follow when he noticed the newspaper still lying on the divan. Now what should he do? The question was decided for him by a beautifully gowned woman, apparently a resident of the hotel, who took the seat just vacated by the vanishing gentleman. She had several newspapers. The agent was genuinely excited, for he knew that here in the flesh was the much sought Madame de Victorica and that she would take the special newspaper with her.

Soon the counterintelligence men moved in for the arrest. The lovely "Marie de Vussier" was taken on a Presidential warrant on a charge of conspiracy to commit criminal acts against the government. Her denials suddenly melted when she was confronted with certain articles taken from her room. Innocent enough in appearance, beautiful white silk scarves had been found by the ink lab to have been impregnated with enough of the German "F" ink solution to have enabled her to write many more messages with special ball-point pens, also in her room. The newspaper had contained more than $20,000 smuggled into the country for her.

With her arrest, her confidence was shattered and so was her health. In statements she did admit to a knowledge of the German sabotage machine operating in the United States, and was specific on a point that Peaslee would pounce upon years

174

later. According to her, the Black Tom explosion was definitely caused "by an Austrian." Kristoff? She also alluded to that agile and highly successful saboteur whom the Army's Corps of Intelligence Police later were to call "Dynamite Charlie."

She was indicted on charges of attempts to commit espionage, but by now her health was such that she was confined to hospital as a prisoner. She was never brought to trial. Instead she faded swiftly despite every care. It was the end of the trail for the once stately Madame de Victorica, a trail that, ironically enough, ended at the "Gate of Heaven." She lies in Grave 8, Plot B, Range 8, Section 43 of the cemetery of that name in Hawthorne, Westchester County, New York.

Some authorities, even the Corps of Intelligence Police records, allude to her as the Beautiful Blonde Woman of Antwerp, so famous in the spy history of the times. It is almost certain that Madame de Victorica was not Elsbeth Schragmuller, the legendary "Mademoiselle Docteur" and shadowy head of the Antwerp spy school for the Germans. Allied intelligence signally failed in putting the identifying finger on this woman, probably one of the most famous in spy literature. Not surprising, then, was the appearance in first one country, then another, of an alleged Beautiful Blonde Woman of Antwerp. Schragmuller was blonde and whoever experienced the impact of her personality firsthand seldom forgot it, but accounts vary as to her actual beauty. It is possible that the truly beautiful Frauline Maria von Kretschman received belated instruction at the Antwerp school, even as it is now believed that the more famous but infinitely less talented Mata Hari did. But as we have seen, de Victorica was actually in league with Nicolai on active assignments when the sinister Schragmuller was still a university student. Colonel Nicolai later turned de Victorica over to German naval intelligence, foreign service headquarters of which was located in Antwerp. Thus the romantic appellation for de Victorica on Corps of Intelligence Police records may have been purely coincidental,

175

since it was from Antwerp she sortied and received her orders.

In any case, while she doubtless justified von Bülow's estimate of her early in her career, she probably accomplished little enough against the United States. The operational control was too remote, resulting in such fatal errors as the muddled postal arrangements and failures of co-ordination. This was compounded by the inadvertency of the switched envelopes. Her dedication might have hurdled even this had it not been for counterintelligence links that exist among the democracies and the co-operation of all antiagent facilities.

Van Deman Rises Again

DESPITE the events just recounted, the Chief of Staff of the U.S. Army saw no valid reason for organized military intelligence. To examine this state of affairs, it becomes necessary to shift attention for the moment from the offensive to the defensive aspect.

With America in the war, Allied countries sent missions to Washington to effect liaison and co-ordination, for now everything would hinge on whether the unchecked U-boats could bring the Allies down before America could train and arm, and get to France. Each country sent a trained intelligence liaison officer. If they were astounded to find no equivalents in the United States establishment they hid it. They were sent to Van Deman, but he had neither authority nor organization; the meetings "resolved themselves in conversation."

Van Deman sought permission to beard his nemesis. Tall, silver-haired Scott listened coldly to Van Deman's plea for re-establishment of the Information Division as the Second Section of the General Staff. The major, his lean body quivering with suppressed feeling, was shown the door followed by Scott's commentary that since our allies had full-blown intelligence organizations, he could not justify our setting up one.

Van Deman brooded. Strength rose in him from the rightness of his cause and the courage of his convictions. He called on Scott again, appealing to the old soldier's pride in service. Van Deman told Scott that it was beneath the dignity of the United States Army, which they both loved, to seek every crumb of intelligence information from allies and offer nothing in return. The allies had gathered it at great effort and often at cost of blood and honor—the Zimmerman affair showed that.

The old general's exasperation grew with every word. Then he cut in. Henceforth Van Deman would cease his efforts to bring about the Information Division, and that was an order. As if he had read Van Deman's mind, he made an amendment: Van Deman would under no circumstances bring the matter to the attention of Secretary of War Baker: that was an order, too!

Too good a soldier to disobey a direct issue, Van Deman swallowed his disappointment and retired in good order. He was defeated for the time being. But his conviction never wavered: Intelligence for the Army had to come. Uncorrected myopia was intolerable whether in the individual or the body politic. And deliberate, cultivated myopia was, in Van Deman's view, tantamount to criminal betrayal of trust. Yet surely the failure was his own: Bell and Scott were fine and utterly patriotic soldiers; the record showed that. Somehow, somewhere, Van Deman had failed. Furthermore, Van Deman had to admit that he was almost alone in his convictions; the majority of senior officers would have wholeheartedly agreed with Scott's views. But their attitude was incomprehensible to Van Deman, as it would be to many of his successors confronted with the same wall of indifference and opposition through decades to come.

Now everything was involved in the race for time. Van

Deman was almost in despair. He had exhausted the resources of his fertile military mind. But fate was preparing to operate outside the confines of staff manuals. How could Van Deman have envisioned succor in the form of a woman? Van Deman elected to keep her anonymous in the records but states that she was one of the best-known and respected novelists of the day and that she had been preparing a series of articles on life in training camps. In Washington she was handed over to Van Deman. Other officers were busy waging war, paper or real.

Well, why not? he mused grimly. He'd asked for it: she wanted information and he was the champion information officer of the United States Army. They toured various military installations in and around Washington. It was a fine day and she was an interesting woman with a penetrating mind. Suddenly Van Deman was all attention. His ear had caught the word intelligence. And she meant what he meant: military intelligence. She had a confidante in European intelligence. From him she had a good basic knowledge of the subject and what they were doing over there.

What were we doing, if he might say without breaching security? What we *weren't* doing poured out of the frustrated officer in a storm of words that surprised even him. And then he sobered. She must not print that, must not let our enemies know of our weakness. She wouldn't, she promised, but added that it was high time the Secretary of War was approached by someone who didn't have to ask permission of the Chief of Staff to do it. The end of the day found Van Deman in much better spirits than at its unpromising beginning.

In the manner of a soldier he refused to rely on one shot doing the trick. He had learned that Secretary of War Baker frequently breakfasted at his club with an official of the Washington police. Van Deman knew the latter slightly. He approached him and to his relief found a most receptive listener. The police official himself had been experiencing qualms about

178

security matters in the nation's capital. What he said to Baker at the next breakfast session was just between them, but it was potent.

Baker wanted an immediate and accurate briefing on the intelligence situation between this country and our allies.

Within forty-eight hours the order went out to the president of the War College that an intelligence organization was to be set up without delay. On the third of May an intelligence branch of the college was established, with Van Deman as its director.

It was a signal victory, but it was not enough. Only the re-creation of intelligence as the Second Section of the General Staff would provide a structure adequate to the demands that inevitably would be made upon it. Realization of his fondest dream would not come until the twenty-sixth of August, 1918. On that day intelligence was reconstituted as the Second Division. "G2" has remained there ever since.

But by that day of realization for Van Deman, the pattern of retribution had already emerged. A General Staff Division normally was headed by an officer of general's rank. It was not a requirement, however. The Chief of Staff had authority to make the decision. He did: the new Second Division was to be headed by a brigadier general. But Van Deman was a colonel. He could have been promoted to put the best man in the right place, but mysteriously his name had been dropped back some forty places on the official promotion list. Under those circumstances there was nothing for it but to relieve him of duty to make way for a man of general officer's rank. Those wise in the ways of the Army would draw their own conclusions: maneuvering out of channels, even inadvertently, could account for such things as that.

Meanwhile the government in London was anxiously seeking any straw that would sustain hope and courage. It came in an odd form by wireless in clear language. The German

179

intercepting station at Neumünster pulled it in, too, but did not discern the double meaning in the text and paid no more attention to it. The message said:

President's embargo ruling should have immediate notice. Grave situation affecting international law. Statement foreshadows ruin of many neutrals. Yellow journals unifying natural excitement immensely.

Oddly enough the message gave deep satisfaction in high circles in London. But it was restrained. There should be confirmation. Neumünster got the second message, too, and ignored it also. It said:

Apparently neutrals protest is sharply discounted and ignored. Isman hard hit. Blockade issue effects pretext for embargo on by-products ejecting suets and vegetable oils.

Lacking at that early date a code and cipher system with London sophisticated enough to withstand the picking of the expert German cryptanalysts at Neumünster, Washington had made a full swing the other way and employed the simple system Kerbey used two wars before. Taking the first letter of each word in the first message and the second letter of each word in the second, identical texts were obtained:

Pershing sails from N. Y. June 1.

On the staff of Major General John J. Pershing was a young major entrusted with intelligence matters. Dennis E. Nolan would go high. On his way up he would serve as Assistant Chief of Staff G2. The only serious contender with Van Deman for the title Father of Intelligence in the U.S. Army is Nolan. Between his efforts in France and Van Deman's in Washington, Army Intelligence burst from its swaddling clothes with impressive speed. It became a famous "triple-play" combination: "From Nolan to Van Deman to 'Action.'"

180

The Corps of Intelligence Police

IT WAS one of these messages from Nolan to Van Deman that gave birth to what one day would be the Army's far-flung Counter Intelligence Corps, and therefore to the present-day development, the Intelligence Corps. The message went out over General Pershing's signature and had the force of a personal request from him. Consequently it received appropriate attention in Washington. But Nolan originated the idea. General Scott was headed for retirement, so it was Acting Chief of Staff Tasker H. Bliss who read the message from the chief of the fledgling American Expeditionary Force in France. It was an urgent request for fifty specialists of noncommissioned status and fifty officers to perform intelligence and counterespionage duties in his secret service section overseas. At least all fifty of the noncoms should be most unusual men, so unusual that when Van Deman confronted with his recruiting problem one of the descendants of Allan Pinkerton, in the New York headquarters of the famous detective agency, Pinkerton told him, "There ain't no such animal."

Van Deman's first requirement was sterling character. This was to be reiterated a score of years and another world war later by Brigadier General "Wild Bill" Donovan when recruiting for his Office of Strategic Services, the OSS. It reaffirmed the axiom that it is better to train men of sound moral character in the devious ways of clandestine operations than to try to make reliable agents out of sharp characters. Next, Van Deman wanted linguists; they must be able to read and write at least French, and preferably both French and German. They should be cosmopolites capable of smooth, unostentatious living on their own amid foreign populations. Finally, and it was this that generated Pinkerton's impatient estimate, they should be men of experience in police theory, methods, and field operations.

181

Van Deman eventually got his men. Qualifications were another matter. First Lieutenant (later Colonel) Royden Williamson who was to command them found the recruits to include "a delegation of Cajuns from Louisiana, a sprinkling of French Canadians, a coterie of Harvard men, a French deserter, and even an active Communist." Despairing of ever satisfying Nolan's lofty requirements, of getting fifty even moderately capable men, Williamson resorted to an expedient that has made successors wince: he advertised in New York and New Orleans newspapers for men for the intelligence service.

He herded them together and started them off for Fort Jay, New York, for training. But since no one quite knew what "training" entailed, Williamson was ordered to Washington to find out. The people who were to instruct him were as surprised and as ignorant as he was: Van Deman was already doing the work of ten men in getting the parent intelligence section organized and functioning, and could not help.

In October, Williamson rejoined his company, to find them lacking everything except close-order drill—even warm clothing. But ready or not, orders for overseas shipment came.

Meanwhile, General Bliss and his General Staff assistants had been having their own troubles. There was no precedent in the Army for this sort of an organization. Not even a name. What should it be called? The staff studied the Pershing message. No one wanted to mention secret service. Intelligence, then? There was the reference to police experience. Intelligence Police? That sounded right. Only time would show what capabilities for misunderstanding and mischief the semantics contained. The final designation of Corps of Intelligence Police was what went to General Bliss for his approval. Where "corps" came into it there is no hint. Evidently it was plucked out of the air to indicate a particular army unit and not the specific organizational structure of that name which implies a certain size and prerogatives. The unit would be a corps in name only; this lack of formality would make difficult indeed

182

the path of the Corps of Intelligence Police and its successor, the Counter Intelligence Corps.

The crowning anomaly came in August, 1917 when General Bliss approved a staff memorandum providing for official establishment of the proposed Corps but somehow overlooked the draft order that accompanied it. Only an order could really do the trick. But the records in Washington defy researchers to uncover one. During the ensuing forty years many devices have been employed to overcome the fact of official illegitimacy in the birth certificate, and to surmount the troubles of a Corps that was not a corps. For instance: the fifty noncommissioned officers, how and in what branch were they to be assigned? Van Deman finally prevailed upon the Quartermaster Corps to loan ranks. Eventually thousands would be borrowed from recalcitrant branches of the service to give status and authority to the members of the organized reserve who served.

Williamson embarked his men on a cold October day minutes after jettisoning his unwanted Communist. They arrived at Saint-Nazaire, France. Stories that they were promptly put under arrest by the Marine Corps guard there are without foundation. Stories that, after tramping endlessly under a cold December moon to reach Pershing's headquarters at Chaumont, their very first assignment consisted of digging latrines in frozen ground, are true.

Before transferring attention to the U.S. intelligence situation in Europe, however, it is necessary to complete the sequence of events in America. An English historian on the subject dismisses the American effort at this time as "insignificant," a presumption on his part, since the records were unavailable to him or anyone else outside the Corps of Intelligence Police. There were conspicuous failures, an admission that must be made for any intelligence organization anywhere, yet the fact remains that the only German secret agent condemned to death in World War I in this country was trapped by Van

183

Deman's personnel. That agent, thoroughly dangerous, could have been a passenger in a rowboat in the Upper Bay of New York harbor the night of the explosion at Black Tom. The work of American agents was astute, mature, and professional and out of all proportion to the degree of training accorded them.

Gunpoint

THE outbreak of war impelled German agents of all categories into Mexico whose neutrality, as has been illustrated, had a distinctly pro-German bias. Smoked-out and concentrated, these agents comprised a natural target for American counterintelligence. Washington authorities sharply denied permission to the CIP under Pershing's command to place secret detection agents in technically neutral Spain where the German secret service openly based its anti-Pershing operations. Unaccountably, however, the same controls told Captain José A. Lipscomb of the CIP office at Nogales, Arizona, to recruit discreetly an agent for undercover work in Mexico. Lipscomb conferred with an astute, imaginative special agent in his ménage named Byron S. Butcher. Unlike enthusiastic amateurs of later years, who, especially in Korea, recruited practically anything in sight for the sake of quick and generally useless results, Butcher never confused quantity with quality and recruited one man, a colonel in the Mexican Army. Colonel Paul Bernardo Altendorf was actually a soldier of fortune who loved life and adventure. To prolong the one and enjoy the other, he had developed qualities of calculated daring and flexibility of mind and action.

Butcher briefed him. Mexico City itself seemed the likeliest hunting ground, though the northern state of Sonora under the military rule of pro-German General Calles was hardly dull. Opposite Nogales, Arizona, was its twin in names,

Nogales, Sonora, a focal point for dangerous line-crossers. Lipscomb and Butcher would take care of things locally while Altendorf importuned Calles for permission to make an official trip to the capital.

Mexico City proved to be an agent's paradise. From lowly bistro to fashionable clubs, Caucasians, whose Spanish contained a heavy admixture of German guttural, moved—and drank and talked freely. Altendorf was an accomplished imbiber and a natural mixer, whatever the level. In an amazingly short time he had become friendly with one Kurt Jahnke. He and Lothar Witzke were considered by London to be the most savage and dangerous sabotage combination in existence. If fourteen million dollars' worth of exploded munitions and a vast waste of wreckage at Black Tom were actually their work, then Washington was inclined to agree with the British estimate.

Jahnke liked his bottle and he liked Altendorf. They made a good drinking pair. But Altendorf could hold his. He learned from the garrulous Jahnke how well the latter knew the United States: he had served in the Marine Corps, he explained with a wink. It was good training, and he got around. Later he revisited some of his service haunts. In San Francisco he went straight to the authorities and told them he had overheard of a plot to blow up Mare Island Navy Yard. Then, said he, he went out and blew it up himself. Naturally, the authorities never suspected him. Sixteen children were among the casualties.

Did he always work alone? Altendorf wanted to know. No, there was another. This man was soon going to smuggle himself into the United States and there co-ordinate a whole program of sabotage to be carried out with the connivance of certain international labor organizations. On the way he would, incidently, take care of an annoying matter at Nogales, Arizona. A pair of American army people playing at being cops were taking their game too seriously. Lothar Witzke

185

would eliminate Lipscomb and Butcher before rendezvousing with his henchman for the big show aimed at crippling the American war effort.

A big job and Witzke could do with help. For one thing, getting across the border would be facilitated if he could be put in touch with General Calles. Altendorf hardly could believe the way the cards were falling. He offered cooperation: he knew the country; he would escort Witzke to Calles and then return to Mexico City for duty.

A few days later he was retracing his steps northward, this time in the company of Witzke. Altendorf never underestimated this man. Witzke was shrewd, ruthless, certainly well educated, daring in the extreme, and utterly dedicated to his country. If he had a weakness, Altendorf had not found it, until one night near the end of their journey. As with Jahnke, it was the bottle. Out of it came Witzke's boast of having engineered the Mare Island explosion and his and Jahnke's involvement in the far greater ones on the east coast, specifically one in which they had rowed over to a place called Black Tom the night of July 30, 1916. Altendorf knew about Black Tom and it made his skin crawl to realize that opposite him was one of the men responsible for it. If ever in his life he had played carefully, he would do so now. He considered. The town they were now in was one of the few in which there was an American consular representative. He would have to get to him. The problem was how. It seemed flatly melodramatic to Altendorf that he should resort to the old business of plying his companion with drink so he could execute his plan. It was indeed a scene in the best thriller tradition that the saboteur's head finally went down on his arm in drunken snores, while Altendorf slipped into the night. Fortunately for him, in the time he had he was able to convince the startled American official of his identity and status and to prevail upon him to send a carefully worded telegram to Nogales, Arizona.

Back in the hotel room, Altendorf faced an aroused Witzke

across the table. The German's eyes focused on his with difficulty. But they focused, and their cold regard was reinforced by the round ring of the pistol barrel down which Altendorf peered. He pretended amazement, wounded honor, and all the rest. He knew it was a poor enough defence for his life against the drunkenly suspicious Witzke. After all, Altendorf argued with a loose tongue, with all that liquor in him, a man might go outside, mightn't he? He dropped his own head on his arm. The show of indifference worked. Witzke later spoke feelingly of his regret at not having pulled the trigger when he had had Altendorf at the end of his gun.

The next day they parted, Witzke to go to General Calles, Altendorf ostensibly to go back to Mexico City. Altendorf displayed a poor sense of direction. That night he swung aboard a freight train heading north and left it in the Nogales, Arizona, yards. Lipscomb was waiting. He explained that they had acted promptly on the telegraphed warning and that Butcher was in Nogales, Mexico. Altendorf was alarmed. Lipscomb reassured him. It had all been arranged with the Mexicans: Butcher would pose as a Mexican emigration official to keep a watch for Witzke and thus learn his plans for crossing.

The next day Witzke appeared. He presented a passport in the name of a Russian, one Paul Waberski, who had lived in New York and San Francisco for the last fifteen years. His accent was convincing. The Mexicans regarded all Russian passports with suspicion, but Butcher had prepared them and Waberski was cleared. A couple of days later he crossed the border and this time it was his turn to look into gun muzzles. Lipscomb and Butcher were behind them.

A personal search of Witzke was disappointing. The only questionable articles found were double passports but he could not be held long because of that. Any other trifling charge which might be manufactured against him he would also doubtless be able to beat. There was a hurried consultation in

187

the back room where Paul Altendorf was concealed. Altendorf knew that Witzke had baggage. It must still be on the Mexican side. There were further arrangements with the Mexican authorities, and the bags came into Lipscomb's possession. These provided ample evidence. There were complete code formulas and a letter in code. The data was rushed to Washington. One of the documents, when broken, said: "The bearer of this is a subject of the Empire who travels as the Russian under the name of Pablo Waberski. He is a German secret agent. Please furnish him on request equipment, protection, and assistance; also advance him upon demand up to one thousand pesos in Mexican gold and send his code telegrams to this Embassy as official consular dispatches."

Witzke denied everything with unbreakable calm, even when confronted with the decoded message. Nevertheless, he was convicted and sentenced to be executed. As with Otto Keuhn a world war later, the forgiving nature of Americans would see to it that he did not die, and like Keuhn, he would be eventually freed to go home. In Germany, naval Lieutenant Lothar Witzke was decorated with the Iron Cross, First and Second Class, for his outstanding work in the United States.

Sometimes spy-detection had its whimsical side. During the Witzke chase CIP agents in Washington were coming to grips with what they had good reason to believe was an enemy penetration of vital war industries. A man with a German name, dubious background, flashy clothes, and sports car to match, allegedly represented the steel industry and in such a capacity made calls on many people in a position to know much about the American war effort. The CIP discovered that the man had two well-furnished apartments at a distance from each other in Washington. Determined to nail a lid on the case, CIP made arrangements with the law for a surreptitious search of one of the flats. They found numerous well-bound cardboard boxes with some hint of index numbers on the fronts. Could this be code data? They were torn open. In "dry" Washington they found forty-two cases of a famous brand of liquor and dozens of pairs of sheer stockings, equally hard to come by in the wartime capital.

Solution?

WHILE out of chronological sequence, it might be best at this time, while the Black Tom details are still fresh in mind, to summarize the case. The German government after fighting the claims bitterly and, according to Peaslee's claim, fraudulently, unexpectedly offered to make a substantial settlement out of court. This was not to be regarded as an admission of guilt according to Berlin, for the charges had never been proved. Nevertheless, it was time to bring the matter to an end.

Berlin's position was based on the fact that the claims judges and the army of legal experts still felt there were loopholes. Once more the hunt for Kristoff was initiated, and again he was found in prison, a different one for a different crime. He was about to be released and promised to meet with a Peaslee operative to make a statement. He never appeared and then the Germans reported his death. The body was exhumed and, except for one feature, it appeared that the corpse was indeed that of the man who apparently had hidden away that night to await the rowers, Jahnke and Witzke. However, the dental work of the corpse did not correspond to that of the Kristoff who had been in prison. Nevertheless, Kristoff was never heard of again.

Now to Mena Edwards. They relocated her too, older, of course, and no longer the "Kodak Girl." As a matter of fact, she had lost that job almost right after the Black Tom explosion because the company felt that she had displayed too much interest in things German and had too many German asso-

189

ciates. The latter had been true, she admitted to Peaslee agents in reiterating statements made not long after the explosion.

Through a girl friend named Vera, who had said she was French but later admitted to being a German agent, Mena had been invited to a certain house on West Fifteenth Street in New York. She was introduced to a sharp-eyed but very attractive blonde woman referred to as the "Baroness" Martha Held. Number 123 seemed to be some sort of a club. There was liquor and there were amiable girls to entertain gentlemen callers. These were not mere drifters or tired businessmen, she discovered. Two of them were von Papen and von Boy-Ed. One night no less a personage than the famous and highly controversial Count von Bernstorff came. There were others who preferred anonymity. Only German was spoken and there was much talk from time to time about explosions and fires. Even bombs were displayed. She had heard the name Black Tom and even a date. On that date she decided to get out of town. She was visiting with a friend when the great roar came late in the night and although they were many miles away, they could see the huge fire. Mena became frightened and wondered if she might not be implicated somehow. But she attended a big celebration at Number 123 to mark the success of the Black Tom effort. She decided to break with the crowd, but she lost her job anyway. She mentioned other names from time to time, and in consequence of this and other data, Peaslee went burrowing after Jahnke and Witzke. The former now was found to be a respected member of the Prussian Diet and unapproachable. Peaslee thought Witzke to be the key man, anyway. But where was he? Astute detection uncovered him in Maracaibo, Venezuela. He refused extradition and curtly denied participation in all except Black Tom. That, he admitted, was "another matter." Now the case seemed to turn upon the mysterious Graetnor whom the deceased Kristoff claimed hired him for what were no longer doubted to be sabotage trips. Here they got a little help from Witzke and more from another former German agent named Fred Herrmann. Graetnor was discovered to be no less than von Rintelen's old Baltimore principal, Hinsch, and it was to Hinsch that Albert had at one time transferred funds due to pressure from Hinsch's operatives who had taken part in the Black Tom explosion. Kristoff was a Hinsch man. Intercepted 40 O.B. messages showed that Witzke was involved too.

Then in a sequence the equal of any cloak-and-dagger fiction piece, Peaslee's people were able to uncover a series of secret ink messages written on pages of such pulp magazines of the day as *Blue Book* and *Adventure*. They bought up whole stocks of these magazines in used-book shops. They had uncovered one of the principal channels of communication the espionage-sabotage ring had used in those years of sinister doings. When developed, these messages mentioned the names of all these principals in indisputable association.

But the court still remained aloof. Kristoff, Jahnke, Witzke, Albert, Hinsch, *et al,* were indisputably linked to the great German sabotage machine, but were they linked equally solidly to the Black Tom explosion itself? The judges believed not. Practically everyone excepting the defence attorneys did. American intelligence has assumed that to be the truth. And shortly afterwards, as we have seen, Germany offered settlement out of court.

The CIP in France

THE record of the Corps of Intelligence Police in Europe was better than anyone had a right to expect, considering the nature of its origin, the want-ad level of many of its charter members, and the almost total lack of training facilities. The way of the pioneers was made harder by official fog obscuring the direction in which the organization was intended to develop. The designation was Intelligence Police. Did that

191

mean they were adjuncts of the Provost Marshal and his Military Police? Nolan said emphatically not. But the Provost thought they were superfluous, and his successors thought so to such a degree that at the critical mid-point of World War II, a generation later, the Provost Marshal General succeeded in killing off the Counter Intelligence Corps within the continental United States and taking over many of its key people. The Corps survived that, too, and emerged stronger and better trained. In any case, "soldiers first and intelligence personnel second" appeared early in World War I as a motto to apply to those people, and it was destined to stick. Accordingly, Corps of Intelligence Police members were required to wear uniforms at all times. The Allies, wise in the ways of secret service, promptly refused to allow the men in their training schools. The order was altered. But the anonymous operative in civilian clothes in the morning might still have to be a sergeant in uniform in the afternoon because he had drawn some camp duty or was due at the pay table. It was all very revealing to the Army and any enemy agents in the vicinity.

In combat intelligence, the Corps sustained one of the highest ratios of casualties to numbers engaged, in the whole AEF. In the rear zone—roughly 80,000 square miles—some 3,700 cases involving security problems were gone into, with enough legal evidence established in 229 cases to neutralize the principals who were involved. But the Corps men soon learned that card-index toil, like taxes, was inevitable; more than 170,000 names were catalogued. These would prove of greatest value in checking nearly four thousand loyalty complaint cases. Run of the mine stuff? Certainly. Most counterintelligence work is just that kind of dull, incessant, but essential, grind.

But drama comes to spice the brew, as it did for Sergeant Pedro Padilla. It was a particular thorn in the side of the CIP that in neighboring neutral Spain, German agents operated openly to effect espionage and sabotage against the American forces in France. German gold was flowing freely to recruit laborers who would be funneled into AEF construction projects. The missions of the recruits ranged from espionage to any other act that would damage the Allied war effort. It was amid these conditions that reliable CIP informant agents in neutral countries would have proved invaluable. But Washington remained adamant. Barred from working to stem the poisonous flood at its source, CIP could only seek to detect it after it already was established within the AEF and then act to counter its corrosive work.

Through a civilian informant came a hint that a dangerous situation existed in a camp of Spanish laborers at a plant construction site in western France. The informant hinted darkly that there would be short shrift for anyone who tried to penetrate the ring.

CIP was breaking into the "big time." There could be no amateur clumsiness here, or a man would pay with his life. Great care was taken in selecting an operative. One candidate who seemed eminently fitted for the job was Sergeant Pedro Padilla. Born in a poor section of Madrid, he had had the hard idiom of the slums burned into him. He was approached and the idea appealed to him. There ensued a careful period of preparation. Padilla's knowledge of the Spanish slums was the subject of a detailed "refresher course." Every contingency was thought of—except one.

Padilla presented himself at the camp as a day laborer seeking work. He was told by a sharp-eyed interrogator to come back again. Padilla reviewed the situation. He was positive that he had not slipped. He improved on his waiting time by observing the Spaniards in the camp. Working from data supplied by the informant, he believed that he had isolated two or more of the principals whose confidence it was his assignment to win. They were a rough, hard-bitten lot.

He was a little nonplused to see some of those very men present when he made his next appearance at the labor office.

Once more the job interrogator studied him with a cold stare. Then quickly the man reached out. He seized Padilla's hands and turned them palms uppermost.

Too late Padilla realized that his preparation had one serious defect, a point which case officers ever since have carefully taken into consideration when building cover stories for their operatives: Padilla had sought work as a day-laborer yet on his soft hands there was not a single callous, not a single scar, and his fingernails were not at all the broken, dirt-begrimed nails of a man whose fingers were concerned with daily rough work.

The interrogator's black eyes fixed him with open suspicion. The Spaniards around him closed in. Padilla's mind was working fast. He explained: He had understood that there was house painting to be done. He was a painter. Obviously, he had been misinformed. He would have to seek elsewhere. But the others had different ideas. He was told to wait. And then again. By various devices they detained him until closing time. Padilla had played waiting games before. He gave no sign of his anxiety but pretended friendship and hinted that he might be useful to the right people.

Then came darkness and he was taken to a cellar with thick walls through which no sound could escape to the outside. One after another the Spaniards took turns. It was a third degree that Padilla knew could have but one result if he failed to give answers that only a true *Madrileño* would know. His brain reeled with fatigue. But he came up with the right answers. By the break of the dawn he thought he might never see, but he realized that he had convinced them.

Now the situation was quite reversed for they wanted him to work for them. They outlined the situation. Bit by bit he accumulated vital information on their methods, their lines of communication, and their contacts, and then Padilla the laborer disappeared.

Sergeant Padilla the CIP operative turned up at CIP headquarters, and there ensued tremendous police raids at the Spanish camp and other points. The communication line to Spain was thoroughly wrecked.

Trap-door Trap

WITH the end of the war, the Corps was assigned to handle all security matters at the Paris peace talks under the shrewd direction of the newly promoted Brigadier General Van Deman. One of the most promising leads of the whole spyridden conference period consisted of a trap door in the American official billets building which gave upon a dark, mysterious passage and which surveillance showed had been repeatedly breached. Van Deman himself went into action. Tracing the tortuous tunnel to its terminal, he was astonished to find himself in a famous night club where the entertainment program was long and greatly varied and the chorus girls' costumes short and simply varied. Further inquiry showed that spies did not know of the tunnel, but tired American peace talk delegates did. While the mystery lasted, it gave the lean security chief some anxious moments; when it was solved, he had other moments in which to reflect on the frailty of human nature.

American Spy in Russia

LITTLE known is the fact that about this time Washington put a spy into Russia. Even less known is it that the spy was a woman, and that initially, she drew the pay of a lieutenant in the army and then, because the quality and quantity of her reports deserved it, the pay of a major. She did not possess a commission, but she was officially listed in the confidential record of General M. Churchill, then the G2, or military intelligence chief in Washington. Accredited to the *New York Evening Post* and the *Baltimore Sun* as a correspondent, the lady, whose present name is Mrs. Arthur M. Blake, went to France and first worked closely with General Van Deman. With the commencement of political chaos in Germany, she was sent to Berlin and on one occasion, because of a mistake in recognition signals, found herself caught in the street in a cross-fire between German soldiers and Communist irregulars. She flattened herself on the pavement and bullets whined over her head. But she lived to go on to Russia.

Forty years later, I interviewed Mrs. Blake. She sat erect, her slender body still charged with nervous energy and her mind as sharp and discerning as it had always been. This amazing woman smoked cigarettes chain-fashion and told me of her writing forbidden things and smuggling them out of Moscow by means of Jewish refugees fleeing across the border into Finland.

"I knew this procedure could not continue indefinitely, though," she said. And sure enough, one night there was a banging on her door. Three secret police agents stood there. She was given a few minutes to dress and accompany them. She was held in solitary confinement in prison for three weeks, a treatment calculated to soften her up and lead to confessions. But she revealed nothing. Instead she learned from her captors that, as she had suspected, one of her messengers had been trapped trying to get across the border and had been searched to the skin.

"Probably I could thank the desperate need of the Russians for American food supplies that I was not treated too badly," she explained. "On my petition to be taken out of that awful hole and put in a big cell with others, they complied."

This incarceration lasted for eighteen months. And then she was freed through the success of negotiations by which all American prisoners were to be released in exchange for American aid. Before her departure, her hosts offered tremendous

196

inducements if she would become a double agent. These included a fine estate, lately the property of Czarist nobility, and free education for her son, still in America. Her reply was politely but firmly negative. Perhaps the Muscovites would not have been so amiable could they have foreseen that this apparently frail woman would accomplish the most improbable feat and enter Russia a second time on an espionage mission.

Mrs. Blake returned to Washington, made a lengthy report, and again got a journalistic assignment that accomplished her entry into Russia, this time by way of Japan, Sakhalin, and Manchuria. Again she was under secret commission by G2. It was while she was in Irkutsk, Siberia, that new political upheavals shook the country, and once more she found herself the guest of the police authorities. The Siberian climate and the almost total lack of amenities, difficult to tolerate for even those far more rugged than she, made heavy demands upon her constitution. But she survived four months of this ordeal before the State Department got her freed once more. In the United States again, she thereafter confined her activities as far as Russia was concerned to journalism and books.

The Shameful Years

THE two decades that followed the armistice of 1918 were for the United States, suddenly elevated into a position of world leadership for which it was eminently unprepared, years of political disillusionment. From the standpoint of organized intelligence in this country, they can only be regarded as The Shameful Years.

If any lessons had been learned in Washington in consequence of what had gone before, that knowledge was not evident. In a matter of months nearly all of the 452 CIP's in Europe would be discharged. The G2 in Washington would see this organization of nearly three hundred reserve officers and a thousand civilians, plus about two hundred CIP men

197

distributed over the country and elsewhere, diminish to a handful. At the lowest point of the 1920's and early '30's, the CIP actually dropped to six noncommissioned officers, all of whom were eligible for retirement or transfer.

It was during this period that the Soviet Union established its espionage system in the United States. It was then also that Japanese developments in espionage were achieving their highest level.

True, America was heavily burdened with postwar problems in a shattered world and was soon to plunge into the Great Depression of the '30's. Radical retrenchment had to be the order of the day. But it was more than that. There was a recurrence of all forms of indifference and often open hostility to anything concerned with intelligence—even a return of the attitude that spying was un-American. It was during this period that Secretary of State Stimson summarily obliterated America's "Black Chamber," one of the finest cryptography laboratories in modern times, ranking next to the British 40 O.B., and its British Cryptograph Service.

With the end of the '30's and the outbreak of war in Europe once more, the United States authorized some increases in budgets and personnel for intelligence work. It was only a start, and Pearl Harbor was just months away.

VIII

Cataclysm

As THE rain of bombs and torpedoes in Hawaii marked the beginning of World War II for Americans, it quite as definitely marked the end of American adolescence in matters of intelligence. As Pearl Harbor stunned the nation, it quite as surely unified it. As the attack was an outstanding tactical surprise by the Japanese war party, it was as surely a strategic error of the first magnitude. For now there could be no stopping the American war effort, backed as it was by vast reserves. With its more than three thousand casualties of all kinds, Pearl Harbor was a human catastrophe and as such was certain to give rise to the most searching of political questions, some shocking in their implications. Was Pearl Harbor allowed to happen by those at the very highest level for the purpose of unifying the country? This would have been playing for stakes on a scale incomprehensible to ordinary minds. Yet the coldest objectivity, in the light of the accumulated mass of evidence twenty years after the event, demands recognition of the possibility that it was a bartering of a few thousand killed and

199

wounded, a dozen ships, and a few hundred planes for the assurance of ultimate victory—absolute and unconditional—for a nation galvanized into action.

If this hypothesis is true, intelligence, one way or another, was quite incidental; and the millions of words of testimony in a score of investigations with their frequently contradictory findings have been so much grandstand play; the ruined high-ranking officers mere political scapegoats. If it is not true, however, then the continuing controversy on points of intelligence that Pearl Harbor generated has both value and relevance.

The black hands on the full-moon face of the clock in Aloha Tower on Honolulu's waterfront were just beyond the point of midnight on Saturday, the 6th of December 1941, or, rather, the first few minutes of Sunday the 7th. Here and there in the city, groups of white-clad sailors began drifting back to catch late liberty boats to their ships in Pearl Harbor. At the big naval base itself lights were going out, but there still was plenty of illumination for maximum security.

In Manila, five thousand miles to the west, at the point where Taft Avenue becomes a confusing delta of streets and lanes in front of the post office building and the Quezon Bridge, the clock on the city hall tower showed the time against the bright, hot evening sky: just after 6:30 P.M., Sunday, December 7th. There was the usual cacophony of motor horns interspersed with the sharp hoofbeats of the ponies drawing *calesas* and *carromatas*. The usual brightly-clad throngs of Filipinos were strolling on Dewey Boulevard now that the heat of the day was waning.

In Washington D.C., halfway around the world, it was hardly daylight on a winter morning. It had not much in common with the other two places except the date, Sunday, the 7th of December. It had just turned 5:30 A.M. and those on night-duty watches in scores of government buildings, civil

200

and military, were beginning to anticipate the arrival of their reliefs.

More than five hundred miles north of the Hawaiian Island of Oahu, with Honolulu on its southern coast, six huge carriers and a considerable number of lesser ships slid rapidly without lights through the dark Pacific waters. Below the flight decks of the Japanese carriers were more than four hundred warplanes. Some were fighters, some dive bombers, some conventional bombers, and others modified for low-level torpedo launching. In the radio rooms of several ships, receivers were tuned to Station KGMB in Honolulu. . . . News in English and soft Hawaiian music.

Past midnight in Honolulu. For some time Rear Admiral Husband E. Kimmel had been in his bed. The Commander-in-Chief of the Pacific Fleet was known as a martinet and a driver. When awake, he pushed himself and everyone else relentlessly, but when it was time to rest, he rested. He had good cause to let worry destroy his sleep for he had no illusions about the inevitability of armed collision between America and Japan, and when it came it would doubtless involve his Pacific fleet. Quite possibly the involvement would come in the very first stages of conflict. Studies and estimates prepared by both army and navy staff officers on Oahu months ago had listed a surprise attack on Pearl Harbor as well within Japanese capabilities. The estimate had envisioned the use by Japan of six aircraft carriers and supporting vessels. The carriers would release their warplanes about two hundred miles northwest of Oahu. The strike could be destructive unless there was time to man ships and planes and antiaircraft batteries, and deploy both air and surface units. The study had been sent to Washington. Admiral Kimmel had also urged that he be kept fully and promptly informed, but since August there had been little information from Washington.

201

The Admiral had naturally followed the tense diplomatic negotiations in Washington closely. Unquestionably the times were critical. Last Thanksgiving weekend had come the President's "war-warning" message. It had opened with the ominous words, "This is to be considered a war warning. . . ." Then it stated that "an aggressive move" by Japan could be expected in the next few days. But Washington said this was likely to be directed toward the Philippines, Thailand, or the Kra Isthmus between Thailand and Malaya, all these places thousands of miles distant from Hawaii.

Within the last forty-eight hours there had been several messages from Washington pointing up the crisis. Japan now was known to have advised several of its major diplomatic posts, including Manila, to destroy at once certain secret-code machines and other material that might require time for disposal; only certain simple codes, which could be easily disposed of, would be kept. The American State Department followed with instructions to certain American Pacific posts to destroy everything of a classified nature not urgently needed and to be prepared to make disposal complete if there was a sudden greater emergency. That afternoon, Saturday, Admiral Kimmel himself had been ordered by the Navy Department to give similar instruction to the more isolated naval posts in the Pacific.

There had been a staff conference that afternoon on the general situation. Kimmel's operations officer had held to his opinion that a surprise attack on Pearl Harbor was less than a remote possibility. But there was a very disturbing point: His intelligence officer, Captain E. T. Layton, frankly admitted that his office had once more "lost" the major units of the Japanese fleet, in particular the carriers. With radio direction finding still an inexact science, his monitors nevertheless believed they had enough data to justify a surmise that the fleet still was in home waters. For the second time in thirty days the Japanese Imperial Navy had suddenly changed call signs for all units. Layton suggested this was a prelude to some major operational move. Now Layton's radio monitors had the tedious task of reidentifying fleet units with new call signs. One help in this was the recognition of "fists" previously known to belong to operators on the radio staffs of certain carriers. (A "fist" is the individual way in which a particular telegrapher taps his messages.) This had been done in a number of cases. Now application of radio direction techniques gave rise to the plottings that apparently located some of these major units in home waters, probably in Yokosuka or Kure Naval Base areas off Honshu. There was some identifiable radio traffic which would place one or more carriers in the Carolines, however. These islands were south of Japan, west of Hawaii. Melbourne and Manila had this on their boards, too. But Layton, a good intelligence man, had reiterated that his locator sheet was full of surmises.

The Admiral could not have been happy about the condition of his fleet at Pearl. He was severely undermanned and there were many green officers and ratings alike in the personnel he did have, both ashore and afloat. True, there were upwards of ninety vessels of all types. But it was an unbalanced fleet for the air age. He needed more modern carriers to provide an effective air umbrella. Not a single carrier was with the fleet at the moment, although three were assigned. The battleships had a heavy punch but they were slow. He needed many more heavy cruisers and more light, fast cruisers. There was a tremendous amount of modernization to be accomplished and endless training to bring the fleet up to anything like battle efficiency. In no case could the fleet be considered a match for the Imperial Japanese Navy should it come against him in a general surface action. Apparently Washington had not considered this a strong possibility, as President Roosevelt had recently weakened the Pacific fleet even further by detaching a number of major units and many destroyers for service in the Atlantic. The studies only recently sent to Washington

203

expressed Admiral Kimmel's views of that time: If Japan planned to hit him, she would do it with aircraft and submarines, not a major surface force.

It was known that one of the most experienced intelligence officers in the Navy held strongly to the same view. Captain Ellis M. Zacharias had expressed himself on the point on several occasions. There were rumors that lately he had been almost insubordinate in his determination to impress upon his superiors his conviction that Japan would hit Pearl Harbor in a surprise air attack, and very soon.

Admiral Kimmel had been weary when he dropped into bed. He intended to get a good night's rest and be up early Sunday morning for a game of golf with Lieutenant General Walter C. Short, the Army's commander for the Hawaiian Department.

General Short had gone to bed early, too. There had been a quiet evening with service friends and he had found it a little boring. It had gotten off to a bad start because he had kept Mrs. Short waiting for nearly an hour owing to business with Colonel George Bicknell, the Army's counterintelligence chief for the islands. Bicknell had phoned just as they were about to leave and asked Short to postpone his departure until he could have an urgent word with him. During the course of the ensuing party, the General had been preoccupied. Maybe he had been rather unfair to Bicknell, but these intelligence people could be aggravating with their alarms and excursions.

When Bicknell arrived at Short's quarters at 6:30 that evening, he had asked to see the General alone. Then he had produced the transcript of a transoceanic telephone conversation between a Japanese-born Hawaiian dentist and a Tokyo newspaper. The FBI had monitored the call and referred it to a Nisei in the Corps of Intelligence Police for translation. Dr. Motokazu Mori and the caller in the distant *Yomiuri Shimbun* office had talked of whether there were airplanes flying around Honolulu, about searchlights, about the number of sailors on liberty, and then, most curiously for a call that was costing as much as that one, about flowers. Mori said that the number of flowers in bloom were among the fewest of the whole year, but that the hibiscus and poinsettias were in bloom.

Bicknell's people at counterintelligence felt sure that this high-priced talk about blooming flowers was a code to inform on the status of the American fleet at Pearl. The sparseness of blooming flowers could mean that the carriers and heavy cruisers were gone, while battleships and cruisers, hibiscus and poinsettias, were in port. It did seem odd that such a conversation would be indulged in over the transoceanic circuit unless it had something more than cultural significance. Still, Mori's wife was a correspondent in Hawaii for the Tokyo newspaper and it was not unthinkable. Conscious of Mrs. Short's impatience, the General had decided that little could be done at the moment, but that he would think it over further.

He had thought about it at the party. Did the telephone conversation have any connection with President Roosevelt's solemn war warning of the week before? Of course he had considered the possibility of a Japanese attack on Oahu. He had agreed in general with the recent Oahu studies. After the President's warning he had ordered a Class Three Alert for his command, the lowest of three possibilities. This alert called for an increased security guard at all installations against possible sabotage. The air arm was under the Army then, so that meant shifting parked aircraft at Hickam and Wheeler fields to group them closely for ease in establishing guard perimeters. Of course that would make them better targets, too, but if an assault were imminent, surely Washington would have supplemented its war warning of a week previous. In any case, General Short had radioed Washington some days before of the precautions he had taken in consequence of the warning, and

205

there had been no reply from the Chief of Staff, General George Marshall, to say that this was inadequate.

General Short was depending, too, upon Admiral Kimmel and his squadron of long-range Catalina flying boats to keep a close watch on the sea approaches. Furthermore, Admiral Kimmel's intelligence people presumably knew what they were about in keeping tabs on the Japanese carriers.

He was not depending wholly on the Navy for an early warning. Five Signal Corps Type-270 radars were now spotted around the island, and while these big units were new and their crews newer, they had shown in tests with friendly airplanes out of Oahu that they could pick up definable echoes and state direction, position, and speed of approaching aircraft at upwards of 150 miles. As a result of the President's "war" message General Short had directed that these units be manned the whole Thanksgiving weekend. It was only reasonable that if the Japanese were going to hit unexpectedly, they would take advantage of the American habit of relaxation over weekends. There also had been a front-page story in the *Honolulu Advertiser* that the Japanese fleet might hit on Thanksgiving. Where the newspapers got their information was not his business. But there had been so many cries of wolf that not too many appeared worried by it. As a matter of fact, the same paper had only that day, Saturday, declared the Japanese fleet to be "moving south." General Short's chief signal officer had gone to Washington. Among other things, he was trying to get more training money and some spares for the expensive tubes in the new radars. But in Washington, Lieutenant Colonel C. A. Powell was given the impression that the budget people considered too much money was already being spent on air-warning measures. To save the only tubes he had, Powell's assistant in Oahu had given the word after an eventless Thanksgiving Day weekend to go off the twenty-four-hour scanning alert. Instead there would be a three-hour dawn scan Saturday and Sunday mornings, December 6 and 7.

At the Japanese consulate in Honolulu a robust, round-faced Japanese named Nagao Kita who loved his *sake* and a good time paused to consider the state of things. Consul General Kita's mind dwelt upon the recent messages from Tokyo warning him to be prepared to destroy all classified material, keeping only a new "Hidden-Word" code. When he should hear on his short-wave receiver certain words stated, or repeated, at certain points in a news broadcast, he would know, for instance, that relationships had been broken off with Russia, or England, or with America. That would mean war, of course. Other phrases might reach him via overseas cables before matters got to such a pass. They would have specific meanings. There were not many of them. It looked as if Tokyo was stripping for action. He had been quietly destroying classified material for some time now, so convinced was he that things could not go on as they were between the United States and Japan. He had no code machine, therefore did not have to worry about that. His laboriously encoded messages to Tokyo went out via ordinary commercial means. There had been many of them lately, for ever since the directive of September 24th, Tokyo had been patricularly insistent upon detailed reports of the status of the fleet at Pearl Harbor. The September message had directed him to consider the American naval base as a grid of squares for reporting purposes. He would report the vessels present in each grid, and whether they habitually occupied the same grids when in harbor. He would note whether the ships were in the stream, at buoys, or in docks. He would particularly note whether ships were tied in pairs parallel to each other. Such detailed reporting meant careful work by young, dedicated Takeo Yoshikawa, known as "Vice-Consul Morimura."

"Morimura" was not sure when the war would break out, or where, but he felt that it would be very soon and that it would involve Pearl Harbor. Possibly he had already asked Consul General Kita to send the last message that ever would

207

be sent on the fleet data he had so patiently and meticulously been collecting for months. His final messages had been encoded and transmitted only an hour or so ago. It said that in Pearl were nine battleships, three Class-B cruisers, three seaplane tenders, and seventeen destroyers, and more light units were just coming in. He previously had noted the absence of carriers and heavy cruisers but he did not know where they had gone. Yoshikawa was especially pleased that he had been able to correct an erroneous report about balloon barrages above the base. He had expected such a barrage this weekend, but at dusk he had made a final trip around Pearl City, near the base. And later he had gone to his favorite observation place at the Japanese Shuncho-ro restaurant high on the Alewa hills back of the base. Here the view was excellent as he sat on the *tatami* mats sipping drinks and visiting with the amiable *geisha*. There were no balloons with trailing cables to foul low-flying aircraft. He thought it important to notify Tokyo because now the way would be open to use torpedo planes against ships in the shallow waters of the base. Such an attack could reduce the outer of the ships moored parallel, while bombing should take care of the inboard ships.

Yoshikawa had played a lone game. He had avoided even Italian or German officials. There was a German civilian, though. For operational purposes Yoshikawa referred to him as "Kalama." Japan was relying heavily on Kalama to provide information about the status of Pearl Harbor if all other means of communication should be cut off; the Japanese Navy would not want to risk an assault on an empty base, then or later. That Saturday morning Kalama had made one of his rare appearances at the consulate. He had driven up in his old yellow car and left an envelope with Vice-Consul Otojiro Okuda. Okuda gave it to Yoshikawa. In the envelope was Kalama's simplified code for signaling to observers at sea information on the status of Pearl Harbor. A light burning in the dormer window of his house at Kalama (the operational name for him was not too veiled) had significance depending upon the time of night it was turned on. At one hour it would mean ships of a certain type present, at another, certain other types of ships, and so on. Failing this, he would try the same thing with his automobile headlights pointed to the sea. In daytime, the kind and spacing of laundry on a clothesline of his other house at nearby Lanakai Beach was to accomplish the purpose, or the numbers and position of numbers on the sail of his Star sailboat. Bonfires at a certain location on the hills of Maui Island facing the sea would also serve, different hours meaning different things. Then there was the offer to try transmission of data by short wave. Kalama was a former German naval cadet and he knew Morse code. There were also arrangements for inserting certain false advertisements in the KGMB classified advertisements broadcast daily. Thus the American radio station would obligingly tell Japanese monitors at sea of conditions in Pearl Harbor.

Kalama was free to move about; he was trained in the German Navy; he had a daughter named Ruth who ran a beauty parlor heavily patronized by U.S. navy wives. Yoshikawa allowed himself a stray thought or two about Ruth. She had those appealing sort of eyes some western women had, and the form, too. He could not see any resemblance to either Kalama or his wife. But Yoshikawa did not presume to be an expert on western genetics. All he hoped was that Kalama would prove more useful than he had so far, submitting only one or two reports of ships in Pearl. At one time Yoshikawa had delivered to Kalama in a little shed at the rear of his house $14,000 in crisp new hundreds and twenties. For appearances' sake he had pretended to be a steward from the *Tatuta Maru,* just in port from Japan. That was late in October.

The steward trick was useful. Only a few days ago a "steward" from another ship had called at the consulate. He had left a little ball of rice paper with some ninety-seven questions

209

penned thereon. They dealt with details of Pearl Harbor and the habits of the American military there, and with the Army and Air Corps people. The "steward" was really Lieutenant Commander Suguru Suzuki of the Japanese Imperial Navy. Yoshikawa had been able to supply most answers in detail. As to the air installations, he had sometimes hired a small commercial airplane and flown above them, occasionally dipping low for a photograph. But he had found American airmen, soldiers, and sailors much more security conscious in their talk than he hoped they would be. Also he had been unable to get onto the base at Pearl, even when he had gone disguised as a Filipino laborer, and he had nearly gotten shot by a sentry that time.

In Manila, General Douglas A. MacArthur knew of those insistent messages Tokyo had been sending concerning the fleet at Pearl. He and Admiral Hart of the American Asiatic Fleet, based at Cavite across Manila Bay, knew that Tokyo not only wanted reports of ship movements but now reports of lack of movement, and that all reports were to be accompanied by utmost secrecy. They knew this because in the Signal Corps laterals of Malinta Tunnel at Corregidor there was a duplicate of Tokyo's famous "Purple" encoding machine. Together with others for London and Washington, it had been built by Signal Corps wizards by sheer deduction of what the Tokyo prototype had to be like to send the kind of encoded messages it turned out. The whole decrypting business was so marvelous that Washington gave the operation the code name of "Magic." Not since the famous American Black Chamber had Washington had such a complete understanding of what Japan still thought were her topmost secrets. It was a cryptanalysis triumph to match Admiral Hall's 40 O.B. in World War I. And it was most secret. Oddly enough, and for reasons never brought to light, neither the Army nor the Navy in Hawaii had been given a Purple machine, and Manila had no authority to relay what it knew to Short or Kimmel.

On the receipt of the war-warning message just before Thanksgiving, MacArthur had put his establishment throughout the Philippines on full-war footing twenty-four hours a day. Extensive maneuvers in concert with a new division of Filipino soldiers had just been completed. They showed promise, but there was a long way to go. In his headquarters within the Walled City of Manila, the General was glad he had insisted that at least half of the newly-arrived Flying Fortresses be deployed six hundred miles south to Mindanao. Air Corps boss General Brereton had been unhappy about that. There was no protection for them down there, even from the weather, and no maintenance facilities. Well, those could be provided in time and six hundred more miles of distance from Japan's splendid bomber fields on Formosa certainly was protection greater than they could have at Clark Field, north of Manila.

The assistant G2 of the Air Corps headquarters in Manila had been to a lawn party in north Manila that Sunday afternoon. Mostly personnel from the Army's Philippine Department headquarters in Fort Santiago were in attendance. It had been pleasant, but hot. There had been a careful avoidance of war talk. Now in the cool of the evening, the intelligence officer walked along Dewey Boulevard. Out to sea there was the usual scattering of freighters anchored in the magnificent harbor. Then he frowned. No "Red Ball" ships. He grunted. Hell of an intelligence estimate that was—no ships showing the rising-sun flag of Japan, therefore, war must be close! Still, it might be a contributory indication. He looked farther south and saw the familiar shapes of Admiral Hart's Asiatic squadron, the *Houston,* the *Marblehead,* a scattering of old "four-stacker" destroyers, a couple of oilers; he couldn't see the submarines. But some were there, no doubt. Not much of a match for the mighty pagoda-masted superdreadnaughts that Japan was supposed to have, but still, something. Against surprise he was inclined to put faith in the Signal Corps Type-270 radars, new as they were. Only one actually was in operation, on the west coast of Luzon, at Iba. Already it had detected Japanese aircraft formations maneuvering off the coast on the night of December 3rd and 4th. There had been a single unidentified plane very high above Clark Field on two early morning occasions as well. The Fifth Interceptor Command Chief, Brigadier General Harold H. George, had said the visitors now had the range and navigation data they wanted and that the next time they'd "come right in without knocking." The junior officer wondered if they'd try it tonight. Iba was operating on a twenty-four hour schedule and so was the Interceptor Command Air Warning center at Nielson Field.

In Tokyo and Yokohama whole busloads of Japanese sailors were enjoying special tours arranged by naval authorities. To anyone inclined to give it a thought, it was obvious that the fleet was in. At naval bases south of Yokohama there was unusual activity in the transmitter rooms of the powerful base wireless stations. Oddly enough, some of the operators were strange to those surroundings. Normally they would be with their own ships, the carriers especially. Both apparently unrelated circumstances were parts of an elaborate deception scheme. To local observers, the fleet was in. To Captain Layton's radio monitors and radio direction-finder operators on Oahu, there was recognizable wireless traffic on fleet matters emanating from the general areas of Yokosuka and Kure Naval Bases off Honshu: recognizable "fists" doing business in Japanese home waters. There had been an especially detailed wireless exchange between one base and nonexistent carriers in the Carolines. The radio deception was so realistic that one Japanese admiral, fearful that so much traffic would

212

inform unfriendly ears of too much, issued a testy reminder for radio security precautions.

Now, however, one of the stations at Kure was preparing an authentic broadcast to Admiral Nagumo, about four hundred miles north of Oahu. He would not acknowledge, since his fleet was observing absolute radio silence. The message was a summary prepared by Kure naval intelligence of Yoshikawa's last advices from Honolulu: the exact listing of ships and that there was "nothing unusual." It would give Admiral Nagumo all he needed to "Climb Mount Niitaka," the code phrase for attack.

In Washington the four American-built Purple machines had been operating in almost nonstop sessions. Two of these marvels were with Communications Intelligence in the Navy Department and the other two in the Signal Intelligence Service Branch of the Army. There had been such an overload all day Saturday that several messages, some already several days old since interception, and some recent, had to be put on a deferred basis for the latest one coming in. As a result of catching and decoding a "pilot" message from Tokyo to the Japanese negotiators in Washington, Magic people knew that this weekend they should get what would probably be one of the most critical messages in U.S. history, Japan's reply to America's toughest one of November 26th. The pilot message said that Japan's reply would come in fourteen parts. Thirteen would be in one transmission, then there would be a delay until Sunday morning for Part Fourteen. A time-of-delivery instruction would arrive at that time too. Could there be much doubt but that the carefully delayed Part Fourteen, to be added to the previously received thirteen parts and all subject to a special time of delivery would have enormous significance, and that top-level Washington should be on the alert for it? But curiously enough, there had been irregulari-

213

ties in distribution of the thirteen-part decoded document quite unprecedented in periods of crisis.

All thirteen parts had been decoded and processed by Saturday evening. Distribution had been made to President Roosevelt. One of his top advisers, Harry Hopkins was with him. He saw the President study the long message, then look up and say, "This means war." The President then asked to be connected with Admiral H. R. Stark, Chief of Naval Operations. He was told that the Admiral was attending the theater.

In charge of the Far Eastern desk in Army Intelligence (G2) was bluff, gravel-voiced Colonel Rufus S. Bratton. This experienced intelligence officer was responsible for seeing that the Army Chief of Staff, General George Marshall, got all priority Magic material without delay. He observed proper channels and first telephoned his own chief, Brigadier General Sherman Miles. Bratton could only obey his G2's instruction not to bother General Marshall with it now, but see that he got it in the morning. Bratton stared at the message in his hand. There was a lot of diplomatic repetitiveness in it, but it still seemed of the most urgent importance. Repeatedly he had expressed to navy friends his conviction that Japan would strike at Pearl Harbor suddenly and hard one day, and now he thought that time imminent. Pearl should be warned. But only those at the very top of the military and civil hierarchy had authority to do that. And he had been told not to bother General Marshall.

At least one other intelligence officer had been very worried that Saturday and had slept badly into the dawn of Sunday. He was Commander A. H. McCollum, Chief of Naval Intelligence. Imaginative, quick-minded, sometimes impatient with less agile minds, McCollum had been sufficiently disturbed by Magic revelations on December 4th of Japan's order to destroy code machines that he prepared the draft of a special warning for all Pacific posts. But he had been overruled; the Roosevelt war-warning message was deemed sufficient. Since then Mc-

214

Collum had been unable to rid himself of the thought that code destruction was one of the final acts of a nation entering upon a shooting war.

It was one o'clock in the morning of Sunday, December 7th in Hawaii. At the navy yard it was even quieter than usual for a weekend. In some of the all-night joints on Hotel Street in Honolulu and in night-duty offices of the military establishments no one paid particular attention to Station KGMB's program of dance music.

One of the receivers tuned to it was on the second floor in the Dillingham Building in downtown Honolulu. This was the Contact Office of Colonel Bicknell's intelligence organization. Actually it was his Corps of Intelligence Police unit. Together with the Office of Naval Intelligence, this office had painstakingly compiled a "pick-up" list of Honolulu residents of Japanese descent considered as potential troublemakers should war break out, and no one in either organization seemed to doubt that contingency. A year before, the FBI had come to Honolulu armed with a presidential order making it responsible for all security matters outside military installations. The CIP and ONI had turned over all pertinent records, but had retained a copy of each. The two offices had gone on a twenty-four-hour duty basis many weeks before. Now at CIP the duty officer and duty agent worked on these files; it made the time go by.

At the Japanese consulate, intelligence agent-*cum*-diplomat Yoshikawa was finally slipping into restless sleep after listening a long time for signs of unusual air patrols from Pearl or the Army's fields. He had heard none.

On the opposite side of the island, the Windward, or northeast side, another man had gone to sleep. His face in repose showed wide, high cheekbones and a suggestion of massiveness that was not borne out by his 145-pound body. From his nose to his mouth were heavy lines, softened now with sleep.

215

On the secret file at the Dillingham Building his name was Otto Keuhn. On the Nazi party lists in Berlin he was called Otto Bernhard Julius Keuhn. His "wife," Friedel, whom for American records he said he had married in 1920, had been working in the Nazi welfare department; one "son" Leopold was a stormtrooper, another "son," Eberhard, did nothing much. There had to be a "daughter," too, German political intelligence said, and so there was. Her name was Ruth. The records said Ruth Kaethe Suse. All these dated from 1933. But German intelligence planned a long time in advance; there was no waiting until the situation became exigent. This "family" would go to Germany's new ally, Japan, ostensibly to learn the language. When it was sufficiently instructed, it would await orders, probably for settlement in Hawaii. The Keuhn "man-and-wife" team sailed from Germany in April, 1935. Keuhn made discreet contacts in the United States and got the names of Germans he was to see in Honolulu. He boarded the *Tatuta Maru* for Hawaii. In Honolulu he received further instructions from a Dr. Hoerman. The two Keuhns were to go on to Tokyo. At the Imperial Hotel there they would find Professor Hisamatsu. He would "teach them the language." But their instructions did not start then. Instead, there was a surprise visit to Shanghai, from which city Friedel unexpectedly sailed back to Germany and Keuhn returned to Honolulu. Now it was arranged that Keuhn should have an "inheritance" to explain why he had so much money for travel and later "investments" on Oahu. Friedel was lucky, too, so lucky that when in 1936 she came back to Honolulu she had enough to buy two or three houses on the Windward side of Oahu, one at Kalama. Meanwhile Ruth and her "brother" Eberhard arrived, while Friedel brought another "son," a little fellow named Hans. Leopold stayed in Germany as a functionary of the party.

The property the Keuhns had bought on Oahu commanded a fine view of the sea. It was important that it should. Conversely, an observer on a vessel at sea could pick them out distinctly with a glass if he knew just where to look, even from the low deck of a submarine.

There had been other trips to Japan and numerous lessons. Ruth had captured an American husband. But her madonna-like face and limpid blue eyes were troublesome to other Americans. Ruth seemed to have a penchant for army and navy officers. There had been domestic words about it, increasingly sharp of late. Ruth was spending more time with her "mother" in the beauty shop at nearby Kailua. There was much chatter by navy wives about the comings and goings of husbands in the fleet.

At different times Otto Keuhn had received large sums of money from Japan, his "inheritance." His visits to the consulate had made Kita nervous. So Yoshikawa came to see him at Kalama instead.

In Manila it was 7:30 Sunday evening. Hawaiian-born Japanese Richard Sakadida was on duty as a desk clerk at the Nishikawa Hotel. He was glad that the day was cooler. He was worried and the heat was more bothersome than usual. The truth was that he was not keen about going down to Mindanao. He was doing well in Manila, he thought. He believed that his cover story still was intact: He had grown bored with life "on a rock" in Hawaii and had shipped as a deck hand on a Japanese freighter; but Manila looked so good, he had jumped ship. Now the childless Japanese couple who owned the hotel liked him so much they wanted to adopt him. He hated to deceive the Fugii's. He had grown attached to them. Maybe that was one reason Captain Nelson Raymond of the slight body and the bright brown eyes in the Army's intelligence section at Fort Santiago decided it would be better for him to change locations. Raymond was right, as usual. What would happen if Sakadida were disclosed as the Corps of Intelligence Police agent he really was? Colonel O'Rear, the frosty-eyed G2, had told him that he had been very helpful. He believed he had. For one thing, he had helped a number of Japanese in Manila to fill in their alien registration forms. Some had quietly asked his advice on whether they should conceal the fact of previous Japanese military service. Sometimes Sakadida had said yes. It looked better that way. But the full list he had compiled and turned in to Captain Raymond on one of those nighttime "car contacts" in the Tondo district was accurate in every detail. Tonight he would get ready to go to Mindanao.

Now it was nearly 3 A.M. in Honolulu. That would be nearly 8:30 Sunday morning in Washington. Part Fourteen of the Japanese diplomatic message was in, together with the time-of-delivery instruction. They were being processed. Colonel Bratton surely would want to see these.

At 8:30 he did see Part Fourteen. Even if he had been expecting it, he was thoroughly shaken at what he read: ". . . The Japanese Government regrets to have to notify hereby the American Government that in view of the attitude of the American Government it cannot but consider that it is impossible to reach an agreement through further negotiations." This was virtually a declaration of war. He waited impatiently for the two additional interceptions.

It was approaching 3:30 A.M. in Hawaii. The small minesweeper *Condor* was on patrol just outside Pearl Harbor. Station KGMB was still sending dance tunes out over a thousand miles of the Pacific. In the *Akagi's* radio room they were still listening to the program. Surely if Honolulu suspected anything, there would be some sign. More than three hundred miles south of the *Akagi,* just off Oahu, a submarine radio operator was listening to the same program. On the deck of his big submarine were two midget subs that were to make an attack at dawn against Pearl Harbor. There were three

218

other midgets in the vicinity. In fact, one was watching for a chance to get inside the submarine net at Pearl. Far out over the Pacific toward San Francisco a formation of four-engine American Flying Fortress bombers was droning toward the speck in the dark seas that was Oahu. It was specifically for such bored crews that Station KGMB intended the all-night program, and the flyers appreciated it as they listened.

At nine o'clock in the morning at Washington, Colonel Bratton read the first of the shorter interceptions. He knew now that he must see General Marshall. Immediate action was imperative. The message he held directed the Japanese negotiators in Washington that they must deliver the fourteen-part message with its final break-off in Part Fourteen at exactly one o'clock in the afternoon. When was the classic time to launch an attack, Bratton asked himself. Dawn. At one o'clock Washington time, where would it be breakfast time at important U.S. military possessions? Not in Panama, for there it would be 11 A.M. Not in Manila, for it would be in the middle of the night. But at Pearl Harbor, it would be 7:30 Sunday morning, just the time to pipe sailors to mess decks and call soldiers to mess halls. Colonel Bratton put through an immediate call for General Marshall. To his dismay he was told that the General was out for his usual horseback ride. Bratton left word that he had to get in touch with him most urgently.

On the Navy side, Admiral Stark arrived at his office at 9:25. His intelligence people put him in touch at once with the whole string of messages. Then they urged him to send a special warning to Pacific areas. He declined.

It was just about this time, about 4 A.M. in Hawaii, just outside Pearl Harbor, the *Condor's* watch officer saw something that made him take a sharp second look. He spoke to the quartermaster beside him and they both peered. They agreed that they were seeing a moving periscope leaving a wake as it moved. Since this was an area where submerged travel was strictly forbidden, the officer made a signal on the blinker light to the destroyer, *Ward,* also on patrol. At that moment, the stranger apparently caught sight of the *Condor* through her periscope and veered away. The *Ward* began to alter course, too, but she didn't know about the visitor's change, and she went in the wrong direction.

On the farthest northwest point of Oahu, at Opana, army Privates Joseph Lockard and George Elliott were just as glad to be inside the SCR-270 Radar Station. Funny how it could be chilly out there on Opana when it was still muggy in down-town Honolulu. Elliott was brand new at the game and he was glad to have Lockard as an instructor. The only trouble was that from the time they had opened up at 0400 hours there had been hardly anything on the 'scope except the permanent echoes from the nearby hills on Oahu, and therefore nothing to plot. Usually there were planes about. The same condition prevailed at Fort Shafter, where atop a Signal Corps ware-house there was an information center and master plotting map. Lieutenant Kermit Tyler from Wheeler Field drew the duty this morning. He might as well have stayed in bed for all the activity there was. He couldn't leave until 8 A.M., al-though the plotters could go at 7 A.M. Tyler suppressed his indignation in philosophizing that this was the Army.

In Tokyo, Sunday night was still young in the paper-lantern-lighted Yoshiwara district. The sailors were making the most of it, even if some thirty-one ships of the fleet actually were not in at all but at this moment were less than 350 miles north of the Hawaiian Islands.

Now it was nearly 11:30 in the morning in Washington. The telephone bells in Bratton's office jingled. Bratton's fingers fumbled as he took off the handset. It wasn't like him. His associates always thought him pretty solid, if not stolid. He started to give General Marshall a hint as to what he felt was so urgent, but the Chief of Staff stopped him. Not over the telephone, Marshall said; he would come to the office within the hour.

Almost at that moment at Pearl Harbor the crew working the antisubmarine nets completed the opening operation to admit a tug that had been working with the *Condor*. It took some ten minutes to swing the boom. The crew decided that since the *Condor* was due in soon, and another tug was due out shortly after that, they would leave the net open. Outside, the *Ward* was still poking about on the *Condor's* sub alert call but making no contact.

From the deck catapult of the Japanese light cruiser *Tone* north of Oahu, a reconnaissance seaplane was shot into the dark. Eight miles away, to avoid the possibility of collision, another roared away from the cruiser *Chikuma*. The chronometers said 5:30, Hawaiian time. In an hour they ought to be over Oahu for a final look at Pearl Harbor. Throughout Admiral Nagumo's darkened fleet there were signs of intense activity. In only half an hour, at 6 A.M., the first wave of 353 planes would take off. The next wave would go at 7:15. There still would be a formidable reserve to give the armada protection.

General Marshall arrived at his office at 11:25 Sunday morning. Bratton and his chief, General Miles, followed him to his desk. They betrayed their anxiety by suggesting that he give attention to the all-important Part Fourteen and the time-of-delivery directive. But General Marshall waved them off while he went through the long fourteen-part message.

221

As he read, the flight decks of Japanese carriers north of Oahu pounded to the fiery roar of scores of heavily laden aircraft in takeoff. By the time he finished reading, the formations were leveling off and heading straight for Oahu. The General put the papers down and all present agreed that the only interpretation was that Japan intended to open a shooting war some place in the Pacific within an hour or so. He pulled paper toward him and drew up a message for the Philippines, the Carribean, and the Hawaiian Department. As finished, and signed by him, it said:

Japanese are presenting at one P.M. eastern time today what amounts to an ultimatum. Also they are under orders to destroy their code machines immediately. Just what significance the hour set may have we do not know but be on the alert accordingly. Inform naval authorities of this communication.

It was now 11:58 A.M. Washington time, or nearly 6:30 A.M. in Oahu when the message to warn Admiral Kimmel and General Short was ready for encoding.

At that moment, Elliott was concentrating on the 'scope at Opana Point. There were two blips. They were very faint, about 130 miles out to the northeast. A little later the Shafter information center telephoned that they might as well close up shop. The truck would come at seven and take them back to the Signal Corps camp a few miles down the coast. But Elliott said he would just as soon play around with the Type-270 and familiarize himself more with it. It was all right with Lockard. So they kept the power going.

Curiously, about that time (the records are vague as to exactly when) there were registrations on the 'scope of another Type-270, the one operating off the China Sea coast of Iba, in the Philippines. To Lieutenant C. J. Wilmer, in charge of the Iba detachment, it looked like an echo from

222

a whole formation of aircraft, just as those on the night of the 3rd and 4th had been. At the nearby airstrip the young pilots of the Third Pursuit Squadron under Lieutenant H. G. ("Hank") Thorne scrambled from mosquito-netted bunks. Air crews were rushing through an abbreviated preflight check. The humid night hammered to the roar of the new Allison in-line engines as the Third took off over the dark China Sea. The radar plottings had given them the point of expected interception, but this early radar computed only a horizontal plane. A little later the Iba plotting board showed that there had been a horizontal interception. But not long after that the Third came back in and landed. The explanation was that the two formations of opposed aircraft had been at different altitudes; the chances were that the American flight had passed under the Japanese and neither had seen the other in the night. Now the P-40's stood on the tarmac cooling off, their guns still loaded. The point buzzed in Hank Thorne's mind: In view of Washington's instructions that Japan must make the first overt move, how could General MacArthur have been able to explain it had the two formations collided in gunfire, as they fully expected would be the case? World War II almost certainly would have opened off the Iba coast of the Philippines that night. As it was, the blips now showed fainter, then disappeared; the strange formation had gone back out to sea. In the smoke-blue room of Fifth Interceptor Command at Nielson Field, the plotters under youthful Captain "Bud" Sprague wiped their brows, relaxed, and wondered when "they" would come in again. In the Air Intelligence vaults in the other wing of the headquarters building there were stacks of greenbound books. Boldface type on their covers said they were Bombing Objective Folders. Some were marked Formosa and others with names of the main Japanese islands where it was known that Japanese air installations existed. The folders were far from complete and many lacked photographs. But

223

they were a start. Air intelligence had existed in the Philippine Department only since March and, as a going concern worthy of the designation, since June—five or six months, perhaps.

Back at Pearl Harbor the submarine net was still open. A navy tug was going out to take over a barge from the supply ship, *Antares,* which was in sight now. So was the *Ward,* still nosing about. Above her a Navy PBY Catalina patrol plane was doing a tight turn as if she had spotted something. She had. And almost at the same time so did the *Ward.* For several minutes a black object that seemed to be caught on the *Antares*'s towline had puzzled the *Ward*'s lookouts. Now they realized that it was not on the towline at all, but on the near side of it. A moment later they knew it was the conning tower they had been seeking all this time, and that the submarine it belonged to apparently was proposing to sneak in past the net with the tow when the tug took it in. There were shouts aboard the *Ward.* The gun crews jumped. Ammunition passers were waiting with three-inch shells in their arms. At the same time the PBY dropped two smoke bombs to mark the location of the conning tower. The *Ward* heeled hard over and bore down.

At 6:45 A.M. the *Ward* fired the first shot of World War II for America. The shot went over. Thirty seconds later another three-incher crashed into the conning tower at the base. The *Ward* whipped on, the sub in the foam of her wake. And now the sea rose in a mighty heave of fire, mud, and water. The *Ward*'s salvo of four depth charges was going off, and the strange submarine was right in the middle of it. Aboard the *Ward* and the PBY overhead there were awful misgivings. Supposing she was American, despite her unfamiliar shape? The PBY dropped depth charges and the sea erupted again. A mile or so away the *Antares* thought it was target practice. But at three minutes to seven the *Ward* radioed headquarters

224

that she had "attacked, fired on, depth-charged, and sunk a submarine operating in the defensive sea area."

Five minutes later Lockard was staring like a man hypnotized at the 'scope face of the 270 at Opana. Elliott had been fooling with the set and it was possible he had put it out of commission. Here was an echo bigger than anything he'd ever seen. He checked. The 270 was in perfect order. He called numbers and Elliott plotted them. This was a big formation of airplanes just a shade east of due north and they were about 137 miles out, coming in fast.

Elliott grabbed a direct-line phone to Shafter information center. It was dead. The plotters had just closed up and gone home. He tried the Army line. Finally Private Joseph McDonald answered. Elliott gave him the data and told him to see that someone in authority got it. McDonald thought he was alone but when he turned he saw Lieutenant Tyler in the plotting room. Relieved, he went to him.

Tyler considered, shrugged, and waved McDonald away. McDonald called Opana. This time Lockard answered and in an excited voice said that the formation was coming in fast, about 180 miles an hour. He asked to speak directly to Tyler.

Tyler listened, and as he did, he remembered something: Station KGMB was broadcasting for that formation of Flying Fortresses coming in from the mainland. For some reason they probably had got up north a bit and now were rolling south, but fast. He said to Lockard, "Forget it."

Back at the 270 Elliott and he continued to plot the time and space relationships. At 7:25 the formation was sixty-two miles out. At 7:30 it was only forty-seven miles out. Nine minutes later, at 7:39 the echo was confused with the permanent echo from the mountains on Oahu. They prepared to close down. For some reason the truck was late.

It was just then that Admiral Kimmel's office informed him of the *Ward*'s attack. After a welter of calls and messages, it

225

appeared that the PBY had reported the same thing to proper authority and furthermore, there had been a second sub sighting by the *Ward* and she had released depth charges again. Kimmel said he would be right down.

Meanwhile a Japanese-born messenger for RCA in Honolulu had checked in to get his first batch of messages of the day for delivery. He thumbed through them and planned his route. There was one for the commanding general at Fort Shafter. That's all it said on the envelope. No "urgent" or "priority" or any other notation. It would be delivered in the course of his route, then. While he sorted, the operators at RCA were getting excited about reports of "dogfights" among airplanes and "bombs bursting" over Pearl Harbor. That might be, but he had his job to do. He started out but before he got very far he encountered road blocks put up by excited National Guardsmen. They told him to get out of there because in his messenger's uniform he looked too much like a Japanese paratrooper for his own well-being. He decided that he agreed and discontinued his delivery trip.

The duty officer for the Corps of Intelligence Police Contact Office upstairs in the Dillingham Building for the 7:30 shift was Lieutenant Gero Iwai. The slender, quick-speaking Nisei officer relieved the night D.O., checked the log, and checked in the day duty agent. The morning was warm and the air seemed to "bump" in a queer sort of way. At 7:55 the telephone rang. Some early bird with the wrong number, he thought as he reached for the handset. Then he straightened. The voice was that of his commanding officer, Colonel George Bicknell, and he was talking fast. Bicknell lived on Aiea Heights overlooking Pearl Harbor. But this morning the view was filled with smoke and flame and screaming airplanes. He told Iwai to get the emergency plan into effect at once. Everyone must report immediately. Iwai grabbed the roster of personnel with telephone numbers and started to dial. At the same moment the Honolulu police radio came into action. The receiver vibrated with orders for all police, all firemen, all rescue teams, Red Cross, and everyone in Civil Defense to report to their stations immediately.

The CIP duty officer got good results on his calls until he tried Lieutenant H. H. Henderson out near Hickam Field. He tried for a long time but the lines were congested.

At about 8:10 he heard the commercial stations broadcasting. This was no training drill. It was an attack by Japanese warplanes and Pearl Harbor was in flames. War had come.

Now the CIP officers and NCO's were beginning to arrive, bursting with questions and stories of what they'd seen. With them were men from the Federal Bureau of Investigation. The pick-up would go into effect at once.

By nine o'clock the office was operational. Teams of CIP working together or with mates from the FBI, Honolulu police, or the Office of Naval Intelligence, went out according to the pattern long drawn up for this event and began to bring in potential troublemakers. Among the first were Dr. and Mrs. Mori who had had the interesting transoceanic telephone call about flowers the night before. Iwai himself and an FBI agent named Polkinghorn made that pick-up.

Former Ensign Takeo Yoshikawa, known as Vice-Consul Morimura, had awakened early despite his late night work, and he was at breakfast. He felt curiously at peace with himself. He believed he had served the Emperor well. He recalled how heartbroken he had been in 1933 when the naval surgeons had told him he had ulcers and would have to be retired from the Imperial Navy. But he had never lost hope and never ceased to study all things pertaining to naval forces, and—believing as he had that some day Japan would collide with the United States—all things about the U.S. Navy especially. Then, his heart had soared with joy when in 1936 he had been invited to serve on as a civilian specialist in intelligence.

His training had been rigorous. For years he studied every detail that had been accumulated from Japanese agents acting as merchant seamen, ship suppliers, tourists, language students: anything that would give them opportunity to study U.S. ships at close hand in Honolulu, Manila, and in American ports. There were pictures, profiles, special reports, and books.

Then came the day in April 1941 when he was sent to Honolulu as a "junior diplomat." He had been an indefatigable worker collecting data supporting the plan for a surprise attack that he knew had been in conceptual stages for more than ten years.

His thoughts, and his breakfast, were suddenly interrupted. The morning air reverberated with heavy explosions. Repeatedly they came. Consul General Kita rushed in. They both had the same idea. But was it true? There was a sure way to tell, the Hidden Word code. He snapped on the shortwave radio. Radio Tokyo was on the air with news. If the attack was real, if war with the United States had broken out, they should hear in the middle of the newscast the phrase "east wind, rain" once repeated. The explosions continued and over Pearl Harbor the sky was darkened with a huge blanket of fiery smoke. Then the words came: *"Higashi no kaze ame . . . higashi no kaze ame. . . ."*—east wind, rain!

The two men hurried into the consulate office. They must now burn the last code and all other classified material. There was no time to waste. People already were gathering on the other side of the street. Soon volunteer soldiers surrounded the consulate.

There was an insistent knock. It was a reporter from a Honolulu newspaper. He was sent away. As the door was shut on him a low-flying airplane roared past. The rising-sun symbol was clearly seen on its wings until it plunged into a smoke cloud.

At 8:30, Honolulu police and the FBI came. All the staff

was herded into one room and the building searched. They were put under house arrest.

On the Windward side Otto Keuhn wondered if the Intelligence Police, or anyone, would come and arrest him as an alien. Perhaps it would look better if his wife and Ruth went to the Red Cross or some such place and offered their services.

Now the Honolulu radio stations were doing their best to convince a still incredulous population that the attack was genuine. An official radio warning went out from Pearl Harbor to all units that might be coming in. "Air attack on Pearl Harbor. This is no drill." It was an "action" message over the signature of Admiral Kimmel.

In Manila it was the middle of the night. On the hook of Cavite across Manila Bay to the south, the Navy's three tall radio towers pierced the moist night sky. Now the antennae snared a message "in the clear" that made the scalp of the navy operator copying it tingle. It said: "Air attack on Pearl Harbor. This is no drill." Downtown in Manila monitors whiling away the time at a commercial radio station heard the same thing and wondered what it meant. They decided to call Clark Field, seventy miles north. Clark had no knowledge of any attack. Clark would have, though, as soon as the official wheels went into action at Cavite. To give air protection to the remaining two squadrons of B-17 Flying Fortresses, their crews were ordered to take them aloft and "stay there until further orders." They could do it; the big planes had long-range fuel capacities. As it worked out, the planes had greater capacities than their crews. Around noontime the men got hungry, since they had been aloft since approximately 4 A.M. They radioed Clark for instructions but failed to contact the control tower and landed anyway. They parked in neat rows as they had always done. While they were eating, the attack came from the north and west. Frantic warnings from Nielson Field had not reached them and fighter patrols had run dangerously low on fuel and had come in for replenishment. It was as if the enemy knew it would be that way. They caught the fighters on the ground, too. Nearly the whole B-17 force was wiped out in minutes. Half of the fighters were gone, including most of the Third at Iba, and the faithful SCR-270, as well.

Richard Sakadida had stared into the bright, moist sunshine of that Monday morning in Manila after the word of Pearl Harbor had got around. He had been forced to the bitter conclusion that he, an American secret agent, for his own protection must now report himself as a Japanese national. If he didn't he would most certainly be taken, maybe shot, by the Filipino soldiers or the Philippine Constabulary that everywhere was rounding up Japanese according to their own black lists. The Japanese would believe him. He had been in the act of drinking a toast to the Emperor with one of them when the radio had announced confirmation of the Pearl Harbor rumor. Sakadida would be interned. Later he would be released by one of Captain Raymond's agents. He would go on to make counterintelligence history for the U.S. Army as one of its most versatile spies with the occupying Japanese.

It was ten minutes before two o'clock, Washington time at the Naval Communications Center. Over the direct circuit from Pearl Harbor radio station, "EOEHME" in official parlance, a message was coming in. "Air attack on Pearl Harbor. This is no drill." The center personnel was incredulous but wasted no time in delivering it.

As word spread through official Washington, there was an immediate reaction in the office of General Marshall. He wanted to know exactly what had happened to his warning message that had been ready for encoding at noon, less than two hours before. Since a minimum of three hours, and more probably five, would be required to assemble air crews in the middle of the night, to man surface ships and get up steam,

230

as well as all the rest that must be done to bring about even the first stages of preparation to meet a major attack on Oahu, it occurred to some that the question was academic, a hurrying for cover, as it were. In any case it was later revealed that at noon the normal Army Signal Corps channels between San Francisco and Honolulu had been practically unusable due to atmospheric disturbances, so the officer in charge of the Army's Message Center had the message sent via RCA. There was no priority marking on it. It also developed that the Honolulu RCA messenger boy was finally able to get through repeated road blocks and all the confusion to deliver the non-priority message to Fort Shafter just before noon. After decoding and the rest of the routine, it was in General Short's hands in the middle of the afternoon, more than seven hours after the first bombs fell. He did not think much of it as a warning.

All through that appalling day in Honolulu the CIP, the FBI, ONI, and the Honolulu police went about gathering in the Japanese on the pick-up list. Lieutenant Colonel Byron M. Meurlott was directing CIP for Colonel Bicknell at the Dillingham Building. Night came and darkness closed down on the scenes where more than 2,400 had died and nearly 1,200 had been wounded, many badly. But so far, Meurlott had been unable to isolate a single genuine case of sabotage or co-operation with the enemy by Honolulu Japanese in the torrent of reports that had come in and were still coming in. All over the city, guards were trigger-happy and would fire at any moving shadow without the formality of a challenge. Wearily he gave inward thanks that the security people had worked so well and that the potential organizers of trouble among the huge Japanese population were mostly in the stockade. It was nearly midnight. He reviewed the lists. Suddenly he stared at a card. He was incredulous, but there it was: Apparently no one had picked up Otto Keuhn, potentially one of the most dangerous of them all!

The only man in the office was a dead-tired CIP agent

named Ernest Halford. Halford strapped on a forty-five from which no one had cleaned the cosmoline and felt his way to his own battered old station wagon; the two old Model-A Fords of the detachment had both expired under the constant grind that day. It was midnight as he picked his way through the blacked-out streets. Never had a night seemed darker to Halford as he felt his way along the heights over Nuuanu Pali. His eyes strained to make out coastal configurations on the Windward side. At last he drew up at the Kalama house of Otto Keuhn. The German made no resistance, nor did Friedel. With them and the two boys in the station wagon, Halford crept along to where Ruth lived nearby. He told her to get ready. She looked at him with her big soulful eyes, then without a word went to comply. Her husband, a veteran of the First World War, followed her with a glance in which there was no sign of affection, nor of concern as to what might happen to her. To Halford he muttered that for a long time he had been suspicious of his wife; he was relieved that now she was being picked up.

Early that afternoon in Washington, President Roosevelt asked Congress to declare war on Japan. There was no hesitancy in Congress. In common with Americans everywhere, there was outrage. President Roosevelt knew now that he took a united nation into war against the Axis powers, a thing he had been unable to count on before the Japanese struck an unprepared and ill-advised Pearl Harbor.

Was Pearl Harbor an appalling intelligence failure, or a deliberate strategic sacrifice of appalling proportions? The man who could have answered the question did not do so in his lifetime. It will be remembered how the spy James Henry revealed to President Madison prior to the War of 1812 that European rulers treated America with open contempt because of their conviction that no President of the United States

232

could align divisive factions in the country for a sustained war effort. They were mistaken, and would be again. Yet it took the memory of the *Lusitania* and the damning evidence of 40 O.B. to unite the nation behind Wilson. Historians have speculated on what it might have taken to unite America against the Axis had it not been for the attack on Hawaii. Although essentially an attack on a military target, more than forty explosions in civilian areas were traced to American antiaircraft fire or the ineptness of excited gun crews at Pearl Harbor. Had military chiefs on Oahu been kept as fully informed as those in the Philippines, for example, would not they have expanded and speeded defence preparations to a point where Japan would have considered the risk of attack too great? Possibly. If they had been ordered into full alerts since the first of December (they had been twice before that year for much lesser crises) would not the defensive front have been sufficient to dissuade the Japanese high command? It is quite possible. Even had there been a five-hour warning from General Marshall instead of a message that was ready for encoding and dispatch less than two hours before the strike, aircraft might have got aloft and ships might have been deployed. Would Admiral Nagumo still have sent in his planes? There are reasonable grounds for doubt. Did Washington deliberately allow a condition of defensive inadequacy to prevail on Oahu in order to insure that Japan would take the bait and commit the "first overt act" so dear to diplomats? It was the adamant instruction to U.S. theater commanders that they take no aggressive action unless Tokyo made the first irreversible step. (It was this which prevented MacArthur from sending Flying Fortresses against nearby Japanese bases on Formosa during those first critical hours of December 8th in the Philippines; he still lacked official knowledge of Japan's act of war against Hawaii, and as yet there had been none against the Philippines.) Many have argued in published statements of great persuasiveness that this was the case. They have pointed out that it is inconceivable that professional military men of the stature of General Marshall, Admiral Stark, and those few others intimately acquainted with what Magic was giving them about Japanese preparations would, on their own initiative, have rendered themselves collectively and individually impotent at the very moment when it was practically instinctive to shout a warning.

It was my privilege to be intimately associated with both Captain McCollum and Colonel Bratton subsequently in intelligence operations of great sensitiveness. Discrimination, imagination, foresight, and general intelligence sense of the highest order characterized both men. It is quite impossible for me to see them in roles of intelligence ineptness. In the late Colonel Bratton's place (he died in 1960), it was not enough to have been rendered professionally impotent at a time of crisis; he was castigated and compelled to forego any hope of promotion as the result of findings of investigating groups. He remained on duty. General Short and Admiral Kimmel were professionally ruined and retired, justly as many believe, on the basis that they proved singularly insensitive to the warnings they did get.

It is reiterated that if top-level secret policy was to permit Pearl Harbor to happen, then individual failures in intelligence matters are purely incidental. To those who have laid the whole catastrophe at the door of intelligence, however, let it be put this way: The absence of an integrated intelligence machine, operating in all its departments of collection, collation, evaluation, and dissemination quite possibly allowed Pearl Harbor to happen, whether by design or by default. The absence of the integrated machine was, in turn, largely the result of indifference by Americans in general and the military in particular, to most aspects of intelligence.

Conceivably, an integrated system evolved over the years would have considerably altered the course of events. A far-flung collection system would have accumulated much data, in turn to be evaluated by experts. A true picture of Japanese capabilities would have emerged, quite different from the erroneous picture of the times, in part attributable to military professionals. A true estimate of capabilities in turn defines the boundaries of the probable intentions of a country. It is within the realm of possibility that Japan would have been revealed as entirely capable of striking over a large part of the Pacific area simultaneously. But it is also possible that such an astounding estimate would have been discounted. If Japan were going to attack the Philippines and Malaya, it was not likely she would be able to strike far-distant Oahu at the same time. Still, the capability to hit Pearl Harbor could not have been ruled out, and when added to everything else, the Oahu studies, the military desirability of neutralizing the U.S. fleet, the conviction of seasoned intelligence personnel that it was inevitable, and so on, the signals might have been too clear to ignore on any level. Surely it is hard to concede that a secret policy of allowing the attack to occur could have been maintained under such circumstances.

But there was no integrated intelligence structure. Collection was sporadic and unprofessional. Military attachés turned in what shrewd Japanese diplomats intended them to, and little else. With the exception of Colonel Mashbir and Commander Zacharias, we had practically nothing in the way of professionally-minded intelligence people of experience who were in a position to do much about it. Van Deman had done much, he could do little more without sacrificing his professional army career entirely. General Dennis Nolan had experienced a most dismal time trying to hold even a vestige of intelligence together for the Army. A new generation of dedicated intelligence reserve officers was just coming up, and in the months before Pearl Harbor, counterintelligence was being rapidly expanded. But there still was only the most desultory co-ordination between services in intelligence matters; even Kimmel neglected to tell Short, who depended on him, that naval intelligence had "lost" the carriers. There was no provision on the highest levels for the proper evaluation of such information as did get up that far. One man's unsupported opinion was as good as another's, better if the former happened to have the edge in rank. The machinery for framing an over-all intelligence estimate of such size and impact—one impossible to ignore without courting political and professional suicide—was simply not there.

It follows that there is little profit, from a national standpoint, in emphasizing individual intelligence failures, although intelligence classrooms may benefit from such studies. They were legion: There was the irony of the personnel and schedule inadequacies at Opana Point, compounded by those at the Fort Shafter communications center. Opana even tracked the Japanese attacking force as they left after the strike, but no one at the communications center knew what to do with the vital information. So whatever forces the Navy and Air Corps had left went searching to the southwest on a false tip instead of northward. Earlier, the failure of Naval Intelligence at Pearl to draw proper conclusions from such data as it had collected about movements of the Japanese fleet was fatal. But technical equipment in those days was not what it is now, and personnel was untrained; intelligence training hardly existed, in fact. We had not gone that far.

Out of the horror of Pearl, of Hickam and Wheeler fields, of Clark Field, came intelligence. True, General William J. ("Wild Bill") Donovan had been told before by President Roosevelt to get on with his Office of Strategic Services (OSS). But now it went into high gear. Naval intelligence and the Army's Counter Intelligence Corps which succeeded the old CIP on January 1st, 1942, developed into first-rate organizations. Tremendous processing and disseminating facilities appeared. From out of OSS after the war eventually came the Central Intelligence Agency—CIA. The Navy's ONI, the Army's CIC and the new Air Force's Office of Special Investigation, OSI, would not be permitted to collapse. Instead there would be the inevitable battling by them for jurisdiction and targets, to be resolved, in theory at least, by presidential directives defining responsibilities and limitations.

On the top level immediately after Pearl Harbor there was organized the Joint Intelligence Committee to sift data and supply the heart of it to the President—the beginning of integration. Subsequently, this high-level structure was greatly expanded and now once each week there is a meeting of the National Security Council. Supplying this body with the best and latest intelligence consensus from all collection and evaluation agencies is the director for the Central Intelligence Agency. Intelligence structures have become enormously complex, perhaps too much so, for complexity in itself is no guarantee of infallibility. Complexity defeats its own purpose, stumbling over its own feet, no match for a single dedicated mind bent upon espionage. In intelligence, to think otherwise is very dangerous, as dangerous as having no organization at all, as the days before Pearl Harbor.

Forgiven but Not Forgotten

IT remains to recount what happened to some of the principal actors on the intelligence stage.

As he anticipated, Takeo Yoshikawa was repatriated to Japan, where he continued to serve faithfully in intelligence throughout the war. For years afterwards he retained his secret. But bits and pieces got out. Otto Keuhn was tried by a special military tribunal growing out of the prompt imposition of martial law on Hawaii following the attack. His conviction followed. It was based largely upon sworn statements given by him to the FBI. His defence was that his concern for getting money to his "son" Leopold in Germany had prompted him to offer his services to the Japanese, even though he said he

237

had no intention of going through with the complicated signal system. The tribunal found him guilty of conspiring to get defence information illegally and of plotting to transmit that information to other countries. He was sentenced to be shot.

The order was not carried out. Almost a year from the date the bombs dropped, sentence was commuted to fifty years in Leavenworth. That was not carried out either, except in part. In 1946 the government agreed to deport him to Germany on the promise that he never would try to come back into U.S. territory. In 1948 he sailed aboard the *S.S. Uruguay* for Argentina.

These successive hesitations in Keuhn's case sprang from legal uncertainties as to the original jurisdiction of the tribunal. Few matters in U.S. history have created such a legal furor as the issue of martial law in Hawaii. Apparently the civil courts were intact and were therefore the only constitutional instruments of the Territory. But from the intelligence standpoint, there is no question of Keuhn's guilt, despite opinions to the contrary. These opinions are not so vocal since some of Yoshikawa's published admissions. These tear to shreds the tissue of lies that Keuhn used to explain away his affluence and Friedel's. The money came from Japanese intelligence. Postwar experience with Japanese intelligence planners convinced me that they are not given to extravagance in such matters. On Oahu they spent freely and they fully expected returns for it. Keuhn had no time to practice his signal system, nor would it probably have proved necessary as things worked out. Hawaii was never seriously threatened again, thanks to the U.S. Navy at Midway.

Ruth and her mother were both interned. They also were repatriated. Ruth went via the *Gripsholm* early in 1943 under alien registration number 5556507.

Contrary to widespread reports, there apparently was no other organized espionage or sabotage on Oahu. Reports that Keuhn was taken while signaling are without foundation. Sec-

238

retary Knox's initial claim that Pearl Harbor was the result of wholesale betrayal by Honolulu Japanese proved to be quite unsustained by facts. Yoshikawa himself bemoaned the fact that his most careful efforts to enlist aid among them met with success in not one single instance. Of course there were the usual activities by consular people, by Japanese "language students" here and there, and by others Yoshikawa mentions. Once again, even though he is a most modest man and claims little for himself, Yoshikawa's postwar statements that he did it all himself is not accepted in intelligence circles. As usual, it was the work of many. But the fact remains that none came from the Japanese of Hawaii, and apparently none from other organized agents directed from Tokyo, other than those who have been mentioned.

Napoleon said that a spy in the right place is worth 20,000 troops. Japan had that spy at Pearl Harbor. The United States did not have him in Tokyo, or Yokosuka, or Kure.

But Russia did have him, of all places, in Japan. By that time, Russia was fighting for her life against Germany and therefore, presumably, ranged alongside the other nations arrayed against Berlin. Her man in Tokyo was one of the most cunning, one of the most successful in all the history of modern espionage. He knew of Pearl Harbor's coming and informed Moscow of the intended attack with stunning accuracy. If Moscow passed the vital warning on to Washington there is no record of the fact, although some in high places have made the charge that there was such a record at one time. If, in turn, they are right, then there is indeed a mystery for the future to unravel.

That, however, is not our concern in this narrative. Let us turn, instead, to the fantastic story of Richard Sorge.

IX

Sorge—Synonym for Cunning

MY OWN association with the Sorge case was incidental and did not occur until years later, during the Allied occupation of Japan, when MacArthur's intelligence section under Major General Charles Willoughby was turning every stone to uncover the truth.

We faced each other across a little sheet-iron stove, so incongruous in the room that in all other respects was thoroughly Japanese. But the weather of that postwar winter of American occupation on Honshu was particularly cold; the glitter of flames in the grate and the pale red of the stove's sides were most acceptable, incongruous or not.

"Sorge was," said the fine featured, kimono-clad Japanese in her flawless English, "almost inhuman in his determination; his inner strength was terrifying."

This woman with the intense black eyes had enjoyed a favored position in old Imperial government circles and in the subsequent postwar era was one of the few "unpurged" of the great Japanese families. All the more authentic, then, was her estimate of the Russian spy. She knew him well.

To the prewar German ambassador in Tokyo, Major General Eugen Ott, Sorge was friend and closest confidant, she explained. And to the ambassador's tall blonde wife perhaps something more. To the embassy staff he was a tough-minded Berlin newspaper correspondent who had mysterious "inside tracks" and was worth listening to. To Tokyo society he was an unkempt man who masked an agile, penetrating intellect behind a seeming contempt for genteel society's "clothes horses" as he termed them. Far and wide in the paper-lantern-lit byways of the night world he was known for his limitless capacity for wine, women, and, if the occasion required it, song.

To Moscow, however, and unknown to all others, he was the most successful Soviet secret service agent on that side of the world. Unless history should show to the contrary, he was Moscow's principal for the entire Far East.

Consider his superlative position for service to his country, locked in a war for survival with Germany: so close was he to General Ott that on repeated occasions of crisis he actually assisted the by-no-means stupid Ott in the drafting of messages of utmost gravity to Berlin; he was privy to a staggering total of secret diplomacy that shaped the courses of Germany and Japan, and the whole world.

His own priceless information reports to Soviet Russia were gotten out of the country by two means: special couriers to Shanghai where contact was established for forwarding either by courier or wireless; his own mobile radio transmitter in the Tokyo area that sent the material to Vladivostok for further relay.

Was one of these messages destined for transmission in his pocket the spring night in 1938 when he came roaring down a Tokyo street on a motorcycle? A turn loomed ahead. There was a screech of rubber. The motorcycle crashed against a

241

wall that, ironically enough, protected the American embassy. The machine came to rest thirty feet away. Sorge's blood reddened the pavement.

"He was fearfully injured," my hostess went on. "No one thought he would live more than a few minutes. Yet he did. And at the hospital he summoned enough strength to refuse to allow any treatment. Instead, he whispered a name and a telephone number. Then, through what must have been an eternity of agony, he waited until that man arrived and bent over him. Sorge's mangled hand fluttered to his chest. The man reached and withdrew a blood-stained envelope. He nodded and got to his feet. 'Take care of him now,' he said and he disappeared. Richard Sorge waited only that long, then he permitted himself to lapse into unconsciousness and there he remained, off and on, for days."

Only moments after the mysterious man had left, the Japanese police impounded Sorge's blood-stained clothes. In his pockets they found a large sum in American currency. If they were surprised, they didn't show it; later when other things happened to stir their minds, they probably remembered. But at the time the Japanese police had no special record on him. They couldn't have known that German-born Richard Sorge's grandfather had been a secretary to Karl Marx and that although young Sorge had been thrice wounded in service as a German soldier of World War I, he had subsequently become a convert to communism and had deserted his country. Certainly they had no idea that his cold-blooded efficiency as a Communist worker had so impressed Moscow that he had been chosen for special training to execute secret assignments in far places.

The first directive sent him to Shanghai. From there he organized a vast spy net and communication line that terminated in Moscow itself. (Of greatest assistance in forming this China Unit had been Agnes Smedley. She was an American writer and also a Communist. But for daring to call her that,

General MacArthur one day would be noisily threatened by Smedley with a U.S. court action, if he "would take his uniform off." The General told her to go ahead, but that he would retain his uniform. She didn't sue. Astonishingly, she was given moral support by the anti-MacArthur Pentagon.) Moscow knew that in Japan lay the fate of the Far East for the next decade. Sorge got his orders from the highest level of the Comintern to lay plans for the Japan Unit. He was soon supplied with key assistants.

One was Hozumi Ozaki, a brilliant Japanese Asian scholar, author, and journalist. He was extremely well connected among the Japanese aristocracy and enjoyed the confidences of princes and Tokyo cabinet ministers alike. One day he would become a principal secretary in the cabinet, and thus become a provider of key information for Sorge's ring, surpassing even Sorge himself. To round out Ozaki's qualifications as a super-spy for Sorge was the fact that he also was a prime figure in the South Manchurian Railway, Tokyo's real administration unit for Manchuria and a wholesale espionage factory. What wasn't known about him was that he was secretly devoted to the teachings of Marx and Engels. In the same South Manchurian Unit was Ito Ritsu of the Japanese Communist Party. He had nothing to do with Ozaki or Sorge, yet on this relatively inconspicuous man the fate of the whole Japan Unit would turn.

Another recruit assigned by Moscow to Sorge was a big, bluff, red-faced man with pudgy fingers. Few would suspect him to be an expert radio technician who could build the finest miniature radio transmitters. His pudgy fingers were also lightning on the Morse key. Upon his arrival in Shanghai, Max Klausen was told by Sorge to lie low in an inconspicuous hotel until he could be set up in a respectable business as a cover. The very unlikely Max, who had been about, promptly fell in love with his landlady. He astounded Sorge with a demand that henceforth Anna accompany him. Anna hated communism but loved Max. Sorge was enraged. The pair was sent to Moscow, where Max was disgraced, then astonishingly recalled to grace and returned to Shanghai, still with Anna. He was now ready for Tokyo. It was he for whom the injured Sorge waited on the night of his accident.

With them would go the next member specially picked by Moscow. Branko de Voukelitch was a tall, erect, one-time Yugoslav officer who was accredited as a correspondent to certain European newspapers. There was still another, a Japanese artist named Yotoko Miyagi. He had been disillusioned with capitalism in California. Together with a Nisei, Mrs. Kitabayashi, he became an ardent Communist. Moscow classified him as useful to form secondary informant nets in Tokyo with Kitabayashi as a key member. They disappeared from Los Angeles.

From 1934 to the end of 1941 the Japan Unit would be responsible for the transmission to Moscow of something like 250 messages comprising more than 200,000 word-groups. Added to this were scores of cartridges of film reproducing countless documents and pages of secret books. These went by courier to Shanghai. The total take was enormous.

The list of scoops for Stalin included these of top magnitude: In 1935, Japan would avoid hostilities with Russia in the foreseeable future, thus freeing Russia to develop her strength for the coming conflict in Europe; in 1936, a military treaty aimed against Russia was being secretly negotiated between Japan and Germany (the "Anti-Comintern"); in 1941, Germany would declare war against Russia in midyear and march against Moscow with crushing force (Stalin chose to ignore this intelligence estimate as he did others of the same kind from different sources). Also in 1941, Japan definitely would not enter the war against Russia via Siberia, thus enabling Russia at her most desperate moment of the war to hurl her Siberian Army against the rampaging Germans, preventing by a margin of hours the taking of Moscow, a turning point in

244

World War II; again in 1941, Japan would make a surprise attack by air on Pearl Harbor, probably at dawn, December 6th.

It was not surprising then, that Stalin should order congratulations transmitted to Sorge and his Tokyo Unit. Neither was it surprising that in Tokyo, Sorge swelled with self-appreciation. To at least one startled female conquest he asserted his value to Russia, not without reason, to be far over that of mere generals and field marshals. The smitten girl kept his secret. He took few pains to conceal from Max Klausen the contempt he felt toward him; arrogantly he withheld funds Klausen believed due him for services rendered. The massive Klausen could have crushed the comparatively slight Sorge but he was nevertheless terrified of the leader. He said later that he was convinced Sorge would kill his best friend for communism, if he could do so safely (for the radioman secretly held Sorge to be a physical and moral coward despite his own fear of him).

Sorge was riding high, but apparently for a fall. It is ironic in the extreme that Sorge's whole great structure should come crashing down through the act of one who was himself a devoted Communist. A secondary cause was born of one of Sorge's own errors. Seldom indeed did he make one. But espionage chiefs are not permitted such a luxury at all.

In one of his rare moments of panic Sorge far overestimated the importance of what was really a routine rotation of Japanese troops in Manchuria. He did not wait to check his usual sources for confirmation of a report that significant reinforcements were going in. Instead he had Klausen send immediate advices, then follow-ups, and finally a series of hesitant qualifications. Klausen was worried about the volume of traffic, if nothing else. So much wireless going out in a code any Japanese interceptor would identify as foreign was sure to get unwelcome attention.

Klausen was right. What he did not know was that Japanese

counterintelligence had been intercepting his transmissions for a long time. His crisp "fist" had been well identified and even the primitive radio direction-finding equipment in Tokyo at the time had narrowed the field of probable locations to the city itself. Japan's code breakers had no luck with the messages, however, and continued tracking by radio direction finder seemed the only course open to them. Tokyo ordered the best available, from Germany.

Meanwhile, Max Klausen seemed to attract trouble as Sorge attracted women. Once when Max proposed to jettison his first transmitter in favor of a new and more efficient one he had built, he and de Voukelitch stowed the dismantled parts in rucksacks and, impersonating hikers, set off for a lake outside Tokyo. Here they intended to sink the parts. When beyond hope of evasion, they realized they were being followed by Japanese police who demanded to know what was in the sacks. Klausen tried to pass it off with banter: They were hikers with big, big European appetites and their rucksacks contained food. The police were not amused and Klausen began to sweat. Then the cool de Voukelitch intervened: They had to admit that most of their "food" was bottled—they were going on a drunk. Then he made as if to unstrap one of the sacks as he invited the police to share a bottle with them. It worked. The Japanese were more frightened at the possibility of being observed violating the law about drinking with foreigners than they were of anything else. They declined with thanks and went rapidly away.

On another occasion while Klausen was carrying the new radio in its suitcase from one transmitting point to another (Sorge insisted that transmission be rotated among their homes to foil detection by the direction finders), a policeman suddenly opened the car door and jumped in. He took the suitcase from the seat, put it on the floor and sat down. Then he questioned Klausen thoroughly. By that time Klausen was a genuine businessman, making enough money eventually to imbue him with capitalistic ideas, and he was able to satisfy the policeman. The latter replaced the radio on the seat and got out, having given Klausen only the routine interrogation to which any foreigner in Japan in those times was liable. But Max had a bad case of nerves and the others began to wonder about him.

This state of affairs was not helped when, during a transmission from his house, Max looked up in time to see a Japanese "repairman" in a bo'sun's chair swing slowly past the window, staring intently in as he went. Klausen jumped up and shielded the set with his body. Soon thereafter "electricians" knocked for admittance. They said they wanted him to pull the power switch to facilitate some repairs they had to make, but Klausen was able to get rid of them without their having detected the transmitter.

Sorge never underestimated the Japanese. Like every other foreigner, he had been under surveillance since the moment he set foot in Japan. But now he took further precautions. He rented a chalet on the Isu Peninsula about twenty miles from Tokyo. Klausen took the set down there for transmissions.

After the war, Hans-Otto Meissner, who had been a junior attaché at the German embassy and an acquaintance of Sorge, claimed to have uncovered positive proof that by this time Japanese counterintelligence had by sheer deduction narrowed down the field of top suspects to a little circle that included both Sorge and de Voukelitch; further, that through the attractions of an alluring Oriental dancer named Kiyomi, Sorge was to be drawn into an inescapable trap. Meissner credits sources available to him in a diplomat's internment camp and elsewhere. These sources were not available to MacArthur's far-flung intelligence facilities digging into the Sorge story, for his own ill-advised order had freed political prisoners from allied nations without screening. Meissner's sources may have been correct. My hostess of that night seemed to think there was something to it; if so, it was poetic justice that Sorge's

247

immediate betrayal was an undiscerned price tag on the last of his list of ever-successful amours.

In any event, the ring was doomed. After nine years of successes unparalleled in the modern history of the Far East, the unit would have had to go back through those same years to uncover the genesis of its undoing. It was Ito Ritsu.

He was, it will be remembered, the inconspicuous man in the organization of the South Manchurian Railways. A devoted member of the Japanese Communist Party, Ritsu had been instructed by Moscow in the formative years of the Sorge ring to make contact with Mrs. Kitabayashi. But here occurred one of Moscow's seemingly inconsequential slips: Mrs. Kitabayashi was not warned. This American Communist who had met the painter, Miyagi, in Los Angeles and been inducted into the party at the same time with him, had become indispensable to Miyagi as a key agent in the secondary net organized in Tokyo by him and Ozaki to serve Sorge. She was under the strictest injunction to ignore any advances by anyone else. Miyagi's precaution was proper under the circumstances. But he was not Moscow-trained; too many subagents knew of both Miyagi and Ozaki being involved in something potent. This was bad; they might plausibly know Miyagi, possibly, for he was on a relatively low level, but Ozaki, a consorter with cabinet members, a confidant of Prince Konoye himself—that his activities should be known, or even suspected by subordinates, was a breach of security which Moscow would never have tolerated had they known of it.

At any rate, Mrs. Kitabayashi rebuffed Ito Ritsu and the little man took it personally. His pride was offended and he vowed secretly to make her smart for it.

Meanwhile, the Japanese counterintelligence had an eye on Ritsu. Japan has always been anti-Communist and when in June of 1941, Ritsu became rather too open in his views on behalf of the party, he was arrested. Japanese police methods were effective and he talked. It must have given the sorely-tried man some solace to put the finger on Mrs. Kitabayashi.

Nothing else happened right away. Then suddenly the police swept her up. She proved malleable. She named names, in particular that of Miyagi.

Another interval, while summer became fall. In October the police knocked on Miyagi's door. Miyagi, far gone with tuberculosis, made a heroic gesture in his despair and stabbed himself. But the police were prompt and saved him for worse days.

In his turn he named names. One of them rocked the Japanese counterintelligence: Hozumi Ozaki, a pillar of the government. They went to his home and found him dressed in full ceremonial robes. They took him away as he was.

Meanwhile Sorge was only slightly less disturbed than Max Klausen at the sudden silence from two key members of their ring. In order to confound radioed detection further, Sorge had leased a fishing smack. On land, cover for Max Klausen's activities often had been noisy *sake* parties participated in by duped Japanese officials. Now Sorge gave *sake* parties out in Tokyo Bay. Below, in a cabin marked with a fresh paint sign Klausen noiselessly sent his precious data to Vladivostok. Japanese technicians came in for a blistering from their superiors when they had to admit that their latest triangulations with the sensitive German equipment put the mysterious transmitter out in the water!

Sorge sensed that the game was up. He gave Klausen one more message of top importance. It was a flat statement that Japan would launch a devastating air attack on Pearl Harbor, probably at dawn, December 6th. Then Max was to close out and go home.

He went home. On the way he encountered Japanese police, who seemed more coldly hostile than ever. But they let him go, for the moment. That night they dragged him from bed. All the fears that had harassed the big, soft man rushed over him and tortured him. Furthermore, business success had softened his communism. Somehow he identified all his troubles with Sorge. He remembered the many small abuses and insults, and he turned on him. Klausen's written confessions were to answer hundreds of questions for the Japanese as well as for MacArthur's postwar intelligence staff.

Then came Sorge's turn. He was apprehended, tried, and with Ozaki, sentenced to death. The others were given long prison terms, except Anna, hater of communism, lover of Max. She got only three years.

In Sugamo prison, Ozaki wrote endless letters to his wife while awaiting the call to the gallows. Sorge wrote a learned legal appeal in Japanese so flawless that it amazed even scholarly Japanese. It was denied. Still Sorge declared that he, a Russian, would never hang. Then he turned to writing his confessions. They were singularly frank and revealing, unemotional and intellectual in concept and content.

The months became years and the war began to go against Japan. Still the final summons did not come. Meissner insisted later that a Japanese dentist had been ordered to make a new denture for Sorge, the man who was to die soon, and that a tailor made him a new suit.

The cold, grey day of November 7, 1944, finally dawned. The great naval battle of Leyte Gulf had been fought and the once mighty Imperial Fleet was now only a shell-shocked remnant. MacArthur had kept his promise and had returned, accompanied by immensely strong forces, to the Philippines. Tokyo was preparing for the final onslaught.

At Sugamo, the door to the gallows chamber opened at last. Ozaki, speaking softly and bowing, paused at the chapel, then went on. The trap was sprung and then reset. There were only Japanese witnesses.

Sorge was escorted to the noose. He thanked his captors for their kindnesses. They were his last official words. Furthermore, the record says, the trap was sprung again and Sorge died at 10:36 A.M.

He did? Meissner is sure that he did not. There are others who insist that the Japanese, anxious to avoid further complications with Russia at this critical time, and knowing Sorge's value as an exchange item, never executed him. Meissner also speaks of a beautiful dancer riddled by bullets in Shanghai in 1947. Her name was said to have been Kiyomi and her assassin a slight man with intense, bold eyes who had watched her dance from the shadows of the café that night. It adds an element of intense mystery to this bizarre tale.

What of the opinion of my knowledgeable hostess that night while Willoughby's agents were charged with uncovering the truth?

"He died," she said simply. "There were certain letters he wrote just a few days before. . . ."

On my notes a purple-ink stamped impression has grown dim. It identified so many of the documents that told of the early days of the ring. It says, "Shanghai Municipal Police." The quiet words of my hostess that night seemed to put a stamp of finality on its last days.

X

Dead-Man Double

IF Richard Sorge was a man of several faces—the loyal German soldier, the anti-German Communist agitator, and the brash Tokyo journalist-*cum*-master spy for Russia—then surely on the other side of the world one of the most successful secret service operatives was a man of no face, in a sense, because he was dead.

Operation Mincemeat had long been a top-secret matter. For reasons of delicacy if not for military security, Whitehall proposed to keep it that way. The public did not need to know the story of the amazing deception of the German General Staff in 1943. But some stories are too good to keep. A few years after the war, security-minded directors of secret operations were shaken by the appearance in book shops of what apparently was a highly imaginative piece of fiction by a man so well known as to preclude any suspicion of evil intent. The story written by the late Alfred Duff Cooper told of a poor wretch whose state of health was so little equal to his patriotic drive that all three services rejected him for war service. He died brokenhearted, only to be used by his country as a

252

corpse to bring about a dazzling deception of the best minds of the living enemy.

Whitehall's postwar perturbation sprang from a guilty conscience, for there had been in fact just such an operation. Called Mincemeat, it had involved the use of a corpse as a device to lead top German planners into a mistaken conviction of where the next Allied blow would fall following the landings in North Africa late in 1942. Mincemeat had been as successful as it was implausible. Surely history lists no *ruse de guerre* more grim. But for years the lips of the man who conceived the bizarre notion and those who were concerned in its implementation were sealed by official secrecy. With the appearance of the fiction, however, the man credited as the originator, Lieutenant Commander Ewen Montagu of the Royal Navy, protested to highest authority. Questions were being asked, insinuations made, and half-truths stated which were both unfair and dangerous. He was directed to tell all. Besides, the secret was slipping out in America, too.

Allied planners agreed that when North Africa was secured, the next logical step was the investment of Italy via the stepping stone of Sicily. If it was logical to them, the strategy would surely be logical to the German and Italian defenders as well. Grim indeed was the contemplation of the casualties that could then be expected, unless by some means or other the German staff could be made to believe that the Allied forces would attack elsewhere due to considerations apart from sheer logic. Then the vast power of the Axis defence would be shifted and put off balance. But how was such a belief to be implanted?

Montagu came forward with his scheme. Spain was known to British intelligence to be at that time a hotbed of pro-German intrigue, just as it had been in World War I. Significant information acquired by Spanish authorities invariably found its way to Berlin. But Walter Wilhelm Canaris's men were no fools; any capture of "lost" plans would be looked on with suspicion and a fatal hesitancy by Berlin would ensue. Similarly a "captured" staff officer loaded with plans would be seen through at once as the plant he was. But Montagu proposed to use a most convincing staff officer, a dead one.

The dead officer, in full uniform, would be equipped with an official courier briefcase. It would be secured to the courier's body by a kind of chain that bank messengers sometimes use to make certain that money transfers cannot be snatched out of their hands. The chain in this case would go around the body and out one coat sleeve, and there be clipped to the briefcase. (American official couriers carrying highly classified material are usually handcuffed to their briefcases.) In the briefcase would be certain wax-sealed envelopes. In one or more of these would be the "leak" of an apparent Allied intention to make for the "soft underbelly of France" by way of Sardinia. But, to add realism to this, the document would disclose that there was provision to use Sicily as the cover operation, to make it appear that Sicily was the real target. Thus the Germans would realize Allied appreciation of Sicily as a logical target, but for reasons yet known only to the Supreme Allied Command, it was apparently unfeasible at that time. There would of course be other documentation in the briefcase, mostly irrelevant. In the clothing would have to be convincing pocket-litter, including personal letters, proper identification, and so forth. The "courier" would have been a passenger in an aircraft that had crashed at sea close to the Spanish coast. His body would drift in and be spotted by the Spanish.

The perpetrators of the scheme anticipated trouble convincing higher authority of its workability. For some time it appeared that it would be just another intelligence brainstorm. Then the imaginations of a few key men were piqued. They asked for details. Bit by bit the plan in principle received attention up the chain of command until the eagerly sought but hardly expected approval came from on high.

The "leak" document was to be a chummy letter of the type seniors can write to one another, apparently nonchalant but bristling with secrets, all out of channel and strictly horrifying from the security standpoint. There would be a friendly "clarification" of certain General Staff cables dealing with the forthcoming offensive against Sardinia, followed by consolation about the usual annoying administrative problems and staff appointments. If it was to appear genuine, the letter should include, very unofficially, of course, a few inter-Allied unpleasantries of authentic flavor. This one did: British distaste for the American penchant for distributing awards and decorations like favors at a debutante's party. As finally signed by the deputy chief of the British Imperial General Staff and addressed to General Sir Harold Alexander of the Eighteenth Army Group under General Eisenhower, it was a very convincing piece of work.

One might think that procuring a dead body in time of war would be no problem, but it was. To be useful when recovered in Spain, the corpse would have to withstand the pathological examination the authorities would surely make upon it; therefore, the man couldn't have died of certain diseases, nor of severe injuries, as these might look suspiciously like an attempt to render the body unrecognizable—it must fit its identity card data and photo. If possible, the courier should appear to have been drowned, although death might have been caused by shock and exposure. The body had to resemble what a youngish British staff officer might look like, not an especially husky specimen, aesthetically inclined rather. As work went on, it was feared it might be necessary to "snatch" an appropriate body from a cemetery. But Montagu and his associates rebelled. Still, if a recently deceased young man was to be used, the surviving relatives could be a problem.

Nevertheless, at last a suitable subject was discovered and the relatives proved solid, loyal British citizens who gave consent when assured there would be no desecration and that in

255

all probability the Spanish authorities would accord a military funeral. Furthermore, the grave could subsequently be visited for proper maintenance.

The young man, who was to be "Major William Martin of the Royal Marines," had died of pneumonia. British pathologists assured intelligence that pulmonary fluid in this case would be convincing instead of detrimental. A "sweetheart" was found for him who wrote him a love letter celebrating their hasty wartime engagement. To back this up, a Bond Street jeweller gave a receipt for an engagement ring. There was a receipt for lodging in a London military billet corresponding in date to a reference in the girl's letter. There was another letter from a worried, indulgent father.

One night, late in April 1943, a Ford pickup truck left London for a northern submarine base. In the truck was a large metal cylinder weighing about four hundred pounds. In the cylinder was dry ice enclosing the fully clothed body of "Major Martin" in the uniform of the Royal Marines. His frigid fingers clasped the handle of a briefcase. The chain had been eased as a courier might do on a long air trip, but was still attached.

A few nights later the British submarine *Seraph* lay off the dark coast of Spain close in to the locality of Huelva. The cylinder was hoisted on deck and opened. The body was taken out and examined. All seemed well. At 4:30 the body was slid into the water. At the same time the submarine's engines spun the propellers in reverse. The wash, combined with an onshore wind carefully planned for, slowly carried the silent warrior out of sight landward. There were salutes, and prayers.

Then the submarine moved against the wind and discharged a rubber dinghy of the type aircraft might carry as lifeboats. Only one paddle was in it. The dinghy was launched upside down, then the *Seraph* disappeared.

In London, intelligence anxiously awaited word. The *Seraph's* skipper sent it and in a short time there was a most gratifying second message, this time from the British naval attaché at Lisbon. He had been notified by the Spanish authorities of the recovery by fishermen of a drowned major of the Royal Marines, one William Martin, whose body had been given a military burial.

Now London took the next step in the *ruse*. The attaché was not included in the deception. It was deemed safe, therefore, to take him into the "confidence" that the news was very disturbing since the major had been carrying confidential papers of the highest order. The attaché would, therefore, while using the utmost discretion so as not to excite curiosity, determine whether an official courier briefcase had also been recovered by Madrid. If not, he was to pursue his careful inquiries on the coast. If the answer was yes, he was to try to regain possession of the case intact as soon as decently possible and forward it posthaste to London.

In due time the attaché reported that Madrid had informed him of the attaché case and that he would soon have it. When it arrived in London, technicians quickly checked secret clues and gave their verdict to tense intelligence officers: at least one of the letters, the vital one, had been opened and cleverly resealed, wax and all.

Lisbon now had the "leak" and Berlin certainly would have it soon, if it did not have it already. The silent warrior had accomplished his mission, and from England went officials and relatives to accord honor and care to his last resting place.

Did the deception work? By specific order of the supreme commander of the German forces, Field Marshal Keitel, the German defences were completely dislocated to meet the anticipated drive into Sardinia and the subsequent invasion of southern France.

Sardinia eventually was taken by the Allies but long after the invasion of Sicily and Italy, accomplished against relatively weak opposition.

Dream "Sleeper"

"MAJOR WILLIAM MARTIN" had well and truly served his country, though dead. Germany, on the other hand, was effectively served by a man who apparently never existed at all.

The element of fear implanted in a people can accomplish some things that reality fails to achieve because reality brings with it at least an opportunity to fight back. The invincibility of German espionage proved a myth which, while it lasted, contributed measurably to the over-all image of an invincible enemy. And to this myth, "The Watchmaker Spy of Kirkwall" ably contributed.

The years have eroded the story until now there is excellent reason to believe that he never even had the status of a dead man. Therefore it would appear that he must be withdrawn from his position as a classical example of the "sleeper" agent, one inserted into an unsuspecting community in time of peace to wreak destruction with the onset of war. It follows, then, that crediting to his efficiency the loss to the British of the battleship *Royal Oak* on the dark, cold night of October 13th and 14th, 1939, is an error: the fatal explosions *might* have been due to some form of sabotage, but almost certainly not to the torpedoes of Commander Prien's *U-47* as a result of the supposed watchmaker's exact directions as to how the *U-47* might run a gauntlet of obstructions and get at the vessel.

The persistent story centers upon a quiet little man who years ago came to a lonely village in the far-north Orkney Islands of Scotland and opened a watch-repair shop. His selection of the bleak place gave him an excellent point of observation of the Royal Navy's excellent antisubmarine shelter at Scapa Flow. The harbor had served well in the 1914-18 war but the defences had been allowed to deteriorate, and the outbreak of war in 1939 found them inadequate against either underwater or air attack. Therefore, the Admiralty thought it best to keep the fleet in movement. But blockship hulks from World War I were still in place and now antisubmarine booms and nets were strung. Strictest blackout regulations were enforced. On dark nights, even the mass of a battleship was indistinguishable at more than two hundred yards or so.

The watchmaker who had become a fixture in the town on the other side of the hills from Scapa Flow had been an outdoor man. He had walked and walked and observed until he had determined that although it would mean a delicate job of piloting, there was a way past the defences for a U-boat.

And then, the story goes, the little man had bad news from farther south, the illness of a relative and he was duty-bound to go. But, he assured his sympathetic and unsuspecting neighbors, he would be back.

In time, the war commenced. In the anchorage at Scapa Flow on that chilling night in October, there were only two navy ships, the *Royal Oak* and an old seaplane carrier, the *Pegasus*. They were separated by two miles and the first watch aboard the battleship could see no sign of the *Pegasus* whatever.

At exactly four minutes after one, watch officers felt a sudden lurch of the deck beneath them and from some place forward there was a muffled thud. This was followed by a thunderous clangor as the anchor chains ran out through the hawse pipes. But no one testified later to having seen the flame-lit geyser characteristic of a torpedo hit. Apparently there was none. Emergency stations rang through the sleeping ship, for it was the belief of the watch that the *Royal Oak* had suffered some sort of internal explosion in the vicinity of the flammable paint stores up forward. But to the surprise of watch officers, ventilation pipes from that area were blowing air forcefully. That could only mean that the damage had been so severe that the sea was rushing in, displacing air.

A searchlight was switched on momentarily. There was no sign of a submarine. Then, eleven minutes later, a second and

259

much heavier explosion shook the 29,000-ton ship from end to end. A cascade of water rose higher on her starboard, or land side, and at least one witness said there was flame. This was more like a torpedo hit. Before the stricken ship could get her breath, as it were, further explosions shook her. Apparently these were from her own magazines. The great vessel seemed to curl over on herself to starboard. In an appallingly short time she went down. The rent hull was a coffin for more than seven hundred men.

The Admiralty disclosed her loss as presumably due to submarine action. This assumption would seem to have been substantiated by Berlin's broadcasted details of the ceremony in which the intrepid commander of the *U-47* was publicly decorated for his achievement in Scapa Flow.

Yet throughout the years the Admiralty has remained singularly secretive about the whole thing. The *U-47* was subsequently lost with all on board, otherwise it might have been possible to check personal accounts of crew members against records. In his excellent book, *Black Saturday,** Alexander McKee presents page upon page of evidence to show that Lieutenant Gunther Prien never made the perilous entry into Scapa Flow that night and that the claims for which he was decorated were sheer fiction.

We are not concerned here with the validity of the claims for Lieutenant Prien, but with the associated claim that the clever sleeper-watchmaker-spy supplied data which made Prien's penetration of Scapa Flow possible. On this point McKee is adamantly negative. After my own pokings-about in Scotland, I am inclined to concur without reservation.

Intelligence operations men of experience agree that few projects are more fraught with danger for an agent than one demanding insertion into a tight-knit community where everyone knows everyone else and all about each other. Add to that

* Holt, Rinehart & Winston, New York, 1959-60.

the natural reserve of the Scotsman and compound it infinitely with the clannishness of the Orkney Islanders in those thinly populated, far northern places, and it becomes apparent that certainly if such a man as the foreign watchmaker of Kirkwall existed, he would have been most thoroughly catalogued by those with whom he sought to make his home. Yet it is quite impossible to find anyone in that closely knit community who remembers such a man. There is a watchmaker. He has been there for years and is a native of the Orkneys. He never had any competition that he knew of and he would most certainly know.

The years accord a better perspective on Hitler's over-all intelligence machine and tend to the conclusion that in the positive intelligence field—espionage—there were more propaganda victories than actual ones. This surely was the case with the efforts of Himmler's civilian agents as contrasted with the military agents of Admiral Canaris. Our own intelligence people developed a healthy respect for the energy and resourcefulness of *Abwehr* (defence) spymasters, and a particular regard for the efficiency of Section 111 B, counterespionage. So did Russia, for that matter, quite early in the war, when she thought to make the Alfred Redl chapter of history repeat itself, and for a while it looked as if she would succeed.

Redl with Variations

IF World War I produced for Britain that genius of naval intelligence, Admiral Hall, World War II produced for Germany one of the same stature, Admiral Walter Wilhelm Canaris who performed the same job for Hitler. Early in the war the astute Canaris held in his hands counterintelligence evidence so grave that he suspected the rot might even reach as high as Martin Bormann, who one day would be Hitler's deputy. This was never substantiated, but there was no question that it did penetrate into the Air Ministry, Foreign Office, and the Ministry of Economics; the poison had gone far and its potential for harm to the German body politic was certainly great.

Ultimately, when as much of the full story as would ever be revealed was familiar to Canaris, he found at the core of the rot clandestine homosexuality which was known to the Russians and fully exploited by them.

German radio monitors in *Abwehr* 111 B, scanning the frequency channels for unauthorized transmissions in occupied Europe, had repeatedly identified an unlicensed note. It was clear and clean but not very powerful, and was heard during the hours between midnight and dawn. After months of the most patient work, the radio direction-finder triangulations converged upon Brussels. Then the mobile teams went to work. The plottings narrowed. They pointed with damning certainty to a house in the Rue des Atrébates.

Midnight of December 12, 1941, was cold and quiet. The sudden thudding of heavy boots on the ground-level floors of three houses in the Rue des Atrébates was like thunder. The doors had flown inward simultaneously; lock-pickers had prepared the way. Another locked door within the central house of the three banged inward. Bright lighting momentarily blinded the raiders. But soon they saw that they had made a rich find. A small, efficient wireless transmitter, that more than one non-Communist country would come to know in the next decade, was fully deployed and its tubes were still hot. The operator had fled but left behind were certain coded messages that he must have been preparing to transmit.

Meanwhile in another room a woman was arrested. She denied any knowledge of irregularities but the *Abwehr* men began a minute search. A secret door in her room was sprung. It led to a room with complete paraphernalia for making passports, travel permits, ration cards, anything needed by agents —what the trade calls a documentation mill.

Another woman was found. From her they learned one very disturbing fact: The language spoken in the house was German; there were also mysterious visitors who spoke German.

Then the *Abwehr* brought in a man. He had been fleeing over the roofs. He confessed to being a Soviet lieutenant. But he succeeded in maintaining that he was only a radio operator who dispatched and received traffic in codes unknown to him. It was probably true for the Russian secret service has always practiced a particularly effective compartmentation to prevent chain reactions should compromise of one unit occur.

There the case seemed to bog down. Canaris was not happy. Reduction of only a single link in a chain is tantamount to failure. But espionage lightning was destined to strike twice in the same place.

A few months later monitors again were picking up a familiar-sounding unlicensed note, and at the same hours. It couldn't be the identical one, for they had the Russian transmitter under lock and key. But once again the radio direction finders were turning upon Brussels. Then the mobile teams got the street address. This at least was different. There was another midnight raid, and again a man fleeing over the rooftops. A transmitter was found ready for use. The man was captured, proved to be the operator, but this time he was German. He might as well have been Soviet, however, for he proved to be a Communist with a long record. Like his predecessor, he had not been anticipating the raid and papers taken on his table included clear-language data about coming major German offensives against the Russians which only four of the highest ranking men in the German military would know in detail. Then in one of those rare breaks for counterintelligence men, they also uncovered a certain Berlin address.

The address led to a German air force officer. The Canaris

men found a link between him and a male stenographer who had once been under a political cloud. That had passed. The Luftwaffe officer had good connections and had gone up rapidly, no one ever suspecting his dedication to Soviet communism. In his important post he met many young men. A few he singled out and they became more than devoted to him. He placed two of them in the heart of a cipher unit that handled the most sensitive foreign intelligence matters. When he suggested to his protégés that they pass résumés on to him, they could only comply. From the résumés he picked subjects upon which he wanted full reports. He got them. Soon they were his willing slaves in any pact, even when they knew that he was passing on every important piece of information he got to his Soviet controllers. And when they learned of the latest Brussels coup by the *Abwehr* they promptly warned the Luftwaffe officer by telephone. The latter collected everything incriminating and made himself scarce. He kept in touch with the hapless code clerks by secret telephone.

One day the officer made a call, asking for one of his protégés by name. To his surprise an unknown male voice answered. Quickly he muttered something about a wrong number, and hung up. The recipient of the call who had just been assigned a new office with a telephone in it, became suspicious. Perhaps there was no reason why he should have but he did, and as a result the *Abwehr* put "tails" on the code clerks. When they next had a rendezvous with the Luftwaffe officer, the trio was bagged.

The resulting exposé revealed Soviet agents in the foreign office and in many other high spots. Also uncovered were a number of secret transmitting stations like the Brussels unit. The *Abwehr* struck, and the backbone of Soviet espionage against the Reich was smashed. Some have placed the number of arrests as low as eighty, others as high as four hundred.

XI

Invitation to Espionage

THE PARADOX of the entire legal apparatus of a democracy battling to save an individual who has been dedicated to its violent overthrow is traditional in this country and England. It springs, of course, from the same concept of a free and just society that is a foreign agent's invitation to espionage. France, on the other hand, wastes little sentiment on its avowed enemies, and reserves for them the harshest of punishment.

Fortunately for us, the vagaries of human nature are infinite, otherwise Western political science might not survive the onslaught to which it is constantly subjected. But it happens that even in strictly regimented countries, trusted agents *do* defect; spymasters develop patterns in their planning which can be predicted by their intended victims; von Rintelens are checked in mid-stride through jealousies in their own camps; secret sex weaknesses send others to destruction. And in democracies, weakness can beget strength; counterintelligence sensitiveness, resourcefulnesss, and agility have been developed to compensate for the absence of such totalitarian tools as police registration of all citizens, travel control, midnight search and arrest, and police-state trials with their powers of life and death.

Even so, in peacetime the odds are all with the militarized nation, or with the dictator of an obedient people.

The Federal Bureau of Investigation's J. Edgar Hoover has estimated the number of Soviet agents alone in the United States in the many thousands. The figure might exceed 300,000 if all types, propagandists, diplomats, certain labor organizers, willing fellow travelers, informers, secret police, and others are included. Only one frail law exists to stem the flood of penetration. Others give it indirect support.

The first is the Foreign Agents Registration Act of 1938, itself a tacit admission of the infested state of the country. This requires any agent of a foreign principal to register if he is engaged in propaganda work or has received training in espionage, has engaged in it, or has knowledge of its being practiced in the country. Presumably this obliging gesture is made by the agent with the Department of Justice immediately as he enters the country. It is significant that in any year only a score or two have bothered to comply, and as might be expected, these originated with countries classed as friendly. But feeble as it is, the law has some usefulness. A dangerous individual charged with such activities can be deported on the basis of failure to register, without the need for establishing an elaborate case against him, one which might not survive the sharpshooting of well-paid legal experts. The Subversive Activities Control Act of 1950 requires listing of all Communist action and front groups with the Attorney General. Details of membership and addresses together with specific activities engaged in could mean serious annoyance for a large class of subversives, including agents and their supporters in the U.S. Until mid-1961, however, the law was circumvented by legal manipulation. It remains to be seen whether even the Supreme Court's narrow decision granting it the status of constitutionality will prove equal to Moscow's determination to wreck it.

266

Both laws are pale ghosts compared with the ruthless machinery of the police state.

Inevitably, then, the country has paid and continues to pay an appalling toll. From the days of von Rintelen to the "atom" spies of recent years and London's Lonsdale and Blake of modern days, the wide-open democracies have sustained an almost unbroken succession of savage blows. With George Blake, too, counterintelligence witnessed something of a zenith in that type of spy potentially most dangerous of all to the state because of his protected position and the enormous difficulty of detecting him—the ideological collaborator. That secret servant of a hostile power can be anyone: your own brother, your closest friend, direct supervisor, or most trusted employee, who, for innermost reasons, has "gone over."

It is this type against which the democracies are most helpless. Every principle of the democratic form, every law designed to give expression to those forms, is at once his most treasured privilege and most steadfast security. Under the aegis of counterintelligence is included the safeguarding of everything of value to the government, from single documents to whole complexes of factories and their personnel. But in every single phase of it, the dependability of the individual is the pivot around which the whole security scheme revolves; without that nothing can resist the ultimate failure of the system. At the Army's Intelligence School it is emphasized that every material device from the simple desk drawer lock to that most ponderously reinforced establishment, the gold depository at Fort Knox, is in the final analysis only a delaying device. Electrical alarm systems, armor plate, thirty-ton doors with time locks, internal and external guard systems reinforced with searchlights, electronic detectors, and police dogs—all depend in the final test upon the loyalty of the individual. True "defence in depth" is the maximum delaying device, all of its components working in concentric circles of protection. Even this will yield to hostile infiltration if the cementing medium

267

of personnel contains flaws. Yet who is to detect in a fellow-citizen the first deeply hidden stirring of doubt in a troubled mind, the first uneasy inner scrutiny of the ethos of patriotism? Nor may it be detected until after the trusted and respectful individual has gone far along the irreversible way of active betrayal. In a democracy, with its guarantee of individual freedom, there is an ever-pressing limit beyond which security measures cannot go without destruction of the freedoms for which the structure exists. Abhorrence of the police state and its methods itself dilutes security efficiency. Few citizens, if any, relish security checks. Most tolerate them at best, and many find inquiry into their private and financial lives altogether intolerable. Surveillance by security agents if it is detected is resented to the point of recourse to law. Even professional intelligence people, knowing as they do the need for periodic security checks upon themselves, confess to twinges of hostility when the time comes for the surreptitious questioning of friends and relatives, the inquiries into family affairs, social habits, use of leisure time, spending habits, etc., to uncover, if they exist, any undesirable tendencies not previously present. It is all so delicate and so highly personal and all the more odious since it infringes upon the democratic freedoms which are the foundation of our country.

Yet following every betrayal of the state there are outbursts castigating security agencies and urging more and more safeguards. Such an outcry greeted the shocking news of the Martin-Mitchell defections from the National Security Agency late in 1960. Then came the hints from Washington that departures from the normal in the social behavior of the two were probable factors in their having become turncoats. In some quarters these statements were attacked as unwholesome and cowardly. In another instance, a large church group petitioned for clemency for a convicted spy whose similarly convicted near-namesake had been charged with obtaining personal data on American government employees to enable the Soviets to exploit sex deviates for espionage purposes.*

As for the Martin-Mitchell case, Moscow attempted a clumsy cover by releasing statements to the effect that the blond, stocky William Martin had married a Soviet woman and was happy with her. Martin stated that Soviet women made more desirable marriage mates. In the United States, official eyebrows went up because there was so little in the record to indicate Martin's competence as a judge of women, regardless of nationality. It was noted that Bernon Mitchell had not succumbed, in a real or putative sense, to the attractions suddenly so irresistible to Martin. There were published statements in the U.S. that security investigators had determined that Mitchell at one time had consulted a psychiatrist on homosexual tendencies.

The defection touched off a flurry of security soul-searching, as well it might, for the two had been accepted into an agency dealing with the ultrasensitive business of code making and breaking. Congress demanded to know how such a dubious pair had been able to insinuate themselves into such critical levels. The records of various security units were checked for derogatory data, but cards in the files of naval intelligence and the Air Force's Office of Special Investigation were unsullied. The FBI, however, admitted to having collected information not so pristine, but hadn't communicated the fact to anyone. It was the old story of faulty co-ordination and it was costly. Implications followed that in high places in gov-

---

* The petition was in behalf of Morton Sobell, serving thirty years for espionage. A namesake, Jack Soble, also convicted, had recruited George and Jane Foster Zlatovski expressly to get compromising information on the lives of Americans at U.S. installations in Austria, especially sex and drinking habits. Morton Sobell, alias "Dr. Soblen," died by his own hand in London in 1962 following a suicide attempt in an effort to enlist public sympathy after he had jumped bail and fled the United States. A near-international incident was created during his sensational attempt to avoid being ejected from England where he had been landed, only temporarily, to save his life.

ernment there were at least a thousand deviates whose betrayals could be as costly, or more so. Yet some of these people were technically accomplished, and came from the best families. Even so, sixty were quietly let out.

Why does the deviate constitute a security hazard? We have seen in the cases of Redl and others that he definitely does. His vulnerabilities are at least twofold. One, of course, springs from his fear of discovery and of being revealed. The other is a guilt-born defensiveness that can result in an antisocial attitude, a frail or even nonexistent patriotism.

The first could be all but eliminated by enlightened social and legal attitudes toward homosexuality, a leap forward from the dark ages which would be at least compatible with advances in the physical therapies. England almost accomplished it in 1960, but, having failed, sat back and relaxed. She shouldn't have. At that very moment in the history of espionage against her and while the Lonsdale and Blake cases were building up to their startling climaxes, a government-employed homosexual in fear of exposure by Moscow was operating with devastating efficiency to pass to his Russian employers the contents of the secret dispatch cases to which he had access. Before the William John Christopher Vassall case would sink into limbo, it would "flap the unflappable" Macmillan government into appointing a super-secret and superpowerful commission for inquiring into the whole welter of rumor and counterrumor involving far more than merely a minor Admiralty civil servant with a predilection for the intimate society of his own sex. There was an insistence, among others, that the authorities had acted just in time to prevent another Martin-Mitchell type of defection involving Vassall and a man of social and political prominence. Vassall, thirty-eight years old when he stood in dock, explained how the Russians had got onto his secret when they got him so drunk during a party in Moscow that he was unaware of what happened next. What happened was gleefully recorded on film by

270

the Russians, who then showed them to the unnerved employee of the British Embassy in Moscow. The pictures revealed him without clothes in compromising postures with others. They were without clothes, too; and they were men. The rest was easy for the Russians, and for seven years, interrupted only when the Lonsdale-Blake cases blew up in London, Vassall served them. Again, like Houghton, but on his own lofty level as befitted a Mayfair playboy, Vassall lived beyond his means and it was this that eventually, if belatedly, brought cold official eyes to study him with interest and suspicion. If Britain needed another hard jolt to make her realize that sex deviates constitute security hazards of the first magnitude, she had it now. But even so, voices were raised in indignant protest against any system which would enable the government to alter its ridiculously inadequate security measures in this respect. It was almost with relief that Englishmen were to read shortly of another conviction for passing prohibited information to a possible enemy of the state: at least the scandal involved people who were refreshingly heterosexual!

If the first area of vulnerability, then, is fear of discovery, the second is more involved and embraces the whole psychiatric spectrum of inferiority complexes. Certainly, though, it would find alleviation in a society that had achieved the first proofs of sympathetic and intelligent understanding. The problem is urgent.

It is something to keep in mind, too, when the temptation arises to credit unfriendly foreign principals with superhuman prescience, unmatchable cleverness, endless resourcefulness, and adroitness beyond countering. History fails to sustain such appraisals. In our own self-created and jealously maintained vulnerabilities lies a significant key to espionage successes against us. Exploitation of social deviations among trusted servants of government accounts for others. Tallied against this is the record of counterintelligence, civil and military, in

271

which, even with its failures, is to be found genuine achievement.

Just how costly the Martin-Mitchell defection really was must remain a secret. But it was no trifle. We have seen that for longer than is generally realized the Russians have been singularly adroit manipulators of the sexual deviate, to their immeasurable profit.

The Weaker Sex!

IN comparison, it is almost refreshing to report the naïve, direct use to which social aspects of biology were put by a trio of desperate American Counter Intelligence Corps operatives in uniform who had been searching for enemy documents during the spearhead advance into the Ruhr pocket in the fighting of 1945.

Suddenly they found themselves too far advanced, cut off, and, finally, in the hands of the Germans. They were disarmed and after the briefest of interrogations, for things were moving fast in those last days, hustled from lower to higher headquarters. En route they somehow managed to dispose of incriminating credentials, thereby hoping to avoid being shot as spies and treated only as ordinary prisoners of war. They felt that their only hope lay in gaining time until the American First Division should overrun the area.

Three times they barely escaped immediate execution. And then the First Division did smash into the town and the German forces fled, leaving the captives in a cellar.

German civilians clung to them for protection from the avenging First. But now the once-sought succor became the gravest threat of all, for the GI's of the First, engaged in mopping-up operations, were firing at everything in uniform in the streets and indiscriminately pitching grenades into every cellar. It seemed sure death no matter what the agents did. Then one of the CIC men, named Robertson, had an inspiration. He searched through the huddle of civilians and hauled out the most attractive girl. Robertson knew no red-blooded GI would fire upon a well-formed girl. He spoke German, and he briefed her fast but well. The girl went up into the street of death, then straight down the middle of it toward the advancing combatants. When she reached the first incredulous, and loudly appreciative, patrol, she told her story. The soldiers asked questions, some of them having no bearing on military matters, and grenade-throwing was suspended for the time being. Robertson later vaguely recalled what counterintelligence training instructions had said about sex in the business—how to avoid entanglements with the *femme fatale* dispatched by the opposition, and above all to shun the sex deviate, but he was quite positive there were no pronouncements on how an agent might use sex to save his life in an emergency.

Such entries in the dark pages of espionage and counterintelligence history are the little breathing spaces between the eruptions of raw drama that shake men and nations. But in the winter and spring of 1960, England sustained a one-two punch that shook it to the base of her thousand-year foundations, the so-called Lonsdale and the Blake cases.

XII

Disciple of Mithridates—1961

ARCHAEOLOGISTS who studied the remains of male corpses buried thousands of years ago in the cemetery of Naga-adder north of Luxor announced evidence that circumcision had been practiced universally upon male children as early as the fifth millennium B.C. The published fact was of some moment to medical historians.

It is unlikely that the statistic was brought to the attention of certain Soviet documentation agents in the mid-1950's. What possible connection could there have been between a reminder of the universality and venerability of the practice and their business of preparing a special agent for espionage against the West? There was, but it would not become apparent for some years. So they proceeded with their meticulous preparation of a cover personality for the dark, square-built individual in their charge.

Conon Molody was Russian-born. But when they finished with him he would be Canadian-born Gordon Arnold Lonsdale. This work was founded upon data long filed away in the document division of KGB, the Soviet State Security Service in

Moscow. Deep in the locked files of the block-long, stone and iron-barred building on Lubyanka Street lay the secret of the fate of the real Gordon Arnold Lonsdale, born in Canada years before. He had been brought to Finland when a boy. Sometime before his thirtieth year he had died, possibly in the war between Finland and Russia. That part of Finland was now behind the Iron Curtain, along with Gordon Lonsdale's original Canadian passport. Such data, such documents are invaluable tools of the espionage trade; they are treasured for future use.

With the long preparation work finished, the Operations Division of KGB instructed "Lonsdale" to say good-by to Galisha, his wife, and their children. He would slip out of Moscow and out of Russia. There began the long separation from his family that would be broken only by infrequent communications by a means familiar to espionage experts. Meanwhile he would go to Canada, establish himself as the long-absent and now adult Gordon Lonsdale. Then, and not until, would he be prepared for the real undertaking. This was a mission which, if properly accomplished, could in one relatively cheap project give Russia parity with the West in another vital branch of the military art, that of underwater warfare defence.

So perfectly did the agent portray the friendly, individualistic, hard-working, hard-playing Canadian that days after his arrest his London friends and his business associates remained in stunned disbelief that he could be anyone else.

That arrest and the subsequent trials which blasted the Lonsdale ring in early 1961, shook British security to its foundations. The repercussions were seismic and they were still reverberating throughout a dismayed West when still another bolt struck.

In some respects the George Blake exposé was even more jolting than the Lonsdale revelations, with its involvement of four other persons known and respected in British communities. To the often-voiced inquiries as to whether there was any connection between the two events, there can be a categorical no. The Blake case will be mentioned later.

While it is almost a certainty that the man known as Gordon Lonsdale would have been convicted by the admirably compiled evidence of his crime against the British state, it was the medical oversight of his original documenters in Moscow that destroyed any hope he might have had of maintaining his claim of being Gordon Lonsdale, Canadian citizen. In a surprise statement in court based on the report given the Canadian police by the doctor who years before had attended the birth of the real Gordon Lonsdale, the man at last in the toils of British jurisprudence must have read his doom. He knew the complete futility of trying to maintain any longer his claim to Canadian citizenship, even under his perfectly valid passport issued by the Canadian government. The minor surgery which had been practiced on so many males since the fifth millennium B.C. had included in a much later day the infant Lonsdale in Canada, the real Lonsdale. This was according to the faded records of Dr. W. E. Mitchell, and substantiated by the old practitioner's memory.

In international espionage, the documentation of agents has achieved fantastic realism. There is no way of telling how often and to what extent impersonation has succeeded. But the check-list of essentials for attainment of a convincing counterfeit is long and ever-lengthening. One more item was added after February of 1961. Even archaeological reports can contain suggestions of value to intelligence men.

The man, Molody, termed "the most dangerous Soviet spy taken in England," or the "director of Soviet intelligence in southern England," was one of a type of high-grade operatives controlled by the six-story center along Dzerzhinsky and Lubyanka Streets. Rudolf Abel, possibly the arch-prototype, had emerged from the same multistep training mill, with its tightly

276

guarded units in at least four locations in Russia. The man was to perform a similar high-grade mission, in this instance against the United States of America. No amateur or adventurer was he, but an exceptionally erudite man who liked to sharpen his mental faculties on the writings of Einstein. Not a "bazaar" linguist, or a stilted product of classroom language instruction, he was genuinely at home in the written and spoken idiom of half a dozen nations. Later on in America he proved facile with such complicated Soviet espionage codes as those utilizing calculus to snarl them after they had already been snarled by lesser methods. He was, in short, the ideal graduate of a complex espionage training course, a course which sometimes took years!

From its files the Soviet center had pulled the passport data of one Emil Goldfus, born in New York City. How the center came to have it is not known, nor is it known by what means Goldfus came to his end. Resurrection is no problem to the center. Tall, slender, resonant-voiced, his deep-set eyes seemingly engrossed with inward as much as with outward vision, the new Goldfus now had to make his way to the city of his "birth." He did this in 1948, via a route that is becoming broadly as familiar in counterespionage as the details are vague —Canada. Oddly enough, to do this he used still another passport enabling him to masquerade as Andrew Kayotis, "a United States citizen." But, by 1948, he was Goldfus, a professional photographer of sorts (excellent cover for microdot activity). He was just another of those countless persons in unprepossessing lodgings in New York, apparently content to struggle for aesthetic expression on an endless succession of painter's canvases. He could paint, too; not too well, for that might have been embarrassing, but certainly well enough to accord him acceptance with his fellow Bohemians. He honestly liked to paint. Possibly it afforded him relaxation from his less artistic role of deciphering the coded instructions that came to

277

him via his Hallicrafters short-wave receiver, a type of machine available to any "ham." Then there were contacts to be made and agent communication lines to be established. Moscow was impatient: It was essential that her lag in atomic research should be overcome.

The story of the atom-bomb spies in America is too well known to repeat, but the reality of its success for Moscow can never be ignored. Whether Colonel Rudolf Abel of KGB, alias Kayotis, alias Goldfus, was the principal behind the diabolically successful espionage that included such puppets as Harry Gold, Klaus Fuchs, the Rosenbergs, David Greenglass, Miriam Moskowitz, is an unimportant question. In the period from 1948 to 1957 he was certainly a principal of top importance, just as, from 1955 to 1961, Gordon Lonsdale was to be a pivot man in southern England.

Unlike Molody (or Lonsdale as we will call him henceforth), Abel was apparently his own communicator. The keenness of his intellect was to a great degree matched by his manual dexterity. In his room were fine carbon-steel drills and other tools. In sensitive hands these could hollow out cavities in cuff links, or split five-cent pieces so that they could be ground out to receive a little patch of microfilm on which was crammed a whole page of typewritten material. Then the coin could be pressed together again and it would look like any other nickel, so much so that one got lost. Instead of going to the agent awaiting the microfilm, it got mixed among countless nickels circulating in New York City. One day it paid a newsboy for a paper. The coin came apart and betrayed its contents of microfilm. Then the meticulously prepared cover for Emil Goldfus, begun years previously in Moscow, began to come apart, too.

But before that, the lean, aesthetic Colonel Abel had accomplished much besides improving his painting. It is quite

278

likely that among the instructions coming over the Hallicrafters was one that he become the guest of honor at a small social gathering on East Seventy-first Street early in 1950. The party was given by a popular young couple, Morris and Lona, later Helen, Cohen. Whether he was already "operating" the Cohens at the time of the party or was there simply to assess some potential agent material, is not known for certain. The record shows that the Cohens were quite *au fait* with Abel by that time, despite the latter's alias for the occasion—Mills, or Milton, "a wealthy British businessman." In any case, he knew them well enough so that seven years later when he was apprehended, due in part to the split nickel, he was found to have in his wallet small pictures of Morris and Helen Cohen. And three and a half years after that, when Gordon Lonsdale was caught in London, the pictures found in his possession of the same people were known to be those of "Peter and Helen Kroger." Colonel Abel's erstwhile host and hostess had formed the hub of Lonsdale's communication net in the London suburb of Ruislip. Nearby was one of the biggest U.S. air force bases in Britain.

A few months after that dinner party in 1950, something happened which made social gatherings by the group out of the question. The suave, quiet-spoken Mr. Mills (or Milton) was seen no more in that circle. Nor were the Cohens. The reason was that certain mutual acquaintances had run afoul of the Federal Bureau of Investigation. Their trial would prove to be one of the most sensational, and to those government officials in a position to assess the damage to the country's atomic program, the most sickening in modern times. It would result in the sentencing to death of Julius and Ethel Rosenberg and the imprisoning of others proved guilty of extracting the vital data and making it available to Russia. Morris and Helen Cohen were known to have been social contacts of the Rosenbergs. A more sinister link would become apparent as

279

the FBI got into the sinuous network. But meanwhile, where were the Cohens?

Both of these people had been the offspring of immigrant parents of average quality. But young Cohen was given a good enough education to show that he was capable of assimilating more. He went to the University of Illinois. Apparently here he absorbed enough of left-wing doctrine to propel him eventually to the Loyalist side in the Spanish Civil War.

Back home again he relocated Communistic friends. A Soviet exposition in New York, somewhat similar to the one held in London after the Lonsdale trial, afforded him closer contacts. Soon he had a job with Amtorg, the Soviet cover organization by which lifeblood is supplied for its espionage program in the United States. This was probably the recruitment point.

In 1941, he married Lona Petka, who changed her name to Helen. Intelligent and lively, she was also inclined toward the left. Cohen's World War II army service was undistinguished but good enough to get him an honorable discharge. He used the G.I. Bill to further his education and became a popular and efficient teacher in New York public schools. There followed the association with Abel. It is certainly possible that it was Abel who directed them to tell friends that they had taken a good job in Hollywood, to pay their bills, close their bank account, and be seen no more in the United States. Moscow had other plans for such useful and dedicated followers.

The FBI concentrated on locating them after the Rosenberg revelations. But the birds had long since flown the coop; the best the agency could do was to send out the routine data—fingerprints, pictures, and so on. Scotland Yard got them, of course. One day early in 1961, the fingerprints were compared by the Yard's experts with new prints just made of Peter and Helen Kroger—against the Krogers' wishes and only after a writ had been obtained to compel them to submit. Now there would be no doubt: The Krogers and the Cohens were the same.

Somehow they had got out of America without a trace. Via Canada again? On a Russian ship—one bound for Australia, perhaps? For it was here they spent many months, even years. What they did there has not been revealed. Maybe Canberra, digging deeper into the voluminous documents of Petrov, the defected Soviet spy leader in Australia, will be able to trace things a step farther.

Far around on the other side of the world, higher above the equator then the Cohens were below it, a smallish man of no particular distinguishing feature was settling into his new assignment at the British embassy in Warsaw. There was a certain cockiness to Harry Houghton that at times annoyed his superior, the British naval attaché. But he had little complaint with Houghton's product as a "writer," a sort of clerk-typist-secretary in the attaché office. The man knew his work, he knew the Navy. He should; Houghton had served in the Royal Navy for more than two decades before his demobilization. He must have displayed more than average abilities to have risen to one of the top spots in the noncommissioned ranks, master-at-arms. He had also turned a pretty penny by smuggling opium, years ago, when serving in a Royal Navy gunboat assigned to the Yangtse station to prevent smuggling of opium. By secreting the stuff aboard his ship, Houghton could dispose of it at a fine profit in Shanghai. His penchant for making a fast shilling, or ruble, persisted. In Warsaw, he was a British civil servant. His attaché superior must have considered ruefully that the man's sagging abdomen no longer could have fitted into his once sleek uniform, for Houghton was going to seed fast from too much drink. As we've seen, the Zlatovskis were recruited to file detailed reports on the sexual and drinking habits of Americans in Vienna. Warsaw, in the Soviet satellite country of Poland, was a dangerous place to exhibit signs of character deficiencies. There is not a doubt in the world but that Houghton's excesses with the bottle, and his indifference to maintaining domestic tranquility with his patient wife, found careful carding on Lubyanka Street under some such head as, "Collaborationist material, without too high a price."

The gregarious, bibulous Houghton didn't last the course. Too friendly with too many Iron Curtain diplomatic representatives anxious to help him enjoy himself, Houghton was marked for return to Britain after eighteen months, instead of the usual twenty-four. MacLean and Burgess had just defected from Britain to Moscow and security personnel were severely rated, but not hard enough to insure that Houghton got steered into nonsensitive work. It would have been easy: a simple administrative transfer. But this wasn't done. Maybe it would already have been too late; maybe Lonsdale had already gotten to him in response to a directive from Lubyanka Street. By that time "Little Harry," as he was known in the pubs he frequented in the vicinity of Portland Naval Base, couldn't have been more ideally assigned, as far as Moscow was concerned.

With success in her atom espionage program against the West already mounting fantastically, the Soviets now had to turn to another area of deficiency. Russia had committed herself to an underwater fleet of unprecedented strength and numbers as the best means of ruling the seas in an air and rocket age. But Western technology had produced sonar devices, highly effective as detectors and locators of submarines. These counterweapons might well nullify the effectiveness of the Soviet submarine fleet. A new priority espionage requirement went out from Moscow.

It became known that other Western powers were co-operating with Canada and Britain in the expensive development program for this and other underwater warfare secret projects. In Britain some of the latest developments would be tested at the Admiralty Underwater Weapons Establishment in Portland.

And that is where, according to the files on Lubyanka Street, Harry Houghton had been assigned.

Now, like a battlefield headquarters marshaling forces for an assault, the Moscow espionage command reached far out and shifted its assets. Lonsdale (who actually may have met, even recruited, Houghton in Warsaw) had slipped away from Russia and in 1954 was in Canada. As we have seen, it was essential for him to establish himself as a bona fide Canadian. The word went out to Australia, too, and the fair-haired, solidly built man and the dark-haired woman, now inclining to overweight, who had disappeared from New York when the Rosenberg explosion occurred, were on the move again. Their trail is involved and the record spotty, but apparently the Cohens went to Europe as Lonsdale crossed to Canada. There is evidence that they were in Austria. If that is true, another lapse in the story could be explained by a period of training behind the Iron Curtain. Oddly enough, they seem to have popped up again in Japan, and once more in Europe. In December 1955, Peter and Helen Kroger, as their valid New Zealand passports showed them to be, arrived in England. Their good appearance so impressed a rather particular land-lord in the Catford district of London that he promptly rented them his home. It would do for them until their chief arrived and gave them instructions in person. Two months later, after a pleasant voyage from New York aboard the *America,* a dark, square-built person, so amiable and entertaining that he had been a favorite with his fellow passengers, a man so healthy-minded that surely there could be no room in it for such dubious business as espionage, landed at Southampton. The Krogers were expecting him. Quite likely the ex-master-at-arms at Portland Naval Base was expecting him too.

Lonsdale had done a good job in Canada. Everything had gone well. Even the delicate business of getting into that country had presented no hitch. Lonsdale never talked

283

about this, or anything else that mattered, but it is thought that he was smuggled in from a Russian grain ship. He had money and paid his hotel bills promptly. Molody was not in the Dominion to spy but really to become Gordon Lonsdale. That meant he had to get a birth certificate. There must have been some uneasy moments when he presented himself at the town hall of Cobalt, Ontario, to seek the necessary document. Someone might remember the real Gordon who had left the little Ontario town north of Lake Erie in 1924 with his mother, but no one did. He had the data the clerk wanted and it was authentic. He must have smiled as he walked out with the certificate; documentation mills are marvelous, but there is nothing like the genuine article. His smile should have been broader when he collected his passport, issued on the basis of the birth certificate. Later when Canadian police checked with the owners of the names that had been signed on his original application as sponsors, they talked to very surprised people. They neither knew Gordon Lonsdale nor had ever seen his application, but their names were in the telephone book. Forgery had done it. The passport was issued by the Canadian government in January, 1955. Meanwhile Lonsdale had been augmenting what the Soviet spy schools had taught him about Canada. He got the idiom. He knew the "lay" of things and what made Canadians tick: they weren't Americans like those in the United States, and they were not British, but a particular brand of pleasant if aggressive, energetic people who knew where they were going and generally got there. Lonsdale crossed into the United States and booked passage aboard the *America*.

It should be said that this was not Molody's first visit to the United States. Months after he had been convicted and imprisoned in England, the FBI disclosed that he had come to America in 1933. Even then it was under false circumstances for he posed as the son of the woman with whom he came over from Russia; actually the woman was his aunt. He had next showed up in Berkeley, California. Molody spent a total of five years in the United States before returning to Russia, where, the FBI believes, he entered military service prior to his recruitment for secret service.

In New York in 1954, there was some slip, as yet unexplained and Lonsdale did not sail as scheduled, but went later aboard the same ship. Apparently the delay was nothing to ruffle his unfailing good humor. In some quarters the postponement is thought to be the result of an instruction from Moscow to get last-minute co-ordination from Colonel Abel.

Meanwhile, in England, things had been happening to give Harry Houghton a freer hand for what was to come. His wife could stand no more of his abuse. She sought a divorce and Houghton moved out. He bought a house trailer not too far from the naval base. Neither was it too far from the home of an attractive, middle-aged woman who worked at the base, Ethel Elizabeth Gee.

Ethel Gee, pleasant and quiet, was the daughter of a respectable blacksmith, and in time she became the only physically fit member of a family circle consisting of her old widowed mother, an aunt, and an uncle. It was upon these, the least able, that the real impact of the blow would fall. But that was in the future, and in the meantime she had passed through a succession of jobs until she had obtained employment at the Admiralty Underwater Weapons Establishment at nearby Portland base as a civil servant. It was a minor post, to be sure, but admirably fitted for the designs of Harry Houghton, whom she met in 1952. She proved a good worker and, in time, was assigned to that part of the organization charged with custody of the secret reports of tests on antisubmarine defences made at the base.

This arrangement was especially agreeable to Houghton, for in the meantime he had been transferred to a fleet repair unit on the base. There is nothing to indicate that this was owing to his past record of social instability, nor his present questionable behavior, for now he made no effort to conceal his friendship for Miss Gee and the house trailer became a well-known rendezvous for the two. At the repair center he had access to an absolute wealth of material, for here were the classified documents and detailed photographs relating to the particulars of every ship in the Royal Navy.

At the hearings and trial in 1961, Houghton claimed that he had met Lonsdale only the previous year. He convinced no one. After hearing his story in Old Bailey court, and following my own lines of inquiries, I join the consensus inclined to the belief that from early 1955 onwards Houghton was passing this kind of documentation over to Lonsdale.

What, then, of his yarn of a Commander Alexander Johnson of the U.S. Navy, allegedly on duty at the American embassy on London's Grosvenor Square? "Alex" was said to have the job of checking on certain data at the Portland base because of Washington's participation in the vital ASDIC program; Houghton could be of no small help in securing this data. Commander Johnson, Houghton claimed, had approached him in 1960, presented properly printed official calling cards, and said he had been referred to Houghton by a fellow American officer attached in Warsaw at the time of Houghton's service there.

If this is an example of Lonsdale's ability to concoct cover stories, there is little wonder that the whole case blew up as it did. A man as wise in the ways of the service as Houghton could not possibly have believed such a cock-and-bull yarn. There is one possible explanation for the crudity: it was not designed to convince Houghton at all, but agreed to between Lonsdale and Houghton to establish credibility with Miss Gee when the time came to gather her into the spy fold. Possibly she needed no such stage setting, for by this time she was in

286

love with him; life was a continuous round of pub-crawling and parties with Houghton.

A most unassuming single room in the lower reaches of that historical London artery known as the Strand was the city base of operations for Peter Kroger. As, in America, Colonel Abel had a genuine love of painting and practiced commercial photography, so, in London, Peter Kroger impressed connoisseurs and laymen alike with his fondness for books. In the premises at Number 190, the Strand, he developed a rare-book business with an increasing clientele in foreign countries. He possessed an uncanny and genuine ability to sift through the gleanings of this part of London where hundreds of thousands of titles are in constant movement among hundreds of dealers and to select those which would go well. Many of them he retained. Of the authenticity of his business there could be no doubt, especially when in the last months, as the net was closing in, he was elected to the venerable Antiquarian Booksellers Association. His friendly smile, his genuine enthusiasm about his books, made for him business and social friends who had a definite liking for him.

At home, dark, talkative Mrs. Kroger got on well with her neighbors. There was only one curious thing: as often as not she would substitute a gin bottle for the afternoon teapot and indulge so heavily that on occasions she would burst into uncontrollable sobbing. But the sympathy of worried friends never elicited the reason. She simply appeared to be under some crushing strain that at times was too much for her. She was, but the source would not be revealed outside Old Bailey courtroom.

There is no record of Lonsdale's having visited Number 190. But the link was definite nevertheless. In due time Peter got his orders: He would have to purchase a house, and it would have to have a number of special characteristics. Probably some of Peter's absences from the shop were not asso-

287

ciated with book auctions; Lonsdale and Kroger must have made long searches in London suburbs for the right place. It was an interesting coincidence that at about this same time Kroger's former associate, Colonel Abel, was making a similar survey with a companion for the same purpose outside the metropolitan area of New York City. But Abel's days were running out and apparently he never did establish that particular communications site for his radio transmitter capable of tying into the Moscow net control. Time and the never-ceasing ferreting of security in England may show whether there was added significance in the final selection by Lonsdale of a house on the outskirts of the South Ruislip American Air Force Base. There are considerations involving radio communication as to why this might be significant, but they may not be discussed here. The frugal bookdealer who complained about his Strand rent of $27 a week and often ate at the cheapest lunchcounters, didn't wince at $15,000 for the house at Number 45 Cranley Drive. It was almost at the end of a dead-end street; a wall and hedges accorded it further insulation: the rear jutted back farther than did the house of the nearest neighbor—innocuous features but as counterintelligence would learn, effective against surveillance. The Krogers moved in, together with truckloads of books. There were other things, too, not apparent either to neighbors or to the many friends and callers that came, for the Krogers were tremendously successful socially.

One of the callers was a darkish, square-built man. He came at odd hours, and neighbors saw him for certain only once or twice. Big American cars are not unusual at Ruislip owing to the proximity to the air force base; the well-used Studebaker sedan that was parked outside the Krogers' house once in a while excited no special comment.

The man who had arrived at Southampton via the *America* had proved as entertaining and popular in England as he had

288

been aboard ship. He blended just the right ingredients of *savoir-faire* and ingenuousness to be the envy of those who had not been around so much and to earn the warm indulgence of those who had. He told tall tales of himself as a truck driver in the giant timber country of Canada. His hairy-chested toughness had a special appeal for feminine listeners, and he never missed a gallery play. It would seem, though, that in Canada he had not been one to "shoot the works" when he came to town; rather, he saved his money: it helped account for the $50,000 or so he laid claim to upon arrival in England. How Moscow had paid this to him in Canada involves a technique Canadian security would be interested to learn.

He took rubberneck tours around England and the continent, too, garnering friends all the way. Americans—women especially—were among them. He never made trouble; Canada could have been proud of her ambassador of good will abroad.

Meanwhile he had taken a flat in central London. It was a small flat and not very expensive for a man with all those dollars to convert to pounds sterling. He didn't seem too particular except on one point: he wanted to be up fairly high, as buildings went at that time in London; he got his space on the sixth floor of White House, off Regents Park. Here he entertained often and well, considering the restricted space. Often his guests were unmarried women of good reputation. For the most part, they frankly admired him and his colorful life as he told it.

One thing was emerging for certain: His tastes were highly contrasted. For two years he pursued with commendable avidity a course in spoken Chinese at a London school. This was demanding and would have been enough to keep an ordinary man going full time. But Lonsdale was not ordinary; his energy was immense. He still had time to develop single-handedly a profitable business on the fringe of London's sturdy underworld—buying and selling juke boxes. Accounting for

289

the Chinese language course is not hard: Moscow had undoubtedly ordered it in preparation for the next assignment, once he had accomplished his mission at Portland Naval Base. But to play a close game with London's "wide boys" was courting disaster, and could have ruined the big game. Intelligence operations control officers puzzled over that one. Cover for another net, possibly?

He abandoned the juke boxes for gum vending machines and this ultimately led to his partnership with a respectable young businessman named Peter Ayers. Ayers had a small manufacturing company that could produce the bubble-gum vending machines. Lonsdale's drive, his persuasive patter, and his nose for the right places to make contacts seemed desirable assets to Ayers, and the company thrived.

And all this time Lonsdale was developing another kind of machine, one that would gather and transmit information in utmost secrecy to Lubyanka Street. How he had time for it all poses another of the sizable package of unanswered questions in the "Secrets Case."

Even then, all is not told, for Lonsdale began turning his attention to larger fields. He found time to make numerous trips to the continent. Some of them were rather extended. Certainly he made some contacts for the company. Doubtless he made others for Moscow, and it is thought most likely he met the faithful and languishing Galisha at least once, probably in Vienna. For her sake one hopes so, because in his travels elsewhere and at his London flat, Gordon Lonsdale never went long without female companionship. Meanwhile he had moved to a luxury flat.

Then he was led on a false business scent. Italy was to be the answer to every businessman's dream of expansion. Italy would certainly buy thousands of bubble-gum machines. All Ayers had to do was expand the shop to make enough of them; and he did. The Italians, however, failed to display the expected enthusiasm for bubble gum. The financial reserve of the

290

company was gone and would never be recovered. Lonsdale lost his own investment, of course, and it is surprising that the record shows him to have been perilously close to bankruptcy at this time. He had taken a big flat elsewhere and now he had to sell a valuable set of furniture to stave off creditors— sell all, that is, except an expensive and powerful radio-phonograph combination; he loved good music, he explained. The unit went back to the more modest White House, again on a sixth floor elevation. Ayers was stunned but still not aware of the deals Lonsdale had been negotiating with others, some of them fairly dubious characters, all the while supposedly promoting the company's product. Ayers was too busy trying to save something from the wreckage to waste time in recriminations, and Lonsdale simply disappeared. The question arises in counterintelligence minds, how did the Russian finance his spy net at this time? Was Moscow suspicious of something awry in his confidential accounts, or did he keep these absolutely straight and thus prevent the axe from falling on his neck, preferring to face the far less lethal London creditors instead? He was in straitened circumstances and had to appeal to others to help him stave off bankruptcy.

In 1960, he got on his feet again. The crisis had sobered him, although he engaged in one more business venture involving a specialized electrical switch. His sense of humor was active: in the interests of increased efficiency for the U.S. Air Force, he brought the device to the attention of officers at the Ruislip base. But overall, there was a briskness to his movements now, a purpose; the tempo was accelerated, like that of the principal in a play which is sweeping toward a denouement. He hinted to friends that he sought to clear up his affairs in England. He might be moving on to other parts.

Doubtless this was true. Lubyanka Street was soon to shift that particular operation into a classification of lower priority, regarding the mission accomplished. Unquestionably another sheaf of directives was being readied that would call for the presence elsewhere of such a successful agent-principal. Moscow was not going to test the axiom that there is a definite and inverse ratio between the productivity of an operation and the efficiency of the counterintelligence forces opposing that operation. There comes a time when the two curves on the graph will intersect, one in a slow descending arc, the other in a sharp ascent. If the time line is extended far enough, compromise and disaster are certain. And Gordon Lonsdale had been working in England since 1955.

Fred Hoskings was a tall man, soft-spoken and methodical. In his little dock-gate office at Portland Naval Base the pale grey winter light from a cold, misting sky filtered onto the sheet of paper he was studying. It was a single sheet and on it in startling black ink were the words, "You dirty Jew." At the bottom in one corner was a crude swastika. Security Constable Hoskings' examination was speculative rather than critical; there was nothing to be learned about the author from what appeared there except that he had been shrewd enough to use a nonrevealing brush to insure anonymity. Rather, it was the remark of the civil servant who had turned the thing in to him. That man, who was not a Jew, explained that he had found the paper on his desk when he came to work that morning; he thought he knew who had put it there, a man working on the base who bore him a personal grudge for some reason or other, a man named Harry Houghton.

The dockyard policeman raised his eyes and blinked through black-rimmed glasses at the cheerless mist. He was disturbed by the positive manner in which the remark seemed to crystalize his own uncharitable thoughts about the man, Houghton. He had felt that way for some time about Houghton. But he shouldn't. As a trained policeman, he should keep unsubstantiated personal feelings out of security matters. But should he? A hunch was a hunch, call it what you like. Constable

292

Hoskings was not authorized to investigate any man off the base; that was a job for the local police. Under the British system, if they suspected security implications, they must notify proper security authorities. Then the whole deliberately vague, formless, faceless civil security personality of the British government slipped into action.

But any man could observe another and tabulate his observations. There was the point that in either one or the other of the two pubs in the neighborhood where Hoskings dropped in for his pint on a damp, chilly evening, there always was Harry Houghton. And it was not just a pint with him. It was plenty and it was hard, and he took more with him to his little blue Renault car. Hoskings knew that car. He suspected that in drink alone the garrulous Houghton was actually spending more than his whole weekly salary at the fleet repair unit.

Then there was Miss Gee. A nice enough little woman. Local girl. She was not much of a drinker, and he suspected that she was more than a little bit worried by her middle-aged boy friend's excesses. But drink or not, she was obviously very attached to him. Actually they made no bones about it any more. Well, a man's private life was just that in England, and no security man, from himself, a constable, on up to the director of home security, could with impunity trespass there. But still there were ways.

To a certain detective of the civil police in the area, Fred Hoskings passed half-a-dozen carefully chosen words: no accusations, no claims, simply, "I don't like the cut of his jib." A personal prejudice, if you will, but it was enough.

The detective consulted with his chief. Surveillance was arranged, not only on Houghton, but on Gee. That was early in 1960. In a very short time the things that the observant Fred Hoskings had noted were confirmed, including the fact that Houghton was spending about $50 a week on drink alone, more than his weekly salary. True, Miss Gee usually paid for her own, but there were other things that bothered the police:

Houghton now had negotiated for a house and in it he had installed furniture that few policemen could have afforded. As time went on, there were expensive gifts for Ethel Gee, and there were trips to London. But by this time Scotland Yard and the military intelligence unit primarily concerned with security and espionage threats, MI-5, had been brought in; a full-time surveillance had been operating on the two. It was found that as a cover story to her aged mother, aunt, and uncle, a fictitious couple had been invented as chaperon. But in London, there was no such couple. There was, however, a dark, square-built man for whom Houghton frequently brought presents of a different kind from those he gave Miss Gee. Sealed envelopes and tightly secured packages. The dark man seemed very pleased to receive them.

Now the dark man came in for attention from security. By this time, it was more than a suspicion that Houghton's activities were adding up to espionage. Accordingly, that total counterespionage machine which, in Britain, has at least six arms and may have as many heads, began to work. The man's every move was clocked and his dossier constructed: Gordon Lonsdale was becoming important.

British security promptly took a very serious view of the whole thing. The Portland Naval Base with its highly secret Underwater Weapons Establishment was a sort of solar plexus of the nation. The Russians would send no mediocre agent to this place. The dark man would know the tricks of the trade. Ordinary surveillance methods would cry out their presence to such a one. There was no time to recruit special surveillance agents of unquestioned integrity and dedication, unless the wives of ranking security men could be induced to serve. It would be a grilling, chilling task and it might last for months. So it was that the eleven-year-old son of a publican in Soho found himself shifted out of his bedroom during daytimes because two trim young women, always carrying with them a

294

black wooden box, used the room from morning till night. This happened after a certain gentleman had visited with the boy's father one day while he was pulling beer at the pub. The box contained a walkie-talkie, camera, and binoculars. One woman peered constantly through the portholelike window of the boy's bedroom. With binoculars she had a close-up view of the inside of a real estate agent's office across the street. There were several phones on the desk. One was Lonsdale's, for this was his London business address. His comings and goings and callers were carefully noted. When he departed, his direction and mode of transport were reported on the radio. A Special Branch monitor, always on the frequency, took the message, turned to a transmitter, and in moments other observation posts had been alerted of Lonsdale's movement toward them. Sometimes a patrol car slipped into traffic behind the Studebaker.

But once the operator at Scotland Yard got a jolt; Lonsdale was headed directly for the Yard. Furthermore, he arrived there as a businessman: it was that automatic electric switch again. He had arranged a demonstration!

But the break came when the trail led far out to west London, where the country is very flat and there are endless rows of semidetached homes and a big American air base. The black Studebaker paused near 45 Cranley Drive and Gordon Lonsdale called on the Peter Krogers. From that time another of the extracurricular surveillance wives went on duty in a house almost opposite. Others working with the regulars checked every movement of the booklover and his compulsively drinking wife.

The new "tailing" system was working excellently. Aside from the housekeeping, family-bringing-up adjustments that had to be made in the homes of the security people involved, the only problem seemed to be an administrative one. Some of the wives were so "senior" that it was thought most indelicate to offer them fees for their priceless work. A box of chocolates now and then or an invitation to pick out a new hat at some modish London shop seemed to solve the problem.

One of the surveillance agents reported that Lonsdale was making a call at the Midland Bank in Great Portland Street. He had gone in with a heavy briefcase, and come out without it. Detective Superintendent George Smith, the senior field man of the security forces on the case, personally arranged for a legal search of the case which was in a safety deposit vault. This painstaking officer, experienced in counterespionage cases, was not overly surprised when he found, among other things, a camera with a special copying lens, a magnifying glass, two film *cassettes,* and a rather special cigarette lighter. The stuff was photographed, then replaced in the case exactly as found. Smith would see it all again one day.

Surveillance was not so successful when Lonsdale made one of his several sudden trips to the continent. Security had its own reasons for not bringing too many into this case; perhaps it was assumed that he was making inevitable and unavoidable contacts with his Moscow home-office associates, but since there was every reason to expect his return, it was best to practice patience and keep a tight case. Surely this was one of the most difficult phases of the whole operation, for those trips almost certainly involved benefit to Moscow, deliveries of materials of the most secret nature from NATO countries. Damage must invariably be sustained while the net designed to achieve the maximum yield is being woven in a manner that will withstand the legal sabotaging of defence lawyers in an ensuing court battle. It is gall and wormwood to patriotic men and a supreme test of counterintelligence fitness. The net was being fabricated, and it was drawing tighter.

Now every innocent-appearing trip to London of the middle-aged lovebirds was recorded in detail. They stayed at the Cumberland, familiar to American tourists in England. Also a woman who ostensibly was just another city worker moved

296

into the flat at White House next to Lonsdale's. She knew his every caller and much more. Other experienced personnel closed in on Houghton, Gee, and Lonsdale as they rendezvoused near Waterloo railway station on the south side of the Thames, across from the heart of the city. In the once heavily-bombed area of the Old Vic theater they greeted each other, not like people meeting initially, but like old friends. Observers noted this fact; it was important later when Houghton was to claim that he met Lonsdale for the first time in mid-1960. He convinced no one.

In August, the United States was jolted hard by the defection of Martin and Mitchell. Shortly afterward, Houghton, Gee, and Lonsdale met again near the Old Vic and decided to take tea in a nearby café. There was a fourth member of the party, but he did not observe convention and sat with his back to the others. On his lap, hidden from the conspiring trio, was a note pad. The man wrote rapidly. One of the others wanted to know if it was true that "they" had "gone over?" The answer was, "Yes, I understand they have." Shop talk, among those in the trade. Then Lonsdale was heard to remark that it looked as if Houghton's briefcase were full. The other quipped that he had more than his shaving gear with him. The remark pleased Lonsdale. He observed, however, that it would mean a lot of work for him that night. Houghton agreed. Doubtless they were discussing the latest batch of documents that Houghton and Gee had filched from the secret files over weekends and had copied before restoring them on Mondays. This had succeeded time after time despite a near thing for the woman once when a call was made for documents in her charge and she was unable to produce them. Gee relied for exoneration upon what would seem to have been a highly defective document registration system. Apparently anyone cleared for classified work could make a withdrawal and remain free from harassment until the papers were needed elsewhere. Then they would be returned. Or they might be passed directly to another worker, who would return them. Periodic checks were made, but they were not bothersome. Now there was an inquiry, and after a fruitless search, the documents were reported missing and no further action was taken. The slackness was salvation to Ethel Gee and a shock for the nation when it was revealed later in the courtroom.

Now that security was on to the broad picture, Superintendent Smith was amazed at the lack of security consciousness exhibited by Houghton and Gee, and apparently tolerated by such an astute operator as Lonsdale. Lonsdale was a master of evasive action and he practiced it to a fine point when preparing for one of the rendezvous. But once with them he changed surprisingly; aside from a few casual checks for "tailers" of the conventional variety, he became singularly insensitive to the presence of lorry drivers blessed with endless waiting time (as double-parking is called in England) or the proximity of loungers.

Oddly enough, such careless behavior is not unfamiliar in espionage proceedings. In my own experience, my lapse into self-generated forgetfulness during a delicate operation was all the more shockingly brought home to me (and my superiors) in a protracted and well-informed wireless announcement from the other side. Of course, the whole expensive undertaking was "blown," and professional ego with it.

On one of Houghton's last London trips, he had some time to kill before his train. He used it, as was his custom, for a drink at a pub. Through the windows of the little Dauphine counterintelligence men could clearly see on the seat the unattended cardboard box and briefcase he was to deliver to Lonsdale. What self-control must have been needed not to smash in and retrieve their country's secrets destined for Moscow and so carelessly attended!

The year 1961 came to a world almost neurotic with anxiety from the never-ceasing, ever more severe crises of the cold war. A new year and for Lonsdale, doubtless another assignment. For Houghton and Gee, what? Transfer to another principal, or a final payoff and time to enjoy the winnings of their treason? The Krogers? Certainly more of the same, either on that assignment or another, unless Helen Kroger's nerves cracked up.

The first of January fell on the first day of the week. London meetings always occurred early in the month. Counterintelligence closed in a step for the showdown must come soon. Such was the feeling of Superintendent Smith and his men, as well as those higher up in the grim, grey buildings along Whitehall. The number of surveillants was increased; now they were everywhere. All avenues of communication were turned against the three, even their telephones. The trained Lonsdale mistrusted the instrument, but even he could not have detected the newest-type taps. Word went out that Miss Gee was heading for London alone. That was Thursday, January 5th. She was never lost sight of on the train or after her arrival at Waterloo. The moving checkers rode with her, the men were spotted everywhere—the two porters at the huge station, the news vendor just outside the main entrance, the loungers on the broad steps, and others, had her in view every moment.

But this time something went wrong. She seemed surprised that no one was there to meet her. In light of later events, it now seems certain that she represented a break in the usual drill and that this time she alone was to make a delivery to Lonsdale. But Lonsdale did not appear. Now Ethel Gee was not the only anxious one. Superintendent Smith wondered if the wary Russian suspected something. Had he seen through the simulated occupations of some of the spotted security men and realized that Gee was marked? At any rate, he was nowhere in evidence and Ethel Gee went back to her room at Portland to care for the aged trio who depended so much upon her. She had already let it be known to others outside that she and Harry Houghton would have married before this had it not been for her responsibilities to them.

Approved technique in an instance of an aborted rendez-vous involves a long postponement. But Lonsdale was in a hurry. Perhaps he was being pressed by Lubyanka Street to close out. At any rate, security men assigned to Portland realized on Friday night that something was astir. Gee worked very late at the office on Saturday morning. Houghton got into his little car. Soon he had picked up "Bunty" Gee. She carried a market basket. They headed for nearby Salisbury on the main rail line to London. They would have to hurry.

Parking was done quickly, Houghton could move swiftly if need be, and they rushed in for their tickets. Returns, so they expected to come back. Security men queued for tickets. Nervously they looked at the clock. The naval officers in line before them were taking a long time getting their tickets to Scotland. Would they never be done? At length they did move aside and Smith's men snatched their tickets, dashed for the train, and barely made it.

Throughout the concourse of the busy Waterloo terminus were men most interested in the incoming pair. When the loudspeakers announced a delay in the arrival of the 12:32 from Salisbury, word went back unobtrusively from the lead man at the gates to the news vendor at the main entrance, and on out via wireless from Scotland Yard to a dark sedan parked not far from the Old Vic theater. In it a grey-haired man sat smoking his pipe. But he was far from relaxed. Super-intendent Smith knew this had to be done right.

The Salisbury train rumbled in. The coaches poured out their human cargo. Close behind the pair from Portland were the two who had been with them all morning. Then Ethel excused herself and went to the ladies' room, leaving Houghton beside a newsstand where he bought a paper and scanned the headlines.

Presently Ethel rejoined him and they started for the main entrance that gives onto Waterloo Road. No less than fifteen men in various guises, all perfectly normal in the scene, began to close in. Everything was going according to plan. Then suddenly, everything wasn't. The next few minutes were unprecedented in the pattern that had been established during the past months.

One moment the two were walking like countless others along the busy thoroughfare, and the next they were sprinting like milers for a red double-decker bus numbered 68. So swiftly did the change occur that only one of the fifteen surveillants managed to swing aboard, too. The bus became one with dozens of others.

What had prompted this? First the use of Miss Gee alone as a courier, then the broken rendezvous with her, and now this. Had it been ordered by a suddenly alerted Lonsdale, or had the apparently unconcerned couple detected their attendants on the train? Or were they simply too early for the appointment and had suddenly decided upon this as a pleasant, safe way to kill time?

For twenty minutes their heavy vehicle jolted and bobbed in the manner of double-deckers until they quitted it at a public market off Walworth Road. For nearly half an hour they ambled and elbowed through the busy stall area, their single pursuer dogging their steps as closely as he dared. He began to feel reassured about them; they did not appear to be uneasy.

Back at Waterloo his fourteen colleagues milled about, not daring to leave their posts, for it was here that they had been told the denouement would occur. Then word flashed around: they were back! They were just alighting from a bus that had come from the market area.

Now the pattern was resumed. The pair crossed the street and headed for the Old Vic. But again there was an interruption for tea in Steve's Café. When they left, Ethel Gee still carried the market basket. She looked placidly domestic.

Then another car arrived and parked near the Old Vic. Superintendent Smith watched a dark, square-built man in a darkish overcoat get out. He was obviously waiting and to kill time he studied posters announcing a season of ballet, with one especially featured. It was "A Midsummer Night's Dream."

Smith put his pipe away. The couple approached the dark man. They exchanged glances but Houghton and Gee went past. Lonsdale fell in behind them.

Smith got out of his car. From across the street other men suddenly seemed to have business on the Old Vic side. Gradually the little knot of people, all moving in one direction, tightened.

Lonsdale caught up with Houghton and Gee. He moved between them and clapped his arms over their shoulders in a friendly embrace. There were startled greetings. It was all very civilized and friendly.

But oddly enough for a casual encounter on a public street between friends, Ethel Gee promptly handed over her shopping basket to the newcomer. The time was 4:30 P.M. Saturday, January 7th, 1961. The moment marked the end of one of Soviet Russia's most productive and most profitable spy operations against the West. At that moment Superintendent Smith moved in and took the basket. He spoke to the trio who were brought up short, staring at him.

"You are all under arrest. I am a police officer."

Now cars whined up alongside and squeaked to a stop. Men appeared from several directions and closed in on the little group immobilized on the sidewalk. Houghton's jaw dropped. He seemed to recoil. Ethel Gee gasped, put up one arm defensively and made a half-grab for her basket with the other. Lonsdale, the disciplined, betrayed his inner feelings by no sign, no word, no act whatever. But surely he must have felt that threatening pall closing in on him which every spy

302

knows and lives with. Smith touched his arm, "It's Scotland Yard for you, boy," he said.

In the basket were two packages. At the Yard it was seen that they comprised the burden of Ethel Gee's late work at the office: document after document of the kind Moscow had been happy to pay well for. Lonsdale had in his pocket an envelope without an address on it. But inside was the equivalent of $350 in crisp notes. Houghton could buy a lot of conviviality with that. At his home, officers with search warrants would find $1,820 more in sterling in a plastic bag. Ethel Gee's modest room would yield the biggest lump, though, more than $13,000. Besides that, it was known that she had been making payments to a savings account in regular, thrifty deposits. Doubtless some was from an inheritance; the rest, from Moscow.

Now, before the alarm could spread, for no one knew whether Lonsdale had cover men to serve should disaster strike, the security men went straight to the Kroger's Ruislip home. Others, as we have seen, went to Houghton's place and Ethel Gee's. Still others went to White House. All had been equipped in advance with proper warrants. But at Ruislip officers wanted to get in before the Cohens, alias Krogers, could destroy important evidence.

The Krogers were expecting company. It was going to be a heavy night's work for them. Helen's amateur efforts with photography, known to all their friends, suddenly had taken on expert purposefulness. There were scores of pages to photograph and reduce to pinpoint size. The microdot process had been invented by the German espionage service in the last war. Then these dots, about as big as the period character on an ordinary typewriter, could be sent to prearranged addresses by one of several means. They might go as periods in inno-

303

cent-looking letters, or in the books that Peter so diligently sent to foreign clients of his Strand book shop, or even on postcards. They were most difficult to detect unless by pre-arranged code their general location was indicated. With a powerful lens they could be read. The Krogers' friend, Gordon Lonsdale, supplied the prototype material which he acquired in the city.

There was a knock on the door. The Krogers jumped up in anticipation. They concealed their surprise when the callers proved to be police officers, a man and a woman. Their pulses must have fluttered momentarily, then settled into a faster tempo. But there was no need. Recent burglaries in the neighborhood were being investigated, the man explained politely; would the Krogers help them in a routine inquiry? The Krogers were noted for their sociability. They opened the door wide. The security agents came in past the especially heavy locks that had been noted previously on that door, the back door, and the windows of 45 Cranley Drive.

Then they sprung their news. The Krogers were under arrest. They would get their coats and hats promptly and accompany the officers to Scotland Yard. Silently they complied. Mrs. Kroger got her handbag, and then, like any thoughtful housewife, said, "Since we may be gone for some time, may I go down and stoke the boiler?"

It was a critical moment but police experience saved it. Yes, provided she either left her handbag with the officers or showed them what was in it before she went.

It was a telling shot. Mrs. Kroger's jaw jutted. Her eyes blazed defiance. She turned as if to make a dash to the basement and the furnace. She proved unexpectedly strong when forcefully restrained. The bag was taken from her. In it were a six-page letter in Russian, a typed sheet of cipher data, and another with three microdots.

But the show at 45 Cranley had only started. The Krogers were hustled off in separate cars, and now a practiced search squad took over the house. First came the photographing of things as they were, then the detailed probe.

Some things were in plain sight. The Ronson lighter was a standard wooden ball type seen in countless homes. But this was a lighter with a difference. Inside was a cavity containing a signal communication plan for the first eight months of 1961, data implying a continuance of 45 Cranley Drive as a transmission center, with or without Lonsdale. Frequencies and time schedules were carefully listed. Column headings were in Russian. There were also what the trade knows as "one-time pads." These are encoding tables. Only one is used per message and then destroyed. They are a cryptanalyst's nightmare. The receiving end has the counterpart pad for breaking the encoded message. Then it, too, is burned.

But where was the wireless equipment? The receiver proved to be the radio-phonograph combination in the living room. It was expensive and powerful and its short-wave side covered many bands. At the back was a plug-in for a tape recorder and earphones. The earphones were connected.

There was a long hunt for the transmitter. Finally it was unearthed from a cleverly camouflaged excavation in the basement. It was a suitcase type of a design familiar to intelligence. Exceedingly compact for its 150 watts of power, it was capable, when used with a proper antenna, of putting a signal straight into Moscow. Now the police had their answer to complaints from people in the Ruislip area of code station interference with broadcast programs at times. The antenna was strung expertly in the attic. Doubtless one of the reasons the Krogers had had the house rewired when they moved in was to insure, as far as possible, against telltale blinking of lights in neighbors' houses when the set was keyed. As to that, the automatic high-speed keying device included with the set was of better design than one which U.S. authorities were experimenting with not so long ago. A tape could be whipped

305

through it in an instant, thus reducing to an unbelievable minimum the time the transmitter would be on the air once the go-ahead had been heard from the other side.

Since Mrs. Kroger had microdots in her handbag, it was probable that the equipment for making them was in the house. In time, searchers discovered the microscope and glass slides. But they had to pore through endless books before uncovering the light-sensitive cellophane used in producing the dots. The precious sheets were stowed between the pages of a Bible. There were also in the house such things as a talcum powder can with a false compartment holding a microdot reader, a flashlight with a false battery for similar storage, a Minox camera, and the rest of the photographic gear for making the dots. A total of about $9,000 in American currency was hidden in various places.

Later, as I was examining that neat transmitter at Old Bailey, I was summarily ordered away by a police guard. In spite of his energetic but belated determination to protect the West against wrongdoers, I could see that it was an improvement over earlier sets the Russians had supplied their agents, and a better one, I think than Colonel Abel had when he was trying to locate a suitable house from which to transmit in America at the time of his arrest. There was the same anonymity of the working components, although one used previously against America had been equipped by Moscow in a spirit of whimsy with RCA tubes. There was that economy of design which suggested the ideas of the Dutch Philips radio engineers who had disappeared against their will behind the Iron Curtain at the end of World War II.

In London, searchers were combing Lonsdale's flat as well. Here was a duplicate of the expensive radio-phonograph combination with the high performance short-wave side. Now Lonsdale's preference for a flat on the upper floors was plain: it gave better radio reception. There was a mate to the Ronson

306

lighter here, too, and inside it, one-time pads. A microdot reader was in the false compartment, as well as a communication schedule. The flashlight, too, was found with the false cell. Over Lonsdale's bed was a Chinese scroll with the usual rolled wooden ends. Unscrewing the knobs enabled searchers to find $1,800 in currency. There were several pages of letters in the room, one signed "Gordon." Innocent as they were, they were key exhibits, for they enabled handwriting experts to show that these and the Russian letter in Mrs. Kroger's handbag were written by the same person, Lonsdale. A typewriter proved to be the one that had done the page of cipher data in the same handbag; the page was destined for transmission to Russia.

The microdots in Mrs. Kroger's bag were reductions of letters by Lonsdale to his wife. Translated, they were mixtures of pathos, resentment, and helplessness, ever the expressions of the spy in a foreign land. He professed affection for Galisha and his children. He lamented the long separation that it seemed would never end. He found hard comfort in having done his duty. At one point he mentioned his true age. Scotland Yard radioed Canada for information about the birthdate of Ontario's real Gordon Lonsdale. The man under arrest was three years older than he should have been. It was the beginning of the end of his cover story. The doctor's subsequent data sealed it.

The hearings at the Old Bailey were a newsman's feast. For once the press was asked to give maximum publicity. It would be a sound refutation of Mr. Khrushchev's pious declamations of espionage "clean hands" at the time of the U-2 exposure. The courtroom had exactly six seats left for the public even after alterations had been made to seat a maximum number of correspondents. There was always a queue for those six seats. Inside, everything was friendly and matter-of-fact. The Krogers, recovered from their initial shock, nodded to friends; but there was some lack of conviviality toward Houghton and Gee. Lonsdale sat stolidly throughout, neck muscles working as from a chewing motion. Could it have been bubble gum?

The government's case was as solid as the history of the British legal system. All five were remanded for trial. At that trial late in March bit by patient bit the prosecution, led by the best legal minds in England, cut away from each of them in turn every splinter of hope and laid the wreckage neatly aside. For Lonsdale, the Lord Chief Justice had, at least, respect—a spy doing dangerous work for his country. He also had twenty-five years for him. To the Americans he dealt out twenty years each. Peter Kroger gasped, staggered backward, and on his face was a beseeching look toward the woman he had known as wife for so many years, and whom he would possibly never see again. The ex-master-at-arms in Her Majesty's Navy awaited his turn. He seemed shrunken in his colorless tweed suit. He trembled visibly at the sentence of fifteen years and the cold words that he would have gotten ten more except that there was no desire to see him die in jail. For Ethel Gee, aging and silent, it was fifteen years. For the three old people who depended upon her in Portland, it was disaster.

The prisoners were whisked away in cars. The newsmen and photographers streamed out after them, and the cold marble foyer was deserted.

Across the street Covent Garden theater was preparing to receive its own crowd. The ballet that afternoon and evening was "A Midsummer Night's Dream."

Moscow knew something had gone wrong as soon as the regular schedules stopped, even discounting the blaze of publicity. But putting to use the radio communication schedules found in Lonsdale's flat and at Ruislip, three wireless monitoring stations across the length of England and Scotland still caught the distant identifying call signs at the times listed. They swung triangulation equipment into bearing. The lines intersected unswervingly on Moscow. Curiously, the Soviet calls continued for eleven days after the arrests. It is customary to continue calls even after a schedule has aborted for some unknown reason, but with the publicity, the reason was known. In that case it is possible that Lubyanka Street was calling other and as yet undetected agents to warn them, and maybe to give new instructions to be effective after the furor had died down.

The battle does not end merely because there have been casualties. Gordon Lonsdale, the Krogers, and Houghton and Gee had become casualties. That was all.

In Gordon Lonsdale and Colonel Abel, the West was shown the top-flight product of the Soviet Union's agent-training facilities. Morris and Lona Cohen represented the higher type of non-Soviet agents recruited in the target country. In Houghton there was epitomized the character-defect type of low-level recruit. Ethel Gee was a fortunate accident for the Russians and might really have believed her impulsive "I've done nothing wrong..." when Superintendent Smith announced the arrest of the trio in Waterloo Road.

Moscow's collection organization is complex and utilizes every type of operator and collector. Some are within the legal framework of embassies, of Amtorg, and of the so-called news agency, Tass. Others operate only within labor organizations. The select circle of operatives for special assignments includes only those who have met years of testing in the party and who have survived years of training. These would have had training in basic institutions such as those at Gorky and Leningrad, as well as the advanced unit in or near the Ural Mountains, southeast of Kuibyshev. Since these Russians have most likely never had the advantage of residence abroad (and therefore are "uncontaminated") it is necessary to expose them to every feature of the target country by artificial means. Whole Western communities are believed to exist at the advanced unit. Here are duplicated the scenes, the language and accents, the customs, and the oddities of the target country of assignment. Transportation units are reproduced, as are such Western peculiarities as coin-operated cafeterias, juke boxes, movies, etc. Businesses are taught. Magazines and newspapers of the area are read in the originals. Only the language of the target area is spoken, written, and heard for months of most rigorous training. Allegedly the instructors are Communist fellow travelers who have disappeared from the Western scene after years of residence there. (Yet there are cracks: Gordon Lonsdale's Slavic weight to certain syllables in his spoken passages at the Old Bailey should have fooled no native Canadian or New Yorker.) So confident are the Soviet masters of their human material by this time that they deliberately brainwash their top-flight agent-candidates so they will even think as Westerners rather than as the party devotees they are. And because they are men like Gordon Lonsdale, they reveal absolutely nothing to counterintelligence, even when convinced that before them lies a life and death in prison. These are men of genuine cerebral quality, of deep cultural roots, of toughest moral fiber.

Only slightly less endowed are the fellow travelers, the Cohens and the Rosenbergs. And they are in far greater numbers. Most of them get training, either from the principal or in special schools back of the Iron Curtain whence they are smuggled. But they cannot be as deeply tested. They are not shock-proof. They may substitute the bottle for the teapot when the strain bears down endlessly.

Then there are the low-level types in the target country. Their weaknesses have been carefully carded, be they sexual aberration, drinking, or gambling. It is desirable if they also

310

harbor real or imagined grievances against their governments or their fellowmen.

Obviously the weak link in the whole carefully fabricated machine is that the least durable, the most vulnerable, member can betray the most select Moscow principal, as Houghton did. It has been said that "compartition," or "cell organization" is peculiar to the Russian system to confine damage of betrayal, as watertight bulkheads seal off a ship from a holed part of the hull. This is not true: Espionage practice has demanded compartition from the very earliest times. Presumably Lonsdale had other agents; he might have been known to one other principal, possibly two, but no more. Doubtless Russian espionage continues to operate in Britain with only slightly diminished vigor, as it did in the United States following Abel's neutralization.

We've spoken of the "life-line" graph of espionage versus counterespionage. Great damage has been done to the West through hostile secret service. But every exposé has taught the West much. Its counterintelligence is to be feared now. Yet there is always a genuine need for education of the public regarding the need for its free operation. Public fear of police-state oppression must be eliminated by the elevation of counterintelligence to a lofty plane; its personnel must be of the highest order so that great power can be safely entrusted to its directors and agents. The answer lies here and not in nervous Congressional hedges and inquisitiveness. The Secrets Case proved that the press can be relied upon for complete co-operation. The public was enlightened, and jolted. More of the same is needed, for only in this aura of public understanding can counterintelligence meet the threat.

Following the Secrets trial, alarmed security officers from various Western countries met in London to see what could be done to insure against repetition. Questions flew. Why wasn't Houghton transferred when it was known that he was drinking hard? It was explained to me, by one of the highest men in security, that in Britain the rights of the individual transcend the rights of the state, a most jealously guarded tradition. Not for one minute would citizens of Britain tolerate checks and maneuvers that American security habitually practices. Applicants for a sensitive job are given an open questionnaire. Some questions may be somewhat personal, but mildly so compared with American standards. "They would do well to answer them accurately," my Whitchall host said, however; "Discrepancies are not looked upon leniently." Once more the British genius for conservative expression.

After the Mitchell-Martin defection (there is some reason to believe that they supplied Moscow with the data that made possible the U-2 incident), Washington tightened requirements that included the use of the lie detector for all those in top sensitive spots. Such a thing is presently unthinkable in Britain, where the centuries-old loyalties of a relatively homogeneous population still is believed the best insurance. Added checks of a quiet kind, however, may be introduced as an enlightened public takes more kindly to the suggestions of counterintelligence.

The Communist party is legal in England. It is not in the United States. Only time can say which policy has the least danger for the host country. But the Cohens proved, if more proof was needed, that in its membership the potential for recruitment and assistance for espionage is endless. This party cannot be looked upon in any other way than as an enemy of the present order.

As the rumble of the Secrets Case receded, following the sentences, there came yet another thunderclap for the West.

A respectable member of the British diplomatic service, a wartime Dutch espionage agent for the Allies and holder of an officer's commission in the British Navy, was revealed to a thoroughly shaken public to have been a diligent spy for Soviet Russia for nearly a decade.

He was a still different type, a most dangerous one. The idealistic agent, the Communistic convert, is convinced in his own heart that he must devote himself to bringing down the present order in the West to open the way for Communist world domination.

George Blake was the son of a British diplomat father and a Dutch mother. The World War II occupation of Rotterdam by the Germans found the young, alert, patriotic Blake eager to serve. Under the noses of the Germans he performed dangerous missions for British espionage. He proved so adaptable, so resourceful and productive that the British determined to extricate him before it was too late. In due time he appeared in England. Accorded a commission, he served in British naval intelligence. Afterwards in this capacity he was sent to Hamburg and served under the British agent who had recruited him originally.

Once out of the service, he studied Russian at Cambridge, then joined the consular service and went to Seoul, Korea. He was captured by the North Koreans and brainwashed—as it developed, effectively.

Back in England once more, he was hailed as a hero and given a new posting. But George Blake was convinced of the correctness of Marxist theory, and his subsequent posting to Berlin insured easy contact and arrangements for passing the data to which he had access. It seemed that the line of communication was never to fail him, nor he it. But the uninterrupted functioning of the arrangement contained the seeds of its own betrayal: Blake had been observed making a contact for which there could be no easy explanation, and from that time on his previous movements were traced.

Meanwhile, he and his family of wife and two children had been sent to Lebanon. This was late in 1960. Blake was to study at the Middle East Center. All seemed to be going well. But in a situation as bizarre as any in the modern game of spy cat-and-mouse, Blake and his family appeared to be the last ones to know that things were not right for them. To an individual, the villagers kept the secret that somehow Blake was an object of suspicion and should be watched. Then came strange stories of illness at home in England that would require one or all of the Blakes to return. They disappeared from the community of Shemlan—and reappeared on the front pages of the avid British dailies.

The sentence handed down by Lord Chief Justice Parker in the Blake case was long, forty-two years. It was the most severe sentence meted out to any person convicted by a British court in this century, and possibly in all British legal history. If he lives, Blake will be free when he is eighty years old.

The sentence probably reflects a measure of the bitterness of frustration, for what defence is there against this type of sincere convert, and who is to detect him?

Surely this is the most cogent question to face Western security today.

Blake was converted or, as we say in the West, brainwashed. There is much misunderstanding about the process, for the term suggests a ruthless combination of physical brutality, mysterious stupefaction of the senses, hypnotic suggestion end-lessly repeated, and so on. We now know better. It is simply the psychology of salesmanship carried to the utmost extreme, coupled with the creation of an atmosphere for utmost recep-tiveness: isolation, mistrust of one's own people, and the apparent sincerity of the proponents.

This is the way it worked on prisoners of war. But working on everyone in the West today are other factors just as potent: weariness with our own problems; loss of basic religious faith; the human propensity to believe that some new *ism* really does have the answers, forgetting that back of it and all like it since time began is simply man himself with all his imperfections.

It becomes a matter of national urgency that each man be able, as Hamlet said, to "bear those ills we have than fly to others we know not of."

XIII

What Now?

WE have seen how the adolescent period of American intelligence emerged into young adulthood with the shock of bombs at Pearl Harbor. During the ensuing war, Intelligence grew hard muscles, a calculating eye, and a head for business.

The next fifteen years was the era of Central Intelligence Agency, or CIA as it is commonly referred to. But even while this book was being prepared, with its introductory suggestions that the time was ripe for reassessment of the over-all intelligence structure, the factors that prompted such thoughts erupted, compelling reassessment in Washington.

Any system of intelligence can be only as effective, as mature, as the soundness and the maturity of the public it is to serve. For twenty years or more, perhaps even since World War I, the American public has generally reflected a receptive attitude toward new ideas, rather in advance of its officials. Oddly enough, it was in the services, especially the Army, that resistance to the development of intelligence and counterintelligence proved most obdurate. Contempt for the whole idea and those who served it was ill-concealed. On all levels, many

316

individuals still hold fast to this attitude. The Army's fine school system, one of the oldest and most important units for training its regular officers, maintained that the whole enormously complicated subject of intelligence could be disposed of in exactly one hour of instruction. But the diehards, once legion, have all but gone the way of the bugle, the drummer boy, and the muzzle-loading musket.

Intelligence itself must take part of the blame for historic opposition. The dedicated few involved with intelligence were so occupied defending themselves and their concepts that they had little time or inclination to think about trying to educate their opponents. Instead, there was a foolish determination to cloak the whole business with mystery. The very individuals whose support was most vital often were affronted by hints that their degree of security clearance was inadequate to permit official discussions! This was especially effective in making an enemy when the rejected individual was a commanding officer of high rank. Generally speaking, however, the higher the rank, the more co-operative the officer. Intelligence planners and operations chiefs could only be elated with the support given by such men as Generals Patch, Mark Clark, Eisenhower, MacArthur, or Admiral Arleigh Burke, to name a few. There were those of the younger group, however, who decided on the spur of the moment that their judgment was superior to that of any of their experienced intelligence men. They caused harm in varying degrees from mild to disastrous. Some of these younger officers responded, in time, to programs acquainting them with the potential, as well as the limitations, of the intelligence program.

As education proceeds, the distrust of the professional army officer for intelligence assignments wanes. But it is still present. Will his whole career be shattered while on some intelligence assignment due to some error, some operations compromise that turns out to have international repercussions, some communication failure, or some costly security breach? Such an officer may become a chronic "no-man" to all operational proposals, with consequent intelligence stagnation in critical times and in critical places.

For decades a dedicated few have sought to provide the services with a professional intelligence service corps whose trained personnel would perform operations and directorial functions. For almost as long a period their efforts met with flat rejection. Eventually, there was an inching forward, and finally real progress. More has been accomplished in the last two years than in the previous fifteen.

An announcement has been made at long last of the creation of an Intelligence and Security Branch for Regular Army personnel. Since the training program has lagged, the next step will doubtless encompass the use of career intelligence reservists to fill up the branch. From there for the most part, will be drawn the new Intelligence Corps. This unit is to include the old Counter Intelligence Corps and various other types of specialists whose work is in classified areas.

Thus, in the senior military service, at least, genuine stature seems to be emerging. The peculiar demands of the Navy continue to be served reasonably well by the Office of Naval Intelligence. The Air Force intelligence organization is complicated and ever more so with the electronic age. Parallel with the technical aspect is its development of the Office of Special Investigation, essentially counterintelligence in aim.

In the Army the development of the structure must be accompanied by an integrated training plan that will produce the true career man. And this, in turn, must be preceded by something still more elemental: a realistic selection plan by which misfits can be stopped before they ever get to the front gate, or, better, before they ever start for it.

The groundwork for integrated training already exists in the proper schools giving courses from a few weeks to half a year in gradually advanced stages. These are alternated with orientation field training with the units they are designed to

318

serve; by this means they "know something besides intelligence" yet are considered to be true specialists.

During the years, when units were called upon for a quota of men for intelligence training, the attitude was that they wanted "screwballs for crystal balls." This approach tended to restrain many brilliant candidates from interesting themselves in such service. Yet the complaints of these same units when intelligence estimates were imperfect were as loud as any. Early attempts to introduce carefully designed testing methods for intelligence applicants were defeated in the Pentagon for vague reasons, some purely administrative. Thus misfits were accepted for training until the mills of routine had ground and they could be dropped. Meanwhile, some dissidents were potential or real security risks. Other candidates were quite inappropriate to the service because of family tensions. The preselection tests must come, and the sooner the better; the country's margin of tolerable delay shrinks rapidly.

Assume then that keen preselection tests have given the schools the best possible raw material for shaping by realistic courses and that time-tested intelligence specialists are assigned to planning and operational positions. One cardinal requirement remains to insure success. Military commanders through whose areas of responsibility these operations must proceed, particularly in time of combat, must be sharply restricted in their authority to block them, once the intelligence operations are authorized. Too many soundly planned and properly mounted intelligence efforts have been hindered or defeated by such officers who, otherwise competent enough, lacked the particular kind of imagination necessary for cloak-and-dagger operation. Or, as has been seen, possibly there was fear by these career officers of damage to their records should these operations go wrong. Intelligence operations are unorthodox as well as highly specialized, yet require the conventional military structure for support and cover. The need for co-operation and forbearance is obvious. Such qualities can evolve only from the proper education of the commanders concerned.

Human factors in the acceptance or rejection of information, even processed and evaluated intelligence, remain a hazard. Pearl Harbor is not the only instance when the signs were, for one reason or another, seemingly ignored by those in top positions. We have seen that Stalin spurned the spy Sorge's reports that Germany was going to attack Russia, even when the alarm was soundly substantiated for him by other competent collection sources. For the United States, the second tragic intelligence miscarriage of World War II concerned our bitter surprise in December, 1944, when a giant German force smashed out of the Ardennes and sent American units reeling.

During a nightmarish two weeks there was too much preoccupation with efforts to dam the break that threatened to flood the whole of Belgium and northern France to consider how the surprise attack could have happened in the first place.

Then the bloody German assault withered before massed Allied strength, and the questions began. For the intelligence family it was a time of trial, and special interest. At the heart of the controversy was one whose name surely qualifies for an intelligence Hall of Fame, should there ever be one. He was Colonel Benjamin ("Monk") Dickson. At the time of the Battle of the Bulge he was intelligence officer for Lieutenant General Courtney Hodges, commander of the U.S. First Army. Before that he had endeared himself to countless members of the Counter Intelligence Corps with his solid, far-seeing, and thoroughly effective planning and implementation work as Second Corps intelligence officer in the chaotic early days of CIC in the North African landings in late 1942. Later he did great service in planning and organization for the CIC and other intelligence units that were to play key roles in the Normandy invasion. He continued on to ever-increasing responsibilities. General Omar Bradley in *A Soldier's Story* paid tribute to Dickson's fairness, patience, discernment, and sense of the authentic in intelligence matters.

320

This man, early in December, insistently predicted that the Germans would launch a massive counter-attack soon and through the Ardennes. Hodges's staff got impatient with him and recommended to Hodges that he be sent back to Paris for a little fun and relaxation. Dickson, only hours before the vast assault erupted, pounded a map board and insisted once more that the blow would come through the Ardennes. And now a woman who had been behind the enemy lines reported an enormous build-up of German strength with monstrous tanks, all at the ready, waiting the command. She was sent up to Hodges's headquarters. Her time was wasted, as Dickson's had been.

The rejection was universal. General Bradley's own intelligence officer disagreed and drastically downgraded Dickson's whole estimate. Even the British concurred; General Montgomery dismissed it with a flat statement that the Germans were now incapable of organized assault.

Before it was over, the Battle of the Bulge would account for some 80,000 casualties of all kinds in the American ranks and an estimated 220,000 German dead and wounded.

Yet who in his heart can blame the Allied commanders for their failure to pay attention? Every sign and symptom favored complete German collapse. Dickson's voice was one crying in the wilderness.

In the civilian field, CIA was the eventual outgrowth of OSS. Over coffee in his apartment overlooking the East River not long before his death, Major General William ("Wild Bill") Donovan referred to his brainchild as "that aggregation of intellectuals, dilettantes, and footpads." (No one else dared so allude to OSS in his hearing, though!) Born of wartime pressure, OSS did all sorts of dirty tricks in all places. Its 12,000 members gathered information (a severe understatement), communicated it, analyzed it, and got it to users; sabotage was performed to order; propaganda was delivered and so were dead bodies. And, as in every intelligence establishment, thousands were engaged in nonsecret work of great value. There were real espionage achievements; there were also inevitable mistakes of every kind, from incidental and accidental to stupid and costly. And there were casualties. A job had to be done and OSS did it all over the warring world except in the MacArthur theater, where the Allied Intelligence Bureau did the job. Here the effort was military and para-military. All departments were included under one wing, although propaganda was later split off. Counterintelligence came under Willoughby, and AIB was coordinated by him. Right and left hands thus were of the same "body intelligence." And that was right, while it lasted; later the Philippine Regional Section became directly responsible to the Chief of Staff, and from then on frictions were natural and inevitable. But the job got done and the statistics imply a worthwhile contribution.

In Europe, the military effort lacked such focus and control. Outfits and agents sometimes stumbled over each other. Individual commanders ran their own shows. The enemy couldn't figure it out; neither could we, which is one way to keep a secret. It all cried out for formalization and maturity.

OSS went out and CIA came in. Originally, it was not intended that CIA should do any clandestine collection. But it was soon evident that a department of dirty tricks would be useful. CIA didn't just grow, it exploded! It got into everything, including other people's hair. It set out to control the entire intelligence effort. In many fields it was doing a tremendous job in a superior way; it sought to do all jobs everywhere. Obviously it couldn't hope to do tactical intelligence for combat units, big or small. The ponderous permission granted the services, allowing them to retain a function that was so obviously a property of command in the first place, certainly irritated more than it soothed. Increasingly there was the conviction that CIA was getting too big for its britches. Crude as the expression is, it nevertheless conveyed a truth, but it took the Bay of Pigs to prove it. Not only was CIA a massive compiler of intelligence, the function it originally was designed to perform, but it had become a Hydra of secret involvement in political intrigues quite apart from its clandestine collection effort. Superimposed on this was the para-military business of recruiting, equipping, training, and directing a rebel force for the assault against Cuban beaches. The task was gargantuan. The complexity of the task did not, of course, doom it to failure, and there was a precedent in our recent history of a similar effort that succeeded. The Allied Intelligence Bureau in the MacArthur theater recruited, trained, and operated battalions of semisecret native soldiers in the Pacific late in World War II, to the great detriment of the Japanese. In fact, in cleaning-up work in the "island-hopping" operations and on New Guinea, these unorthodox forces co-ordinated by the bureau accounted for half the total enemy casualties. But that was a war situation and dependence was put on intelligence collection from a wide range of tested sources. In the Bay of Pigs preparation phase, on the contrary, there is reason to believe that too much reliance was placed on the "wishful thinking" type of report and too little on adverse estimates. Too much reliance was put on the agent of anti-Castro bias and too little on the anti-American variety—if, indeed, the latter was used at all. There is reason to believe, however, that neither the agency nor any of the service intelligence people estimated success for the Bay of Pigs operation unless it was strongly supported, especially from the air. This was not done. Criticism was freely expressed in Washington that the State Department had thrown its weight counter to the military recommendation. Still, the decision had to be made on the very highest levels, and may account for Mr. Kennedy's outspoken statement, "There is plenty of blame to go around."

In any case, CIA may not regain its stature for a long time to come, if ever. Many believe that this is right and just, and the healthiest thing for the country. For one thing, the possibility of bias creeping into estimates prepared by the ten-man United States Intelligence Board may have been reduced. The Board has to supply the National Security Council with the ultimate findings. The President relies on the Council for them and from them makes his own decisions. But if there is bias on the Board level, there may be an unsound instrument on the Council table. As stated, the law seeks to avoid this by demanding the inclusion of minority reports in the estimate. But the fact cannot be overlooked that the Chairman of the United States Intelligence Board is the Director of CIA and the Deputy Director of CIA is that agency's representative on the same Board. Close ties exist between the CIA and the State Department, so close that most citizens do not try to distinguish between them. The State Department representative on the United States Intelligence Board is a civilian. It would require a particular brand of naïveté in Washington to ignore the natural lines of cleavage that often occur between civilian and service representatives on joint committees.

Only a careful study of the secret estimates forwarded to the National Security Council in pre-Kennedy days could substantiate the complaint that while minority views did go into the reports as legally required, they often wound up at the tail end of the critical estimates. The papers are still secret, and the point cannot be proved. But one axiom of intelligence has pertinence here: An estimate, to be of value, must honestly reflect a consensus of all independent and contrasted sources.

Insuring in CIA that the secret tail can no longer wag the nonsecret dog, and buttressing against the possibility of a disproportionately heavy vote by CIA-minded people on the Intelligence Board is sensible. It is also essential to national safety.

The CIA first drew skeptical comment with the blow-up of the U-2 case. This I feel was unfair, but hardly avoidable in a democracy. The agency quite frankly had done a magnificent job and has been doing one for years. Thanks to CIA, our military is no longer as blind as it was concerning the location and nature of many key Soviet war installations. If the history of espionage has taught us anything, it is that there is no gentle way of performing espionage. Nor is there a right time: the only right time is all the time.

I recall participating in a final inspection of one of our Black Cats destined for a dangerous flight. The airplane had been totally, or so we felt, "sterilized"—that is, rendered anonymous through the removal of all marks, plates, numbers, and so on that could identify it with the United States in case it crashed. Infinite care had gone into the matter. One final inspection revealed a bright, shining model- and serial-number plate, bearing the name of a well-known American instrument company! Black Cat flights are no novelty to any of the major powers; only Moscow knows the number of Soviet high-level reconnaissance overflights above United States-controlled territory; we certainly know of many of them.

From a national security policy which forbade even *use* of the word "overflight," Washington now has gone into the business of publicizing the most intimate details of the U-2 episode. The first extreme betrays an overweening preoccupation with the unimportant, indicating lack of true security sense; the second can only result in revelations of technology and concepts that are of vast interest to our antagonists. Old intelligence operators can only shudder!

A cause for sober reflection was the exchange of master-spy Abel for the amateur Francis Powers, who, in the final analysis, was little more than a special pilot. Only the topmost levels can know whether it was worth it; no one else is really in a position to judge. Abel, whose contacts and nets at the time of his arrest doubtless were very extensive, had only to reveal them to his Soviet masters upon his return to Moscow to enable a reactivation of them in the United States. Conceivably this is what the FBI wanted, and it will pounce when the time is right. Powers, on the other hand, may have possessed in-

325

formation deemed vital to the United States, although this is hard to credit. The public was persuaded to accept released statements that the responsible intelligence authorities were satisfied with Powers's explanation as to how it happened that both he and his plane fell into enemy hands; and presumably Congressional questioners were, too. Certainly nothing could be gained from further public airing.

On all levels, in all departments, and with the public itself, it must be accepted that espionage—secret service, more properly—is a game played for keeps. The pink-cheeked youth fresh from an intelligence school is no match for the expertly schooled class of professionals (such as Abel) that the Soviets select from top brackets, train for years, and install in bona fide occupations as covers. This is a grimly adult game. Mere dollars can't guarantee loyalty or courage when a contracted-for agent is compromised and faced with the consequences in a foreign land. Without his loyalty or courage it is futile for us to complain of the result. Without knowing what the facts might be, President Eisenhower spoke eloquently on behalf of Powers. Moscow could hardly be expected to be impressed by either the presidential pronouncements or the spy in view of its own intelligence personnel dictum:

> Agents must be of the intelligentsia; they must not shrink from the last sacrifice at the critical moment.
>
> (Soviet Intelligence Order 185,796)

Now the new Department of Defense Intelligence Agency has come into being. It has been publicly stated that a primary function is to absorb the strategic intelligence missions of the three services; there was no question of tampering with tactical, or combat, intelligence, which are functions of command. Doubtless the existing machinery of the services will play a vital part in the implementation of the defence agency's responsibilities in any case. Apparently it is intended that counterintelligence will remain with the services as far as military personnel and installations are concerned; outside, in the civilian sphere, the FBI has that function, as has been the case for many years. But there will be, in addition, a general policy supervision by the new agency of service intelligence activities. Co-ordination is expected to reduce duplication of effort and cross-operations of the larger classification. All this would seem to be a major stride forward in the often painful march toward maturity. But let there be caution. Interposition of a new "holding company" could once more result in the destruction of independent sources as a means of checking intelligence estimates. Violation of this principle is fatal, no matter what the agency name.

It is no original observation to point out that in government there is a tendency to say, "When in doubt, reorganize." Creating a new agency may seem simpler than attacking basic problems and accords a feeling, however false, of busy accomplishment. Major contributions may result; only time can test the validity of the concept. The nation's civilian intelligence structure would seem to have been trimmed to more acceptable proportions, a laudable move. Now the dome has been placed upon the military intelligence structure to give it line and unity. This, too, seems sound. So much for the aboveground fabric. What will be done now about the basic factors, such things as the stringent pre-entrance testing of personnel? What about integrated training programs for the production of career specialists who are not only capable of supervising but are probably superior to most others for the purpose? What about required intelligence appreciation courses for all nonintelligence personnel? There are other problems, but these are sufficient to occupy us fully now; their solution will advance us a long way toward true intelligence maturity.

Reorganization in itself, unless its purpose is clearly defined, is never justified and can be a confession of chronic frustration. The American penchant for worshiping size for size's sake, and the related aspect of accepting quantity as a synonym for quality in personnel can be adulterants to any plan for advance. If the history of secret service through the ages has shown one thing, it is the devastating efficiency of simplicity, of direct channels of concentrated effort by a few individuals with inherent integrity and unbending dedication forged into usefulness by sound training. We, too, can achieve this. If the new Department of Defense Intelligence Agency can evolve such sophistication in military intelligence and a strengthened CIA does it in the civil field, they will nobly serve a nation in need of such service.

In the meantime, Webster says, "to spy is to watch narrowly." Let us continue to do so.

INDEX

Abel, Col. Rudolf, 276, 278-80, 285, 287-88, 306, 309, 311, 325, 326
Abwehr, Section 111B, 262-64
Admiralty. *See* British
Adolphus, Gustavus, 23
Adventure Magazine, 191
Agents. *See* Intelligence Agents
Aguinaldo, Gen. Emilio, 117-23, 127, 132
Albert, Dr. Heinrich F., 50, 159-64, 191
Alexander, Gen. Sir Harold, 255
Alexander the Great, 19, 169
Alfred the Great, 24, 25
Alger, Sec. of War R. A., 110-11, 115
Allied Intelligence Bureau, 322, 323
Allied Translator and Interpreter Section, 131
Altendorf, Col. Paul Bernardo, 184-88
American Black Chamber, 198, 210
American Expeditionary Force, 181, 192, 193
Amtorg, 280, 309
Anatomy of Melancholy, 5
André, Maj. John, 65-66, 114
Anti-Comintern Pact, 244
Antiquarian Booksellers Association, 287
Anzacs, 34
Aristagoras, 19-20
Armada, Spanish, 24, 28, 29
Arnold, Gen. Benedict, 65-69
Asama incident, 131
ASDIC, 286
Aston, Sir George, 32-34
Attachés as Spies, 10, 125-26
Austerlitz, 43
Ayers, Peter, 290-91

Bacon, Roger, 26
Baden-Powell, Sir Robert, 35
Baker, Lafayette C., 109
Baker, Sec. of War Newton D., 177, 178, 179
Balfour, Arthur, 146
Baltimore Sun, 196
Bancroft, Dr. Edward, 62-63
Bataan Day, 117, 123
Battle of
   the Bulge, 3, 320-21
   Bull Run, 80-82, 100-101
   Leyte Gulf, 250
   Manila Bay, 116-24
   Marne, 163
Bay of Pigs, 323
Beauregard, Gen. P. G. de, 81, 85-86, 96-98, 101
"Beautiful Blonde Woman of Antwerp," 168-75
Bell, Edward, 146
Bell, Gen. Franklin, 128-29, 132, 177
Bernstorff, Count J. H. von, 144, 190
Bicknell, Col. George, 204-5, 215, 226, 231
Bismarck (German chancellor), 49, 51
"Black Cat" flights, 325
Black Saturday, 260
Black Tom promontory, 156
   Explosion, 155-59, 175, 184, 185, 189-91
Blake, Mrs. Arthur, 196-97
Blake, George, 267, 270, 273, 275-76, 313-14
Bliss, Gen. Tasker H., 181, 182, 183
Bluebook Magazine, 191
Bonham, Gen. M. K., 97

329

330

d'Enghein, Duc, 39
Department of Defense Intelligence Agency, 326-27, 328
Dewey, Adm. George, 116, 123
Dickson, Col. Benjamin ("Monk"), 320-21
Dominguez, 76-79
Donellan (Confederate agent), 97
Donovan, Gen. William A. ("Wild Bill"), 181, 236, 321
Dossier system, 50-51
Dual Monarchy, 53-54
Dulles, Allan, 113
Duvall, Betty, 96-97

Eastman Kodak Company, 155
"East Wind" Code, 228
Eckhardt, von, German minister, 144-46
Edward III, 25
Edward IV, 25
Edward VII, 36
Edwards, Miss Mena, 155, 189-90
Eisenhower, Gen. Dwight D., 255, 317
  as President, 326
Elizabeth I, 27, 29, 51
Elliott, Pvt. George, 220, 222, 225
Ernst, Karl Gustav (German agent), 36, 37
Espionage, 1-15, 17, 18, 22, 53, 60, 61, 71, 261, 265, 270, 273, 283, 311, 312, 313, 322, 325, 326
  Defined, 8-9
Espionage civile, 21, 25
Essex Junto, 71, 74
Ethics of Spying, 1-5, 9-10
E. V. Gibbons, Inc., 148, 152
Ewing, Alfred, 140, 141, 142, 143

Fay (German engineer), 150-51
"F"-type, secret ink, 174
"Father of Counter Intelligence Corps," 125
"Father of Intelligence" (US Army), 180
Favre, Jules, 49
Federal Bureau of Investigation, 5, 15, 204, 215, 227, 228, 231, 237, 265, 269, 279-80, 284-85, 325, 326
"Fists," 203, 212, 246

Foreign Agents Registration Act, 266
Fort Jay, N. Y., 157, 182
"Forty (40) O.B.," 138-39, 142-44, 191, 210. *See also* British Naval Intelligence
Flying Fortress bombers (B-17), 211, 219, 225, 229-30, 233
Flynn, William J., 162
Franklin, Benjamin, 61-63
Frederick the Great, 47
Frontinus, Sextus Julius, 21
Fugii, Japanese family, 217. *See also* Pearl Harbor
Funston, Gen. Frederick, 117-23, 132
Fuchs, Dr. Klaus E., 278

G-2, 110, 179, 180, 195, 197, 214, 218
Gaeshe, Emil V., 147-48, 154
Galisha, 275, 290, 307
Garcia (Cuban general, Calixto Garcia Iniguez), 114-15
Gee, Miss Ethel, 285-86, 293-94, 298-303, 308, 309. *See also* Secrets Case
Geheimfeldpolizei, 47-48
George III, 62-63
George V, 150
George, Gen. Harold H., 212
Gestapo, 21
Gideon, 16
Giesl, Baron von, 53-54
Gold, Harry, 278
Goldfus, Emil, 277-79
Graentnor (also Graetnor), 158, 191
"Great Armada," 93
Greenglass, David, 278
"Green House," The, 49
Greenhow, Robert, 88
Greenhow, Mrs. Rose, 80, 82-98, 104, 105, 106, 107, 108
Greenhow, Rose (daughter), 89-90
"Greenhow Prison," 86, 90
Grey Cardinal, The, 23
Gunthrum the Dane, 25

Hague Agreements, 9, 10
Hale, Nathan, 65-66, 69, 114
Halford, Ernest, CIC agent, 232

331

332

Political, 11, 14
Positive, 47, 51, 261
Strategic, 11, 13-14
Tactical, 12, 15
War Office (British), 32, 33
Intelligence & Security Branch (US Army), 318
Ivan the Terrible, 51
Iwai, Lt. George, 226

Jahnke, Kurt, 50, 172, 185-86, 190-91
Japan (Japanese)
Asama incident, 131
Espionage, 125-26, 198
Idiographs in Arizona, 132
Immigration question, 130
Imperial Navy, 202, 203, 210, 227, 250
Intelligence (and counterintelligence), 127, 246-47
"Invasion" of Arizona, 131-32
Sabotage denied, 238-39
Submarines at Pearl Harbor, 218-19, 224, 225
Johnston, Gen. Joseph E., 100-101
Joint Intelligence Committee, 237
Jones, Commodore, 96
Jordan, Lt. Col. Thomas. 90, 97
Julius Caesar, 21

Kalama, 208-9, 216, 217, 232
code, 208-9
Kalb, Baron de, 62
Kayotis, Andrew, 277-78
Keitel, Field Marshal Wilhelm, 257
Kerbey, J. O., 100-7, 180
Kennedy, President J. F., 323
Keuhn
Eberhard, 215
Friedel, 215, 232, 238
Hans, 215
Leopold, 215, 237
Otto, 188, 215, 216, 229, 231-32, 237-38
Ruth, 215, 216, 229, 232, 238
Keyes, Col. E. D., 88-89
KGB, 275, 278
KGMB, Radio Station, 201, 209, 215, 218, 219, 225

Khrushchev, Premier, 10, 307
Kimmel, Rear Adm. Husband E., 201-4, 211, 222, 225, 229, 234, 235
Kita, Nagao, 207, 217, 228
Kitabayashi, Mrs., 244, 248, 249
Kiyomi (Dancer), 247, 251
Klausen, Max 243-44, 245-47, 249-50
Kleist, von (*see* Rintelen), 147
Knox, Sec. of Navy Frank, 239
Konoye, Prince, 248
Kretschman, Baron Hans von, 167, 175
Kretschman, Maria, 168-76
Kroger, Peter and Helen, 279-80, 283, 287-88, 295, 299, 303-4, 306, 307-8
Kristoff, 158, 175, 189, 190
Kundschaftstelle, 53-54

Laelius, 20, 26
Lafayette, Marquis de, 64
Lane, Senator Joseph, 91
La Rochefoucauld, 1
Lawrence of Arabia, 142
Layton, Capt. E. T. (USN), 202-3, 212
Legion of Honor, 40, 44
Lehigh Valley Railroad Co., 156
Lincoln, President Abraham, 82-84, 88-89, 104, 107
Lipscomb, Capt. José A., 184, 196-98
Liverpool, Lord, 71-72, 74-75
Lockard, Pvt. Joseph, 220, 222, 225
Lonsdale, Gordon, 267, 270, 273-76, 279, 282, 283-84, 286-91, 294, 295, 296, 297, 298, 299, 300, 302-3, 304, 306-7, 308, 309
Louis XIV, 62
Lovell, Francis Viscount, 25, 26
Lowe, Mrs. Eleanor, 90
Lubyanka Prison, 21
Lusitania, 145, 233

Macabebes (Filipinos), 119-21
MacArthur, Gen. Arthur, 118, 120, 124-26, 128
MacArthur, Gen. Douglas, 125, 131, 210, 211, 223, 233, 240, 243, 247, 250, 317, 322, 323

333